Key W
for Academic
Writers

Rebecca Brittenham
Indiana University–South Bend

Hildegard Hoeller
College of Staten Island–CUNY

PEARSON
Longman

New York San Francisco Boston
London Toronto Sydney Tokyo Singapore Madrid
Mexico City Munich Paris Cape Town Hong Kong Montreal

To my father Professor Dr. Paul Höller (1925-1996).
Hildegard Hoeller

To my parents, George and Margaret Brittenham,
who inspired me with their passion for reading.
Rebecca Brittenham

Senior Vice President and Publisher: Joseph Opiela
Senior Acquisitions Editor: Lynn M. Huddon
Executive Marketing Manager: Ann Stypuloski
Senior Supplements Editor: Donna Campion
Production Manager: Charles Annis
Project Coordination, Text Design, and Electronic Page Makeup: Shepherd Incorporated
Cover Designer/Manager: Wendy Ann Fredericks
Cover Illustration: © Alamy Images
Manufacturing Buyer: Al Dorsey
Printer and Binder: R. R. Donnelley and Sons Company
Cover Printer: Coral Graphic Services, Inc.

Library of Congress Cataloging-in-Publication Data

Brittenham, Rebecca.
  Key words for academic writers / Rebecca Brittenham, Hildegard Hoeller.
      p. cm.
  Includes bibliographical references and index.
  ISBN 0-321-09436-0
    1. English language—Rhetoric. 2. Academic writing. I. Hoeller, Hildegard, 1960–
  II. Title.

  PE1408.B69855 2004
  808'.042—dc22

                                                                    2003066393

Please visit our website at http://www.ablongman.com

ISBN 0-321-09436-0

2 3 4 5 6 7 8 9 10—DOH—06 05 04

Contents

EXERCISES

1. Read through the table of contents to see which key terms have been selected for this collection. Choose the term that seems most simple and obvious to you and read through that entry. Then choose the term that seems most complex and mysterious to you and read through that entry. Report your findings: what you noticed, what you learned, how the two entries compared.

2. Use the table of contents to create an individualized sequence for yourself by listing the entries you would like to study during a semester in the order that might best suit you as a writer.

3. In a group, list some of the things you would like to know about college writing and college classes that should be included in this book. Halfway through the semester, revisit and update that list of terms, then divide that list up so that each member of the group can write a sample entry on one of those terms.

Alternative Table of Contents
How to Use This Book

We do not imagine that this book will ever be read linearly—from A to Z—but rather that it will be read in all sorts of directions and ways. Because no two writers learn or produce writing in quite the same way, the entries in this book can be read in any order depending on the interests and needs of the particular writers using it, and it can adapt itself to various syllabi or learning plans. Any one entry can provide the basis for a class discussion on its own, can be used as a way to read and analyze an assigned academic essay, or can be used through its exercises to prompt a writing assignment. Each entry contains a list of "related words" that suggests useful links to related topics. The index can also be used to track down an aspect of writing that does not appear in the listed entries (for ideas about "drafting" see the entry on "Revision," for example). The entries and exercises can be sequenced in almost as many ways as the book may have readers: They can be assembled as part of a syllabus to fulfill a targeted set of pedagogical goals or assigned along the way in the order determined by the needs and interests of a particular group of writers. In this section, we list some sample ways in which entries could be combined to address a specific issue, to guide students through the writing of a particular paper or a research project, or to help students focus on such large concepts as "Analysis," "Development," and "The Writer's Authority," which are frequently used in regard to student writing but actually involve a variety of related strategies and practices. Each of the clusters suggests a particular grouping of classes and in doing so tells a different story about how academic writing is produced, about its processes, trajectories, and limits. Many of the clusters speak to differing, even contradictory, pedagogical approaches. For example, the cluster on "The Writing Process" outlines one of the ways in which writers can move from reading and invention through drafting, revision, and editing, "From Summary to Thesis" helps writers focus on stages of argumentation. On the other hand, "The Limits of Reason" helps them to discover the liberating spaces and strategies that appear in and among the formal constraints of academic conventions. In some cases a cluster describes the contours of a potential course, such as "What is College" or "Personal Expression and the Conventions of Form." Other clusters focus on a particular issue, such as "Analysis" or "Grammar and Punctuation," and help to identify which entries might be particularly useful for exploring that issue. These clusters can be varied or combined in any order to structure a course or to create a targeted sequence in a course.

A Writing Process

Analysis

Elements of the Essay

Writers and Their Sources

Grammar and Punctuation

From Summary to Synthesis

Preface

WHY USE THIS BOOK?

This book is designed for college courses that introduce students to academic thinking and writing as well as for independent learners who want to learn more about college writing. As co-authors, we based the approach of this book on two firmly held convictions. *First, we are committed to helping students understand the integral connection between reading published academic essays and writing academic essays of their own.* For that reason, this book is meant to be used in tandem with a collection of assigned readings. Beginning academic writers sometimes find it difficult to make that connection between the finished, polished academic essays they are assigned to read and their own struggles with an assignment, a deadline, with the fundamental problems of writing an essay—such as argument, clarity, coherence, grammar—and even with finding an idea or a desk and a quiet place to write. Even in the classroom this apparent separation is often both temporal—discussing an assigned reading in one class and participating in a workshop on student writing in another—and conceptual—discussions of the assigned readings in one language and discussions of student writing that seem to take place in another, more mysteriously applied language of "thesis statements," "claims," "coordination and subordination" and so on. With this book, we try to overcome that separation on both grounds, temporal and conceptual, by redefining some of the central terms used to describe writing processes and strategies, by showing how those terms apply both to student and professional writing, and by opening those terms to further investigation. We demonstrate a way of teaching and learning that reconnects published academic writing and college student writing.

After all, published academic writers are themselves readers, starting fundamentally with the same processes as student writers; and they too tackle assignments, deadlines, finding a quiet place to work, fear of rejection, writer's block. And when looked at with some care, their polished essays—the impressive products—still reveal those processes. What better way to learn how and why to develop an interpretation, handle counterarguments, work with key terms and transitions than by observing how and why published academic writers do these things? Each entry in this book offers a way of seeing, examines one element of academic writing, performs a sample analysis showing how that element functions in an academic essay or activity, and provides a set of exercises demonstrating how to recognize and analyze that same element in assigned class readings and in student writing.

This approach serves two purposes: First, it shows the academic learner precisely how and why academic conventions, strategies, and habits are used and defines their meanings. It seems easier to begin writing and thinking in such a fashion when one sees the context for it. And second, it makes the published, polished writing much less impenetrable; it teaches how to read such writing not with a sense of distance and intimidation but with a hands-on approach that reveals all the things that went into its making. We may discover a published academic writer who is—like some student writers—struggling with contradictory evidence, or bristling with the desire to speak less academically, or trying to tackle various audiences, and so on. It is a too little stressed fact that most academic writers, whether experienced and published or just beginning to find a voice, both delight in *and* struggle with academic writing.

WHY DO WE ENCOURAGE PLAY?

This fundamental ambivalence is important to us. Once the gap between published academic writers and student writers has been bridged, we can move from intimidation to—not only learning—but also questioning and play. Influenced in part by Roland Barthes' admirable collection of essays, *Mythologies*, in which he interprets everyday events in French culture from mayonnaise to wrestling matches, we have tried to keep the tone and spirit of this book playful, to convey to students some of the rewards and pleasures of textual analysis. And this leads to the second firmly held conviction of our book: *Academic thinking is just one way of looking at the world and learning it is best done when questioning and debating it—even playing with it—at the same time.* After all, academic thinking is a very particular way of thinking that is not self-evidently "normal" or "natural" or useful in all settings. It comes with gains and losses, and it lends itself not only to imitation and emulation but also to parody and investigation; it is, very simply, the language of the academy, of universities and disciplines and their scholars, teachers, and students, a language that changes as these people and institutions change. In studying the rituals and conventions of the academic essay, then, we have drawn on the spirit of anthropologist Clifford Geertz's analysis of "deep play" in Balinese cockfights to consider some ways in which apparently formal concerns like citations and grammar often have at stake fundamental debates about the nature of academic communities. We invite students to view some of these conventions as microcosms of academia's social systems, as places where its crucial modes of communication, its beliefs systems, its deepest desires and fears and its most eccentric quirks are made manifest and available for study.

Each of the entries that follows is thus deliberately provocative, is designed *not* to offer the last word on the subject but to promote discussion and debate. Each entry offers a particular metaphor or way of seeing that is necessarily partial and slanted. We hope that students and teachers will take lively issue with some of the methods, metaphors and perspectives expressed here and will use that disagreement to supply their own terms and definitions to enrich their classroom conversations and the papers produced by them. In the Introduction to this book, "Academic Thinking and the Loss of Common Sense," we offer a way to begin this debate and to establish its spirit.

WHY THE ALPHABETICAL ARRANGEMENT OF ENTRIES?

We chose the key terms that seem to occur most frequently in classes on college writing, terms such as argument, assignment, grammar, plagiarism, syllabus, and titles, each of which has a meaning and usage that is often taken for granted and should not be. We decided on an alphabetical arrangement of those terms because that arrangement opens the book to the most active and varied participation of readers. Precisely by *not* dictating one specific order, one organizational method or one chronology of the writing process, the book allows for the diverse reality of writing—the way one stage of writing often leads back to an earlier stage, or work on one feature of an essay like an introduction suddenly raises questions about another feature, like voice, argument, or audience. It also allows for the realistic diversity of writers and writing processes—one writer may be struggling to create a thesis while another has questions about the difference between summary and analysis, and a third needs help with editing. At the same time, the "related words" feature at the end of each essay tries to emphasize the enormous overlaps between these terms—how the idea of constructing voice is deeply connected to a writer's sense of audience, assumptions and mode of quotation—to show that the relationships between these words are as rich and complex as the culture they represent and maintain.

In spite of the fact that these concepts and features of the essay form are completely and inextricably intertwined, this book singles each one out as a separate entry—why is that? We chose the separate entry format because the meaning of many of these terms seems so "natural" and self-evident within the college context that they are rarely isolated and studied in themselves—why question where the essay form came from when it is such an assumed part of college life? This "naturalness" tends to create an air of mystery surrounding the act of writing academic essays, a seemingly shared but often unspoken agreement about the qualities of a good college paper that leaves many writers wondering if they missed out on some secret code. By analyzing the conventions of the essay, showing exactly how professional writers work with them, and including exercises that show how apprentice writers can make equal use of them, this book aims to dispel that air of mystery.

This presentation of entries is also modeled on Raymond Williams's *Keywords: A Vocabulary of Culture and Society*, which defines in alphabetical order some of the key terms of English and American culture, such as "art, behavior, country, democracy, ethnic, myth, sex, unemployment." He shows both how the meanings of the words have changed over time and what those meanings reveal about the particular social and cultural conditions in which those words have been used. Williams's goal overall was to use this group of terms as keys to the culture, to convey the tangled, interconnected systems of social relations in which words operate and which they help to produce and maintain. Rather than a "neutral review of meanings," he tried to show the "precise historical and social conditions" that had been inherited with each of those terms, and to make his readers "conscious and critical" first that those meanings had been largely shaped for them and second that those meanings were not settled but were "active" and "subject to change" over time (Williams 24).

This book has benefitted from Williams's understanding of how the analysis of a few key terms can expose the governing assumptions, the historical underpinnings, the network of relations through which a particular culture functions. Like him we must say clearly: This is not a neutral review. It is a deliberately slanted and debatable analysis of some of the key terms of academic culture, particularly the terms frequently used to describe the reading and writing of essays. It becomes important to demonstrate that academia *is* a culture with particular languages and social systems of its own. College is an introduction to that culture, to the various scholarly communities that intersect on college campuses and to the thinking and writing produced in those communities. Of course that culture is deeply integrated within the social world at large, in no small part because of the work students and teachers do to connect the knowledge they gain in the classroom to the other parts of their lives. We would like to place this book at the cusp of that integration, to show how the academic world functions as an internal culture but one that is permeated by the very personal dreams, passions, and concerns of its students and scholars. We study some of its key terms to consider what they reveal about the changing social systems of academia, how much of its usage has become outmoded tradition, how much is still maintained through a kind of general consensus, how much leeway there is for individual leverage and for cultural change. Since that culture is actively shaping and reshaping itself continually as social and historical conditions shift, we can only show the state of things as they appear to us and leave as many ends open as possible for teachers and students to make sense of within their own communities and times.

ACKNOWLEDGMENTS

Since this book reflects how we have been shaped as academics, we would like to thank all the students, teachers, colleagues, and the writers we have read over the years who taught us to love academic thinking. In particular, we would like to thank the readers of earlier versions of this book: Anne Cassady, Middlesex County College; Janice Chernekoff, Kutztown University of Pennsylvania; Amanda Corcoran, American River College; Anne Fleischmann, University of California, Davis; Georgina Hill, Western Michigan University; Kirsten Komara, University of Evansville; Barry M. Maid, Arizona State University, East; Jennifer Richardson, Washington State University; Kimberly Ng

Southard, Suffolk County Community College; Kristine Swenson, University of Missouri-Rolla; Deborah Coxwell Teague, Florida State University; Roger Thompson, Virginia Military Institute; Bianca Tredennick, University of Oregon; Randall J. VanderMey, Westmont College; Cynthia Walker, Faulkner University. We would also like to thank our editor, Lynn Huddon, whose suggestions and support were extremely useful.

Rebecca Brittenham would like to thank her first colleagues and mentors in the Rutgers Writing Program, especially Robert Coleman, Steven Dilks, Mary Dougherty, Hugh English, Nancy Glazer, Darcy Gioia, Angela Hewitt, Judy Karwowski, Ray Klimek, Susan Mayer, and particularly Richard Miller for his continuing generosity and encouragement, and Kurt Spellmeyer, whose vision laid the groundwork for it all. She would also like to thank her Writing Program colleagues at Long Island University, in particular Esther Hyneman, Tom Kerr, Xiao-Ming Li, Harriet Malinowitz, Katrinka Moore, Deborah Mutnick, and Patricia Stephens, and her colleagues at Indiana University, South Bend from whom she continues to learn every day, especially Jim Blodgett, Nancy Botkin, Anne Bridger, Joe Chaney, Karen Gindele, Phyllis Moore-Whitesell, Elaine Roth, Margaret Scanlan, Jay Showalter, and Ken Smith. She would like to convey her immense gratitude to George and Margaret Brittenham and to Jonathan Nashel for their unstinting love and support. Finally, she would like to thank her collaborator, Hildegard Hoeller, who is the best and kept making this book happen when it didn't seem possible.

Hildegard Hoeller first learned—and learned to love—the teaching of writing at Rutgers University; she particularly would like to thank Kurt Spellmeyer, Matt Wilson, Dawn Skorzewski, Alice Crozier and many others for being colleagues, mentors, friends. Most importantly, Rutgers brought her together with her co-author and dearest friend, Rebecca Brittenham, without whom this project would be inconceivable. Much of this book comes out of Hildegard's teaching at the Expository Writing Program at Harvard University; foremost she would like to thank Gordon Harvey for his idea about the importance of key terms in the teaching of writing and for his extremely supportive collegiality. Both Richard Marius and Nancy Sommers have been almost unimaginably generous, supportive, and interested, and Hildegard thanks them with all her heart. Harvard, like Rutgers, produced those friends that are always—literally or metaphorically—co-writers in one's life: her deepest thanks to Kerry Walk and Laura Saltz for being such friends and colleagues. Many thanks also Michael Bruner and Brian Seitz who taught her much about teaching and are wonderful friends. As always, many thanks to Hildegard's favorite colleague, friend, and husband, Alec Marsh, whose undying enthusiasm and interest in her work is a phenomenal gift. Finally, Hildegard's deepest gratitude is to her late father, who made her first love academic life—and irony—and whose spirit is part of this book.

Rebecca Brittenham
Hildegard Hoeller

Credits

Introduction
Academic Thinking
and the Loss of Common Sense

It is hard to persuade anybody that losing one's common sense is a good thing; common sense, after all, helps us every day to make sense of the world and survive in it. Yet, to some degree, losing our common sense is exactly what an academic education tries to persuade us to do. And that is why most introductory writing courses are so demanding but also often ultimately exhilarating for both students and teachers.

How and why do academics and college teachers ask people to lose their common sense? Surely not to abandon reason, "to lose one's sense," to act insane, or to reject agreed-upon perceptions of what is and is not reality. Yet, academic thinking often calls on us to replace the tautology—this seems to be the reality we have agreed upon, therefore it must be the reality we have agreed upon, and so on—with investigation of terms, closure with complication, consensus with debate, knowledge with inquiry, assertion with ambivalence, conviction with reflection. There is a great deal at stake in that process: a lot to lose and a lot to gain.

Common sense is, of course, so common and self-evident that it is hard to describe or question; it is, according to the *Oxford English Dictionary,* "the plain wisdom which is everyone's inheritance" (online). Yet, a true academic, anthropologist Clifford Geertz has embarked on the paradoxical journey of investigating common sense, of questioning the unquestionable. Both parodying and employing academic thinking, he concludes that the best way to describe common sense is by

> isolating what might be called its stylistic features, the marks of attitude that give it its peculiar stamp....The terms I want to use in this way with respect to common sense, each with a "-ness" added on to substantivise it, are: natural, practical, thin, immethodical, accessible. "Naturalness," "practicalness," "thinness," "immethodicalness," and "accessibleness" are the somewhat unstandard properties I want to attribute to common sense generally, as an everywhere-found cultural form. (*Local Knowledge* 85)

Geertz's description of common sense helps us to see what exactly we mean by common sense and also what we might be losing by holding on to it too tightly. His list of "unstandard properties"—"naturalness," "practicalness," "thinness," "immethodicalness," and "accessibleness"—reveals precisely how and why academics have lost their senses, so to speak, and have instead gained a sensibility that promises its own "unnatural" rewards. It lets us see how

1

counterintuitive academic thinking is; how, indeed, academic thinking comes at the price—and with the reward—of losing common sense.

I. "NATURALNESS"

Geertz writes: "Common sense represents matters—that is certain matters and not others—as being what they are in the simple nature of the case. An air of 'of-courseness,' a sense of 'it figures' is cast over things—again some selected, underscored things" (85). Common sense tells us that this is just how the world is and that there is no need to question it since we all know that's how it is. In contrast, for the academic the world is a constant mystery; nothing is ever "of-course." Instead, everything demands investigation; academic tones are those of questioning and complication. Media critic Mark Crispin Miller, for example, makes it clear to us that even a soap commercial on television is far from what we think it is; rather, he promises that "just beneath the surface of this moronic narrative" lies some "noteworthy design," which the academic will reveal, analyze, and intepret in order to "lead us to some strange discoveries" (401). Or Robert Bogdan tells us that he began his book *Freak Show* after he watched "a Disney remake of the classic *Treasure Island*" with his ten-year-old son and his friend. When the friend asked his son who the bad guy was, his son replied: "If they look bad, they are bad" (vii). This formulaic simplicity got Bogdan to examine the depiction of "villains in horror and adventure movies" (vii); he noticed that they were "marked by various disfigurements and disabilities." From there he began to see that "Disney and other film producers use disability with great effect to conjure up fear in their audiences" (vii). Bogdan's introduction to his academic study of freak shows from there traces the development of his book moment by moment; each moment simple suppositions were replaced by more complex and astounding insights about the subject.

No surface is able to resist the scrutiny of the academic mind and its world—a world without a solid bottom to stand on, a world full of meaning where none seems apparent, its texts just flying carpets lifting us up to see better, yet making us aware of their thin, magical texture. The flights of academic thinking can be beautiful, their magic qualities exhilarating, their goals lofty, but we always know that we are almost in a fairy tale, that we participate in a tenuous construction of a world that seemed just a minute ago to be, well, just itself—and will perhaps return to that "of-course" reality in the next minute. The academic mind rebels against common sense: Why stay on the ground, it asks, where everything is always already the same, nothing surprises, everything stands guard to a static world, protecting it in its one-dimensional sameness? Why not lose common sense, it taunts, and enter a world that is not self-evident and spoken for, but where everyone (with the right training) can speak surprisingly about it and shake its foundations?

2. "PRACTICALNESS"

"The second characteristic [of common sense], 'practicalness,' " writes Geertz,

> "is perhaps more obvious to the naked eye than the others on my list, for what we most often mean when we say an individual, an action, or a project displays a want of common sense is that they are impractical. . . . [But] it is not 'practicalness' in the narrowly pragmatical sense of the useful but in the broader, folk-philosophical sense of sagacity that is involved. To tell someone, 'be sensible,' is less to tell him to cling to the utilitarian than to tell him, as we say, to wise up: to be prudent, levelheaded, keep his eye on the ball, not buy any wooden nickels, stay away from slow horses and fast women, let the dead bury the dead" (87).

In other words, common sense is street-smart and savvy.

Is the academic practical? No, says common sense, bemusedly invoking the image of the distracted professor searching for the glasses: Everybody else knows they are right there on his nose! Certainly, academics are not practical people in the "narrowly pragmatical" sense Geertz mentions; but they are not viewed as street-smart either. One wonders, how and why can intelligent people be considered dumb about "real" life? Why *are* they sometimes dumb in that sense?

Let me tell you how my father, a physics professor, played miniature golf. Imagine a hot summer Sunday many years ago; my mother, father, brother and I* decide to play a round together even though all of us are terrible players. We are now at the first tee. My mother—a housewife all her life and not an academic mind—swings her club. The ball rolls almost towards the hole. It doesn't quite get there. She approaches and swings the club, gentler now, again. A few more times, the ball is at its expected destination. My brother and I follow, both children at the time. We each play at our own pace, trying instinctively to adjust the power and angle of our swings to the situation of the ball. We all do reasonably well. We laugh at our incompetence, enjoying the narrative of who is winning and who is losing, who is lucky and who isn't; of course, the ones with more luck enjoy it more than the others. Our scores, as random as they may seem to us, are the guiding story of the game, which assigns us different roles; it is why we play.

"Come on Dad, it's your turn!" we cry. "Give me your clubs," my father demands pensively, and we roll our eyes and reluctantly hand them over to him. We don't know yet why he wants them, but we do know that no normal episode is to follow. We look around with embarrassment and see a party approaching behind us, who now have to wait and watch the spectacle of an academic mind playing miniature golf. My father kneels down beside the tee; he puts one bow of his glasses into his mouth as he did all his life when he embarked on impractical (academic) thoughts—those he was most ingenious about. He puts his glasses back on to see the tee, back off, back on. Finally he places the clubs on the asphalt of the tee! Arranging them carefully in angles,

---

*The "I" here refers to Hildegard Hoeller.

he uses them to draw on the course what he computes to be the perfect trajectory (all angles figured out) for the ball. All that's left, according to his calculations, is to hit the ball exactly two strokes along a certain angle in order to put it into the hole. Satisfied with his computations, my father removes the graph made by the clubs (after all he has to use one of them actually to swing at the ball), and he selects one club for its "proper" function. After many deliberations—he snickers as he keeps us in suspense—he swings at the ball. The ball, as if asserting a life of its own, has no intention of rolling along the perfect trajectory computed for it. It lands ridiculously ineffectively right at the first turn, which, theoretically, it should have traversed with great elegance. My father, to our amusement and dismay, collects the clubs again, and takes off his glasses and recommences his intricate measurements.

The score: You figure it out. We move to the next tee, tuning out the whispers and shaking heads of the "common sense" people following us; we are preparing for a very long afternoon in the burning summer sun with our father. He won't win the game through scientific analysis; this much we know.

Not unlike a poet, an academic cares about life in metaphors. In order to see, he needs, like my father, to take off his glasses as much as he needs to put them on. If the balance between the two ways of seeing is lost, so are the best insights. In some ways, the academic always looks at the fragility of those metaphors. Life as he sees it is not enough; it needs to be rendered comprehensible (after having been seen as incomprehensible first). It needs to be theorized, metaphorized, challenged as it tries on different versions of itself. If an academic completely loses sight of the world as we see it, her work is an empty dance of words. If she loses sight of the rendition, her work is flat. It is in probing the mystery between life and an attempted rendition of it that the academic is truly "impractically" skilled. It is not important that my father could not hit the ball as he wanted to; it is important that he saw the possibilities for the ball and did his best to understand the fundamental ambitions of the game. It would have been wonderful if he had hit the ball exactly as he computed, but it did suffice that he *could* have hit the ball as he computed it. His way of playing was utterly impractical for his level of skill as a swinger of the club, but practical in an ideal world; academically, it was insightful and exhilarating as a discovery of the nature of the game. While not completely impractical, the academic is sometimes practical only as an idealist. He wants to grasp the world in images and language, and he can live with the fact that he might not be able to grasp it with his hands quite as well.

3. "THINNESS"

When Geertz tackles the "thinness" of common sense, he compares it to "modesty in cheese, rather hard to formulate in more explicit terms. 'Simpleness,' or even 'literalness,' might serve as well or better, for what is involved is the tendency for common-sense views of this matter or that to represent them as being precisely what they seem to be, neither more nor less. . . . The world is what the wide-awake, uncomplicated person takes it to be" (89). It is almost "thinly" clear how academic thinking tries to be opposite to common sense in this category. If common sense means to look at things as "being precisely what they seem to be," academic thinking might be characterized as looking at things as "being precisely not what they seem to be." Observe how many academic essays begin in that way. Once again Mark Crispin Miller comes to mind with his in-depth view of soap operas and commercials, but more so even, any classroom experience where we were slowly made to see that the poem we thought was about a ladder leaning against an open window is really about sexuality. Or, a commonsense thinker might look at a refrigerator, think of a cold beer, and proceed to drink it. The refrigerator to him or her is just that: a machine that keep things cold. But an academic might consider the larger historical and social context of the refrigerator: What happened to households when people could begin to store food longer? Could the refrigerator be responsible for the disappearance of the market square, the decline in civic interaction, the development of convenience food, even the segregation and isolation of families? Research needs to be done truly to understand the refrigerator and its cultural impact. Like the commonsense person, the academic thinks about herself as wide-awake; however, being awake for the academic means to see things as complicated as they are. Complication is a goal, a method, and a value.

Why is it that academics see what others do not see, complicate what others see as simple? And do they always achieve depth? Just like common sense is not always really thin, academic thinking is not always really deep. And just as common sense rests its validity on its tone of "thinness," academic thinking claims its authority through its claims to "deepness." One digs deeper than someone else, one sees in more complex manners than someone else, one reflects further than someone else, one includes more (all of it crucial to an understanding of the matter) than someone else, one reveals unreflected assumptions of someone else, one asks a complicating question of someone else's conclusion; one is, in other words, deeper than the person before one. Academic thinking is the voice of deepness, probing, questioning, complicating, reflecting. Often it indeed reveals a new dimension to us or shakes the foundations of our beliefs. Yet, academic thinking sometimes is deep only in its tonal conventions, not in its actual arguments. Academic thinking in its poorest form is nothing more than a thin posture of "deepness," just as common sense's "thinness" at its very best points to a deep insight or truth.

4. "IMMETHODICALNESS"

"Common-sense wisdom," writes Geertz, "is shamelessly and unapologetically ad hoc. It comes in epigrams, proverbs, *obiter dicta,* jokes, anecdotes, *contes morals*—a clatter of gnomic utterances—not in formal doctrines, axiomized theories, or architectonic dogmas" (90). Coming in fragmented statements rather than fully developed paragraphs or arguments, it is a conglomeration of often contradictory wisdoms. Nothing, on the other hand, is more deliberate, methodical, and sometimes humorless than academic thinking. While appearing magical in its results at times, it is actually methodical; it is discipline, after all. It teaches us that there is a form to discovery, a form that enables all of us to discover ideas, to be interesting, to contribute to an ongoing search of knowledge. In its form, academic thinking allows all of us to expect surprises, to plan the magic of new learning and insights, and to take the first measured steps towards the unknown. In order to convey its form and method, academic thinking is institutionalized thinking. Experts in various disciplines, trained in the appropriate methods of their fields, teach that method, and with it the potential for discovery, to others. The magic of academic thinking lies precisely in its unmagical, methodical approach.

Marjorie Garber in her book *Academic Instincts* uses the immethodicalness of common sense in order to launch her discussion of an academic argument; she shows, in other words, how her own academic musing differs from common sense because it must explore rather than simply contain contradictory statements. Here is the opening of her chapter on "Discipline Envy":

> Conflicts among the academic disciplines are often compared to turf battles and boundary disputes, likely to inspire the planting of "Keep Off the Grass" signs and cries of "Not in my back yard!" But let's not forget that other familiar proverb about turf: "The grass is always greener in someone else's yard." This Aesop-like saying describes a common illusion and a common mechanism of desire. It's not completely an accident, I think, that the aphorism contains both turf ("yard") and greenness—the color of envy. What I want to suggest is that disciplinary turf battles themselves both inspire, and depend upon, such trespassing. (53)

Note how Garber uses common sense's immethodicalness here to begin an academic argument; while common sense can simply live with two contradictory statements—or at least two statements that do not quite fit together—the academic needs to investigate such a tension. Turning common sense onto itself—making it reveal its contradictions—Garber is able to begin a fascinating argument about disciplines' need to protect and transgress their boundaries, to demarcate themselves and to always desire to be on the other's turf. Hence we move from common sense to academic thinking.

5. "ACCESSIBLENESS"

"Accessibleness is simply the assumption, in fact the insistence, that any person with faculties reasonably intact can grasp common-sense conclusions" (Geertz 91). Here, of course, is where common sense and academic thinking seem to clash most overtly. "One can't understand a word of all this academic stuff," "these people can't see the forest because of all the trees": says common sense looking at academic writing—including Geertz's. "It is precisely the common perception of the larger term *forest* that prevents the individual subject from perceiving the tree in its own entity and as a constituent of the forest; the individual 'tree' is erased by the larger term 'forest,' " counters the academic voice.

Common sense derives its authority from appearing accessible while academic thinking often sounds authoritative precisely because it appears inaccessible. Consider a commonsensical phrase such as "you can't have it both ways" or "each coin has two sides." These sentences seem directly clear to the listener or reader, even though in tandem they begin to pose a bit of a problem, right? Yet, they do not leave the layman stunned as the following sentences might. Consider this one: "Impersonation is imposture: that is, representation is a misrepresentation of the 'representative' to the extent that it effaces his presence in the discourse"(Stephens 239). It appears as if common sense is deeply (or thinly?) invested in being universal, academic thinking in being specialized. Common sense settles for one truth at a time, whereas academic thinking always looks at both sides of the coin, and more if it can! It is inaccessible because it uses specialized language, engages in complex sentence structures and thought patterns, and because it often reflects on its own language, as the quotation shows.

So each form of thinking wants to gain power by being accessible and inaccessible respectively; yet each form of thinking also paradoxically (here is the academic speaking) loses authority by the same token. How accessible is common sense? Does it ever give reasons or is it willing to reason? Its language tells us that what it is saying is self-evident to everyone. And yet, its universality is utterly local, limited to particular situations—as the two quotes demonstrated. One moment at a time, common sense pronounces universal wisdoms: no questions allowed. In that sense, common sense runs the danger of being perceived as both arrogant and facile.

If the "universal" tone of common sense can be seen as arrogant and facile, the specialized language of the academic may be seen as arrogant and pedantic. Why can't things be expressed more clearly and simply? Academic writing seems to exclude some readers because of its difficulty, though only in order to include others so much more deeply (or thinly). At its best, it is thinking about and with its particular audience, and it allows its audience as much insight as possible. In its local interests, its detailed discussions of small parts of our universe, it tries to teach us about that universe; its focus is local but its ambitions are universal. The best academic writing speaks meaningfully to its specialized audience and is able to include a general public. The worst of academic writing is inaccessible to all and pronounces nothing but its own specialization.

In the term *accessibleness,* the two opponents, common sense and academic writing, reveal a bit about their own hunger for power and their blindness about themselves. Clifford Geertz writes, "Common sense, to put it another way, represents the world as a familiar world, one everyone can, and should, recognize, and within which everyone stands, or should, on his own feet" (91). Academic thinking presents the world as unfamiliar, almost unrecognizable, as a shaky construct we have to investigate and understand anew again and again. Neither one makes perfect sense; they have that much in common. And each one allows us to see the world from a different angle, for better or worse.

RELATED WORDS

Assumptions 19   Discipline 57

Audience 25   Interpretation 94

Claims 38   Reading 132

Counterargument 49   Voice 187

EXERCISES

1. Reexamine an assignment given to you in another class in light of this chapter. What is academic about that assignment? What way of seeing the world is implied in the assignment?

2. Look at an academic essay and analyze which parts seem to have the traits of academic writing and which have commonsense traits. Quote or mark passages where you see an example of something "thick," "unnatural," "impractical," "methodical," or "inaccessible"? Why, do you think, does the essay violate common sense in those passages?

3. Take any piece of academic writing and diagnose it as such. Write in the margins where you see common sense violated and in what way. Articulate commonsensical counterarguments and suggestions. What are the gains and losses of abandoning common sense?

4. Enact a dialogue between common sense and academic thinking. Based on a piece of academic writing, write both a defense and an attack, the former in the language of the academic, the latter in the voice of common sense. Then discuss the dialogue in class. What is the fundamental difference between both positions and what can each position accomplish?

5. Using the example of the refrigerator as a model, choose a term and give the most commonsensical definition of it. Then in a group, brainstorm alternative ways of seeing the term in order to complicate, thicken, and enrich its meaning and to make its significance academically debatable and explorable.

Argument
Aunt Anne's Predicament
and the Logic of Persuasion

A narrative tells a story; an argument presents a reasoned progression of ideas. "My Aunt Anne went to the hairdresser to get a perm, and the next day she lost her hair"—that is a narrative. "The chemicals used in the perming process can lead to follicle damage and even hair loss"—that is the beginning of an argument. We can tell the difference in part because of the contrasting expectations these two sentences set up for a reader. The narrative emphasizes a chronology of events; first one thing happens, then another. The argument emphasizes the logical connections between ideas; because one thing is so, therefore another must be so, and yet another and another are by implication so. The narrative gives the entire storyline of the incident and seems to require from the reader nothing more than a slightly shocked or sympathetic response. The argument makes a generalized assertion that seems immediately to raise a series of questions for the reader: What is your evidence for this claim? In how many cases does follicle damage actually lead to hair loss? What about all the people who have been getting perms for years with no apparent follicle damage? As this contrast suggests, an argument can be defined as a claim that has generalized implications or significance for a readership (as opposed to Aunt Anne's predicament which may only interest her immediate family); is open to debate (asserts something that readers might reasonably disagree with as opposed to a simple statement of fact like "the sky is blue," for example); and therefore requires further supporting evidence in order to be convincing, thus providing a sense of purpose and momentum throughout an essay.

The argument is in this sense the core of an academic essay, its thesis, but it is also the chain of reasoning that draws that essay along from thesis to conclusion, link by link, paragraph by paragraph. The word "argument" thus describes both the main point a writer wants to make and the series of connective links through which he or she makes, supports, and develops that point throughout the essay. It is the tensed fishing line that runs through the essay giving it a sense of purpose and direction and keeping the reader hooked.

In constructing an argument, an academic writer organizes and presents information in ways that will most effectively persuade an audience to understand and possibly share his or her interpretation or position in a debate. The argument motivates and controls every aspect of the writing from the organizational moves to the use of logic-based transitions ("thus," "hence," "therefore," "because," "if . . . then," "further," etc.) to the sentence structures, the choice and use of evidence, the vocabulary and tone. For example, architecture professor Daphne Spain opens with a clear assertion of her main argument (i.e., her thesis) in the first paragraph of her essay on gender and workplace:

> This essay examines the spatial conditions of women's work and men's work and proposes that working women and men come into daily contact with one another very infrequently. Further, . . . women work in a more public environment with less control of their space than men. This lack of spatial control both reflects and contributes to women's lower occupational status by limiting opportunities for the transfer of knowledge from men to women. (771)

We might actually break this thesis down into a series of assertions that Spain will have to support and develop through the essay in order to convince us to accept or share her position: that work spaces are separate, that women's are more public, and that there is a cause and effect relationship between those working conditions and the resulting occupational status of women. All of these points seem highly debatable and in need of supporting evidence.

If this is the core of her argument, what are the moves she makes through the essay? Instead of beginning with one of those assertions and then moving on to the next, Spain organizes her essay as a comparison and contrast between the typical occupations held by women and those held by men: We hear first about the women's workplaces and their resulting status (2 pages), then about the contrasting workplaces typically occupied by men (2 pages), and finally how office buildings are architecturally constructed to separate those workplaces (1½ pages). Looking only at the topic sentence of each paragraph (and excluding all the evidence, statistics, and supporting examples) helps to reveal the organizational moves of the essay:

> Paragraph 3: "A significant proportion of women are employed in just three occupations: teaching, nursing, and secretarial work . . . "(772).
> Paragraph 4: "Secretarial/clerical work is the single largest job category for American women . . . " (772).
> Paragraph 5: "Two spatial aspects of secretarial work operate to reduce women's status . . . " (772).
> Paragraph 6: "Like teachers and nurses, secretaries process knowledge, but seldom in a way beneficial to their own status . . . " (772).
> Paragraph 7: "In other words, secretaries are paid *not* to use their knowledge for personal gain, but only for their employers' gain . . . "(773).
> Paragraph 11: "The largest occupational category for men is that of managers . . . " (774).
> Paragraph 12: "Spatial arrangements in the workplace reinforce these status distinctions . . . " (774).
> Paragraph 13: "Just as there are professional manuals for the successful secretary, there are also numerous guidelines for the aspiring manager . . . " (774).

From these sentences, we can see how the essay narrows from its overall assertion to the specific example of secretaries, which Spain analyzes in a way that
prepares the reader for the contrast to male managers. Sentence structures like
"Just as . . . there are also . . . " help Spain to work through the details of
the contrast. At the same time, we can begin to see how the line of argument—
the correlation between "spatial arrangements" and "status"—recurs throughout this organizational pattern and is supported and developed by the extended
examples of secretaries and managers. The purpose of the essay is clearly to
show the problem with these spatial arrangements in the workplace and
thereby to imply a potential solution; the writer's purpose thus supplies a
"problem/solution" structure to the essay. More importantly, it supplies a sense
of momentum; these details about secretaries and managers and workplaces
matter, they take on a greater significance, because they are telling us something
vitally important about the connection between architecture and occupational
status, something that both future architects and workers can learn from. We
might not agree with Spain's conclusions, but we might well take a new look at
the arrangement of work spaces the next time we are in an office building.

Yet, for every degree of control and every erg of momentum provided by
the structure of this argument there are a thousand losses. In deciding to tell
one story, Spain must by necessity truncate or ignore the multitude of other
stories that could have been told but were not relevant to her argument: the
personality differences, race and class backgrounds, and attitudes toward authority that factor into workplace politics in addition to gender; the educational systems that prepare men and women to occupy or to challenge the
gendered roles laid out for them; the individual stories of each one of the
nurses, teachers, secretaries, and managers who become mere statistics in
Spain's article—their families, their fears and joys, their dreams, and desires. All
that must be left out to preserve the integrity of the argument, to give it coherence and keep it moving. This is the predicament of the writer and the true
logic of persuasion. As an argument develops, it becomes in one sense a single-
minded arbitrator setting the standard of value for an essay, deciding at every
juncture what is worth including and what must be eliminated. On the other
hand, the energy and control provided by that argument help the writer to see
and to articulate far more about the one story he or she chooses to tell—in
Spain's case the details of architectural design that would otherwise be invisible
agents in the gender gap. The power of persuasion in an essay comes from a
balance between that arbitrating control provided by an argument and its ability to generate complex layers of meaning, to encompass and build from
counter-arguments and still maintain its integrity.

In other academic essays, particularly those written in humanities-based
disciplines, the line of argument may be less overtly logic-based and more interpretive but the predicament of persuasion remains the same. An essay by the
feminist theorist and TV critic, Laura Stemple Mumford, demonstrates an interpretive line of argument. Mumford analyzes the "paternity plots" in daytime

soap operas—unknown fathers, missing fathers, misidentified fathers—and argues "that the genre of the soap opera is able simultaneously to vent and to contain [women viewers' private] concerns" (258–59). In contrast to Spain, Mumford's argument is based on persuasive interpretations of these examples. Rather than focusing on a statistical survey of viewers' responses to "prove" her case, for instance, Mumford persuades us to share her take on the soaps through detailed plot summaries and the explanatory power of her close readings. Thus, we hear about the character of Natalie Hunter on *All My Children* who mistakenly identifies her stepson rather than her deceased husband as the father of her child (Mumford 256). Working with the details of these and other examples, Mumford persuades us that such shows hold out the "utopian" possibility "that women *can* define the family structure, *can* attribute paternity with impunity, *can* name the father according to their own desires and without reference to blood tests" (258). Like Spain however, Mumford uses the controlling focus of her argument to eliminate other possible topics of interest. For instance, by choosing to focus on the issue of paternity, Mumford clearly excludes the alcoholic mothers and the evil-twin sisters that also plague soap operas and impact viewer reactions. In both cases, the line of argument helps to limit the material that can appropriately be included in the essay and therefore allows for a more complex and compelling discussion of that material.

Further, a line of logical argumentation may be hidden within a narrative. For example in " 'Indians': Textualism, Morality, and the Problem of History," literary critic Jane Tompkins uses the story of her progress as a reader to provide the connecting links for a larger argument about the problem of assembling a true picture of the past. Notice the contrast between the style of her opening sentences and Spain's:

> Paragraph 1: "When I was growing up in New York City, my parents used to take me . . . [to see American Indians]" (673).
> Paragraph 2: "I already knew about Indians from . . . " (673).
> Paragraph 3: "My story stands for the relationship most non-Indians have to the people . . . " (674).
> Paragraph 4: "This essay enacts a particular instance of the challenge poststructuralism poses to the study of history . . . " (674).
> Paragraph 5: "I encountered this problem in concrete terms while preparing to teach a course . . . [about Puritans and Native Americans] . . . " (674).
> Paragraph 6: "For a while, I remained at this impasse . . . " (674).
> Paragraph 7: "My research [on the Puritan/Native American encounter] began with Perry Miller . . . " (674).

As these opening lines suggest, Tompkins organizes her essay as a chronology: first her childhood perceptions of Indians, then her experience teaching a course about Indians and Puritans, then her research on Indians and Puritans, starting with historian Perry Miller and decade by decade showing the debates between historians on this subject. However, through this chronology we begin to see the line of her argument emerging, first with an explicit statement of her thesis—the central purpose of the essay—in paragraph 4, and secondly through the recurring sense that there is a problem involving these various perceptions of Indians, a problem she cannot easily solve ("I remained at this impasse"). Like Spain's essay, this turns out to be a problem/solution structure, and although the storyline of Tompkins' experiences studying this problem does provide the essay's momentum, its driving purpose is the underlying argument that this particular case study of Indians and Puritans reveals the much larger problem of finding a definitive truth about our history and the moral necessity for historians to do exactly that. Here too, Tompkins generates persuasive power by subordinating the huge, multi-faceted question of Puritan/ Native American relations to the controlling momentum provided by her argument about the proper role of the historian.

As these three examples show, the writer's predicament, the necessity of balancing an argument's controlling force against the multiple revelations and counter-claims it generates, against all the things that could be said and all the stories that could be told, is also the source of the writer's persuasive power. Finding an argument allows the writer to structure a progression of ideas, to establish a position in relation to a particular question, problem, or debate by excluding or subordinating all the other questions to be explored and possible positions to be taken. At the same time, that argument frees the writer to make a compelling case for the one interpretation or claim that he or she has most at stake and most wants others to understand and care about.

RELATED WORDS

Claims 38	Research 137
Counterargument 49	Structure 149
Discipline 57	Thesis 176
Evidence 77	Transitions 183
Interpretation 94	

EXERCISES

1. In a group, work on identifying the core argument in several academic essays. Underline the topic sentences and/or the particular places in each essay where that argument reemerges, gets supported and developed. What is the purpose of each essay? How would you describe its underlying structure? What debate does each writer appear to be engaged in? What question or problem is each writer trying to address? Create a chart or diagram showing the different ways in which these writers have chosen to structure their arguments.

2. Write a short paragraph telling the story, the chronological narrative, of a recent experience. Write a second paragraph using that experience

to make an argument, showing the implications of that experience for some larger question or issue.

3.   Trace the line of argument through a published essay by writing down and analyzing the topic sentence of each paragraph. What moves is the writer making from paragraph to paragraph? What transitional words and phrases does he or she use? What is the progression of ideas? What seems to be his or her real purpose in writing this essay? What is at stake in this essay? In your own words, write a short description of the writer's core argument. Perform this same exercise using another student's draft.

4.   Read through your own draft and then write a separate paragraph identifying your sense of purpose as the writer of that essay. What question or problem are you addressing? What debate are you entering and with which writers? What is at stake? What position do you hope to persuade your reader to understand or share?

Assignment
By Definition Not Just a Task

Assignment: "a task assigned to one." If you think this is the primary meaning of assignment, you may be surprised to hear that it is only a half of the thirteenth and last meaning the *Oxford English Dictionary* gives for assignment. The first meaning listed is "The action of appointing as a share, allotment." Then there are: "Legal transference of a right or property," "Appointment Office, Nomination, designation; setting apart for a purpose," "Attribution as belonging or due to," "Allegement, statement of (reason)," and others. Only at the very end do we read: "a task assigned to one, a commission or appointment"; this meaning, the *OED* informs us, originates in the United States at around 1848. So, the meaning that seems closest to the idea of an assignment in a college class is really only a minor and relatively new meaning; and the origin of the word assignment—those other twelve and one half definitions—may help us to get a larger and rather more encouraging perspective on things.

For one, they explain why most writers—perhaps with the exception of some student writers—are eager, even proud, to get an assignment. Most writers want to be given an assignment—whether it be a book review, a grant proposal, a letter of recommendation, an essay for a collection, an abstract, or an entire book—because it means that they have a reason to write, that they have an audience, that they are working in a context, and that someone trusts them to write. Getting an assignment means being given a form of "property," a "share" in things. Someone is "nominating" and "appointing" us and thus signaling that we belong. While an assignment is, of course, a task, it is also a form of inclusion—even honor at times.

Are academic assignments in a college course fundamentally different from these other assignments that professional academic writers receive? Such academic writers typically write in response to "Call for Papers," that is, assignments that are published in scholarly journals, on pamphlets left on long tables at professional conferences, or in e-mail form sent to a listserv. Consider the e-mail "Call for Papers" in Figure 1.

The authors of the call, the future editors of the collection, have an idea for a collection and a purpose: they believe that the reputation of Charlotte Perkins Gilman—a famous American turn-of-the-century feminist—is too narrowly defined and they want to widen it. Therefore, they are calling for papers that expand our view of Gilman; in that sense, they have found an "opening" that allows for new work to be written. They also have an overall purpose to the collection in mind, something approaching a thesis: "The resulting portrait should depict Gilman as both a critic and a product of her times" and thus challenge the "marginalization" of her work, which could have been caused by seeing her as an extreme radical. Finally, the editors describe—even prescribe—how the essays should look and what they should do: They should be in MLA style and roughly twenty pages long, and they should "juxtapose Gilman with other writers and thinkers and explore proximity rather than the usual distance." This assignment, in sum, gives a *motive* for the collection (to challenge a predominant view), a *purpose* (to depict Gilman as critic and product of her time), a *task* for each essay (to juxtapose and stress proximity between Gilman and one other thinker of her time) a *form* (length and MLA style), and, finally, a *deadline:* September 1, 2001. When a writer submits a proposal to the editors, that proposal needs to show how the writer would respond to the assignment and give the editors reasonable belief that the writer can fulfill the assignment and is worthy of it; in other words, a proposal promises both to submit to the requirements of the assignment and to excel at the opportunity it offers. Thus, in the academic world, everyday scholars compete for assignments; later in a writer's career, when he or she is more established, the tables might turn and the editor may invite the writer to contribute and some of the terms may become negotiable.

The nature and conditions of such academic assignments are mirrored and rehearsed in the assignments given in college courses. First, compare the following assignment taken from the composition anthology *Ways of Reading* to

---

Date Sent: Thursday, April 19, 2001 11:35
          "Cynthia Davis"
   From: <CJDavis@gwm.sc.edu>   Add to Address Book
      To: <Cfp@dept.english.upenn.edu>
Subject: CFP: Charlotte Perkins Gilman in the Company of Others (9/1/01; collection)

Status: ❏ Urgent ❏ New

CALL FOR PAPERS
Charlotte Perkins Gilman in the Company of Others
Edited by Cynthia J. Davis and Denise D. Knight

We are soliciting essays for a collection designed to situate Charlotte Perkins Gilman in relation
to other writers and thinkers. A century ago, Charlotte Perkins Gilman was world-renowned.
Today, after decades of neglect, her reputation rests largely on her chilling but anomalous tale
"The Yellow Wall-Paper." The moment thus seems ripe for a reconsideration of Gilman's place
in literary history. One explanation for her marginalization over the years could be an unwar-
ranted reputation for radical extremism. The volume intents to challenge this reputation by
locating Gilman in the company of more mainstream figures. The point is not to scold her for
complicity but to establish these comparisons as grounds for re-evaluation and rehabilitation.
Each of the essays will juxtapose Gilman with other prominent writers and thinkers and explore
proximity rather than the usual distance. The resulting portrait should depict Gilman as both a
critic and a produce of her times.

Please send essays of roughly twenty pages in length (MLA style) to:

Professor Cynthia J. Davis
Department of English
University of South Carolina
Columbia, South Carolina 29208

Deadline for submissions is September 1, 2001. E-mail submissions are welcome.

Cynthia J. Davis, Associate Professor
Department of English
University of South Carolina
Columbia, SC 29208
Please note new e-mail address:xxxx@xx.xxx
ph: 000-000-0000; fax: 000-000-0000

From the Literary Calls for Papers Mailing List
CFP@english.upenn.edu
Full Information at
http://www.english.upenn.edu/CFP/
or write Erika Lin: elin@english.upenn.edu

Figure I   Call for Papers, Charlotte Perkins in the Company of Others

the Gilman assignment above; a compare/contrast assignment also, it deals with two essays, one by literary critic Jane Tompkins called " 'Indians': Textualism, Morality, and the Problem of History," the other by scientist Thomas Kuhn entitled "The Historical Structure of Scientific Discovery":

> Thomas Kuhn . . . argues that discoveries have a "prehistory," a "posthistory," and an internal structure. Tompkins is not a scientist, and there are some significant differences between her discovery and the discoveries recorded in Kuhn's essay. But Kuhn's contribution to the history of science (and the history of knowledge) is the way he imagines a historical and cultural context for the work a scientist does, so to speak, "on his own."
>
> Write an essay in which you compare Tompkins's representation of how knowledge is constructed and reproduced from written texts with Kuhn's representation of the construction and reproduction of knowledge. On the basis of these two essays alone, what are the significant differences and similarities between the practice of science and the practice of history? What are the significant similarities and differences between Kuhn and Tompkins, both of whom could be said to be writing histories? (581–582)

This assignment shares quite a bit in common with the professional example shown here. It, too, defines a *motive* for the assignment (Kuhn himself opens up a question about history), a *purpose* (to reflect on the differences in practice between two disciplines and to reflect on the term history itself after comparing the two writers' approaches to written texts), and a *task* (first compare then interpret the comparison). Should this assignment be adopted in a classroom, *form* requirements such as page-length, format, and a *deadline* would be added.

And the student assignment does not only share the same elements with the professional example of an assignment; it also resembles it in character. After all, the student assignment, like the professional assignment before it, indeed does involve the writer in a larger context, makes him or her part of a conversation and "appoints a share." It transfers "property" if you wish by giving authority to student writers to use an assigned task to contribute their own point of view; and it comes, just as the professional call for papers, with clearly defined boundaries. These boundaries may loosen as students—just like other writers—move through their careers. A senior seminar is more likely to include an open research essay topic than a freshman composition course; just as a student taking a second class with a teacher—and having excelled in the first—is more likely to be able to renegotiate the boundaries of an assignment. The degree to which an assignment limits the writer's own freedom is part of the power dynamics inherent in any assignment. But even the apparently most limiting assignment is ultimately foremost an opportunity for a writer to grow and excel and a sign of some trust in the writer's powers as well as his or her potential. For example, the student assignment is skillful in implying that reading and writing are a way of becoming part of a larger interesting debate about the nature of history. It teaches students how to develop authority, and it does so by trusting them with a relevant task.

Assignments—like all pieces of writing—come in endless varieties according to author and occasion; they differ significantly also based on academic disciplines since disciplines imply different purposes and methods and conversations. But assignments do speak to us about how we can be part of these different contexts; they are a way of inviting us and drawing us in. Since they confer authority onto us—make us authors—it is worthwhile to read them closely: What is their motive, what is their purpose, and what exactly is the task they imply? And what form and timeline is prescribed?

Providing us with all these elements—whether we like them or not—assignments also do an enormous amount of work *for* us. They envision both the product and process of our efforts and hand that vision to us. That is one more reason writers are almost always grateful for assignments. Faced with the assignment, much of the writing of the essay is already done. Faced with the vision implied in the assignment, a pressing question for the assigned writer may not just be "How can I get it done in time?" but also: "How can I best contribute?" "Where am I most interested?" "What part do I want to and can I play in response to this appointment I am given?" and "How can I submit to the assignment *and* make it my own?"

RELATED WORDS

Academic Thinking 1	Discipline 57
Assumptions 19	Introductions 99
Brainstorming 30	Thesis 176
(see exercises, 1, 2, 5)	

EXERCISES

1. Compare two or more college assignments given in two different disciplines. How do motives, tasks, purposes and formal conventions differ? List what this comparison tells about the disciplines within which the assignments are given.

2. Analyze the relation between a student draft and the assignment. Where do you see the assignment reflected in the draft? Where do you not? Mark on the margin where the draft most fully responds to the assignment and where it strays from it. Then consider which elements of the assignment the writer is most responsive to and which ones he or she ignores or neglects. Based on your notes, suggest revisions that help the draft to use the assignment more effectively.

3. Write an essay assignment or a call for papers based on some of the class readings that contains the five elements mentioned: motive, purpose, task, form, and deadline. Discuss it in a group and revise it until all elements seem most appropriate for your class.

4. What do you think was the assignment to which one of the published writers that you read responded? Where do you see signs of the assignment in the essay? Based on your findings, formulate an assignment to which the essay could have responded.

Assumptions
The World Before the Text

Assumptions are both the foundation of a text and its shakiest elements. No matter how reasonable an argument, assumptions are necessary to its beginning and point to the limits of its own reason. Being those things that the author takes for granted and believes his audience takes for granted as well, they are, if you wish, the faith of all texts—something that will not be argued, investigated, or challenged because it is shared by writer and reader. All writers base their writing on some assumptions; there is always, a world before the text, which will not be reinvented—and, at times, not even revisited—and which is worth discovering on our own.

Assumptions have everything to do with human relations. If and when your readers share your assumptions, you share a foundation, a world. In that sense, assumptions are often ideological; they are moments of unquestioned faith in an agreed-upon normality and order of things—the way an essay should function, the way a healthy person acts, the way society progresses through technology, and so on. Most assumptions, for this very reason, are extraordinarily interesting parts of an essay—the parts that ask to remain untouched because everything else is based on them. Yet, it is most often worth our while to go to this buried zone. This is easy when we do not share the essay's assumptions; indeed, in that case, we feel their presence like looming mountains every minute and may resist the essay no matter how persuasively it unfolds based on those assumptions. It is hard when we do share them because they are often invisible. In that case, too, they are worth looking for since they reveal both the foundations of the essay *and* our own view of the world. So assumptions are anchors: They give us a home but they also tie us down. But when challenged they dislocate us—rob us of our home—and liberate us into a freedom that could be eye-opening even to the point of fear.

Irving Rouse's anthropological book, *The Tainos Rise and Decline of the People Who Greeted Columbus,* tries to reconstruct the history of the Tainos—those people, as the subtitle tells us, who greeted Columbus. Like all books, it presents an argument that is—for better or worse—defined by its assumptions. It begins its introduction in the following way:

> Columbus called the inhabitants of the Western hemisphere *Indians* because he mistakenly thought he had reached the islands on the eastern side of the Indian Ocean. He could not use the term *Native American,* which is preferred by today's "Indians," because he was unaware of the continents that now bear the name America. The so-called Indians

were divided into innumerable small ethnic groups, each with its own combination of linguistic, cultural, and biological traits. This book focuses upon one such group, the Tainos,
who greeted Columbus when he first landed in the West Indies. Their habitat and their
characteristics are discussed here, and they are differentiated from their neighbors.(1)

Rouse's introduction reveals several assumptions: He assumes that his audience
knows about Columbus. His questioning of the term *Indian* reveals that he is
cognizant of and sensitive to the term today's "Indians," (that is, Native Americans) prefer; yet, his way of speaking about Native Americans also seems to suggests that he does not imagine "them" as part of his audience even though he
explicitly states later that "my book is addressed to readers who are interested in
the Tainos'cultural history" (48). Rouse's book thus is an anthropologically researched account of "Indians" for non-Indians. His remark that Columbus
could not have given "Indians" the name Native Americans sounds almost
apologetic, as if he was defending Columbus against those who judge him by
today's standard. Indeed, Rouse assumes that his readers know that Columbus
has become an increasingly controversial figure and that his actions have been
judged harshly by today's standards. The title of his book, which describes the
Tainos as those people who "greeted" Columbus, reveals that he saw their role
as friendly and peaceful. And since Rouse devotes his book to the "rise and decline" of the Taino people, he further assumes that the Columbus's encounter
with them, or their encounter with him, led them first to rise and then to fall.
So the first paragraph reveals a world before the text: Rouse's role in an ongoing
debate about Columbus's accomplishments and atrocities, and his assumptions
about his audience's concerns about Columbus as well as their cultural identity.

The opening paragraph also lets us see less well-examined assumptions in
Rouse's argument. For example, Rouse tells the reader that today's "Indians"
prefer the term Native American. How, one might ask, does he know that?
And how does one know what today's "Indians" as a group believe? Contemporary Spokane writer Sherman Alexie, for example, prefers the term Indian
because he considers the term "Native American" a guilty white term for "Indians" (online). Rouse thus is perhaps too quick to assume that "Indians" prefer this term, and perhaps he is unaware of the fact that the term may indeed
encode his own white guilt—according to Alexie.

And Rouse himself clearly assumes, as does Alexie, that naming a group is
a political act; this assumption is made visible by Columbus's initial naming of
the Taino people, but it becomes also visible in Rouse's own argument. How
do we name and define groups? How do we differentiate the Tainos from their
neighbors? Rouse writes: "The so-called Indians were divided into innumerable small ethnic groups, each with its own combination of linguistic, cultural,
and biological traits. This book focuses upon one such group, the Tainos, who
greeted Columbus when he first landed in the West Indies. Their habitat and
their characteristics are discussed here, and they are differentiated from their
neighbors" (1). In this sentence, Rouse reveals the assumptions of his discipline,

another specialized world before the text: Ethnic groups are defined "by linguistic, cultural, and biological traits," and they are best described by their "habitat and characteristics." We can understand the underlying assumptions when we look a little more closely at these formulations. Rouse links linguistic, biological, and cultural traits, but are they necessarily connected? How does biology relate to culture and language? Rouse provides a glossary at the end of his book that allows us to ponder his assumptions. Under race we find the following entry:

> RACE AND BIOLOGY. Two sides of a coin, one consisting of a local population group and the other of the biological traits that define the group. *See also* People and culture; Speech-community and language.(183)

That race is biological and connected to speech and culture—rather than a political or economic concept, let's say—is an arguable claim, one that Rouse, steeped in the conventions of his discipline, is unable or unwilling to question. He assumes that it is so.

Similarly, Rouse assumes that to describe a culture means to describe "habitat and characteristics." Yet why is that so? This, too, is an arguable claim; indeed, it is a claim that many current anthropologists have debated. Why not listen to the Taino legends, for example, in finding out the truth of the people's history? Steeped in a scientific model of inquiry, Rouse needs to objectify the criteria for the description of a culture to artifacts, maps, biological evidence. Making this assumption explicit he explains to the reader how each discipline relies on different kinds of evidence:

> The study of human origins falls within the academic discipline of anthropology. It is done not only by ethnohistorians, whose results have just been summarized, but also by physical anthropologists . . . , archeologists, and linguists. These four groups of specialists have become organized into separate subdisciplines because they base their conclusions on different kinds of evidence, ethnohistorians on the chroniclers' descriptions, physical anthropologists on the Tainos' biological remains, archeologists on their cultural remains, and linguists on their language. Ethnologists, who study contemporary cultures and societies, cannot also participate because the Tainos are extinct.(26)

Rouse thus carefully explains the assumptions behind the description he is attempting and the kinds of evidence he is allowing. Understanding an ethnic group as defined by biological, cultural, and linguistic criteria, he will allow the evidence accepted by physical anthropologists (biological remains), archeologists (cultural remains), and linguists. He excludes ethnological date—that is, for example myth and stories by the Tainos about the Tainos—because he assumes that the Tainos are extinct.

Assumes? How can one question that? He is, after all, describing the rise and decline of the culture. More out of curiosity than suspicion, I* entered the

---

*The "I" here refers to Hildegard Hoeller

word *Tainos* as a keyword into an Internet search engine. To my utter surprise, I immediately found a Website that had written in huge letters: WE ARE NOT EXTINCT! Intrigued by this Website, I searched further and came in contact with Roberto Borrero, a Taino living in New York City and working as an educator for the Museum of Natural History. He as well as many Tainos clearly did not think that he was extinct. So why did Rouse—who had done almost fifty years of research on the Tainos and even met Roberto Borrero— assume that the Tainos were extinct? How could anyone assume such a thing in the face of a living Taino? In other words, Rouse's method—the kind of evidence he selected, and even the very argument of the book itself, that there was a "rise and decline" of the Taino—revealed itself to be an assumption, even a lie when one asked a Taino!

Rouse's method of perception and his description of the "rise and decline" of the Tainos provide answers to this riddle. For example, when Rouse distinguishes various groups of Tainos, his method of distinction and naming reveals important assumptions:

> Columbus was disappointed that the Tainos were less civilized than the east Asians he had expected to find. Nevertheless, Classic Taino culture appears to have been evolving toward full civilization. . . . Classic Taino culture has been termed Formative because it was on the verge of civilization (Rouse 1986: 148). By contrast, the Eastern and Western Tainos were on a somewhat lower level of cultural development, which Julian H. Steward (1947) has called Tropical Forest.(19)

Rouse here surprisingly shares several assumptions with Columbus: that he has the right to name, not as a conqueror but as a scientist; that the Tainos were not as "civilized" as the Spaniards; and that the Tainos could be distinguished based on levels of civilization. He implies that being more civilized rather than less is a good thing, making some Tainos "classic" (as a Shakespeare play) while others are still at a "lower level of cultural development."

So what then does it mean to be civilized and developed, one might ask? While Rouse does not define the term "civilization" in his glossary, his explanation reveals his assumptions about what it means to be civilized and how one becomes civilized:

> Its bearers possessed a good agricultural base and were organized into complex chiefdoms. If they had been allowed a few centuries of reprieve from Spanish rule they might well have bridged the gap across Guanahatabey territory into western Cuba and developed the kind of commercial linkage with the civilized peoples of Middle America that they had already established with the inhabitants of northern South America. This would have made it possible for them to acquire writing, statehood, and other elements of the mainland civilizations, as their fellow islanders, the British and the Japanese, had already done in Europe and Asia. (19)

Civilization then, if one wants to be very cynical about Rouse's assumptions, is something like the spitting image of Europe, which in turn is seen as the center (mainland) of the world and at the spearhead of history—other contemporary cultures miraculously lagging behind. Rouse assumes a model of social evolution in which cultures can be measured against a universal standard of civilization. To understand Rouse's method then, one must understand this fundamental assumption; but Rouse's method, scientific and objective as it may appear, then also shares some significant assumptions with Columbus and his sense of discovery and entitlement.

In that sense, the full meaning of Rouse's argument can only be understood if we discover his assumptions: assumptions about method, about evidence, about the extinction of the Tainos, and about what civilization means. Indeed, his final assumption remains unshaken by his depiction of the horrendous atrocities Columbus committed (150–61) and his depiction of the Tainos as essentially peaceful and self-sufficient people. He remains also unshaken in his belief that the Tainos are extinct, even though he has spoken to people such as Roberto Borrero, "persons claiming Taino ancestry"(161). Because Rouse believes the definition of a culture is determined by specific biological, cultural, and linguistic traits, the Tainos as the object of his study are indeed extinct. Assumptions are, in some cases, matters of life and death!

Challenging assumptions, one's own as well as those of others, is an integral part of writing and reading. Rouse's book is an admirable attempt to scientifically reconstruct the history of those people "who greeted Columbus." Without questioning assumptions, the book is nothing more than a pool of information: "The evidence that Jamaica, with an area only one-quarter greater than Puerto Rico's, was equally populous—indicates, as do several other points (discussed below), that the native Jamaicans were more advanced than the rest of the western Tainos"(7). But once we question the assumptions of the writer, the text transforms and allows us as readers to participate in its meaning: What appeared at first objective, scientific, and dry, now appears as a complex story of a writer trying to tell the "truth" about a people he considers dead. We can engage with the text when we can see what assumptions are defining that "truth" and whether we share them. It must have been interesting to see Borrero show up in Rouse's office—like a visitor from a world outside of Rouse's text—and, according to Borrero, the two men got along, both understanding that Rouse's argument needs to be understood in the context of its disciplinary assumptions. So, this example illustrates that arguments ultimately cannot be understood without revealing their assumptions. And that revealing assumptions is a move towards active and creative reading. The questions asked of Rouse can be asked of all readers: Who is the intended audience? What values, experience, beliefs does the writer assume he shares with his audience? Who is not included as an audience and what difference does that make? What meanings of key terms are assumed and what other meanings suppressed? What constitutes valid evidence for a writer in a particular context such as an academic discipline and what does not? Assumptions are crucial elements of writing, telling moments of silence; they are keys to the heart of the matter, windows into the writers' faiths, ambitions, and blindness. Discovering this world before the text opens paths for readers to participate in a text, to become explorers in their own right.

RELATED WORDS

Argument 9   Evidence 77
Assignment 14   Key Terms 106
Audience 25   Reading 132
Claims 38   Voice 187
Discipline 57

EXERCISES

1. What are some of the fundamental assumptions of one academic text you are reading? What does the writer expect you to know? What beliefs does he or she expect you to share? What kind of evidence is assumed to be valid? What kind of method is assumed? Do you feel included or excluded from the reading? How and why? Which one is the most interesting assumption to challenge in order to engage further with the reading?

2. In a student draft, identify the most important assumptions the writer makes. Are those assumptions shared by the assignment? As a reader of the paper, where has the writer correctly estimated what you already know and what you need explained? What beliefs does the writer expect you to share and are you comfortable with that assumption? After revealing these assumptions, discuss how they could be fruitfully challenged. Which assumptions should the writer rethink in order to develop and clarify his essay?

3. In small groups, list three assumptions underlying the class you are in. Which of those do you share? Which do you not share? How would you question them? And why are they foundational for the class? Have discussion ensue from here.

4. Following exercise 1, list three different assumptions underlying a course in a different discipline or with a radically different teaching style. What do these differences tell you about each discipline or each teacher's teaching style?

Audience
The Listener as the Essay's Other

A writer's imagined audience will inhabit every line of the finished work and will determine many of the choices made along the way. The intended audience becomes a subtle but palpable presence in every piece of writing; by listening hard, we can hear that audience breathing. However, readers' actual responses to a piece of writing depend largely on how accurately a particular reader resembles the audience a writer imagined or intended.

The example of what happens when a piece of writing is read by the *wrong* audience helps to dramatize the difference an intended audience can make in tone, style, vocabulary and content. Anthropologist Bronislaw Malinowski, who died in 1942, has been considered the founding father of modern ethnographic fieldwork. His methods of observing and recording the lives and culture of the native inhabitants of islands off the coast of New Guinea were painstakingly thorough and resulted in several published books and dozens of articles. Note the careful attentiveness to detail in his account of how the Trobriand people organized labor: "When a chief or headman, or man of wealth and influence summons his dependents or his relatives-in-law to work for him, the name *kabutu* is given to the proceedings. The owner has to give food to all those cooperating. A *kabutu* may be instituted for one bit of gardening, for example, a headman may invite his villagers to do his cutting for him, or his planting or his fencing . . ." ("Tribal Economics" 190). Malinowski's work was influential not only because of this kind of detailed research on other cultures and because of the level of trust he was able to establish with the inhabitants he was studying, but also because of the insights he offered on the professional role of the ethnographer. Therefore, when his diaries were published twenty-five years after his death, they caused an immediate uproar in scholarly circles. In sharp contrast to his professional persona, Malinowski revealed himself in his diaries to be haphazard, lazy, frequently interfering and rude to the subjects of his study, and largely preoccupied with the primary functions of his own body and with romantic longings for his best friend's wife: "I have lecherous thoughts . . . I think of E. R. M. when I indulge in lewd excesses of the imagination and adulterous lusts—what would be my feeling if she—?" (*A Diary* 132).

In his published writings we hear detailed accounts of the systems of trade and gift exchange through which the economic system of the islands functions; we get a sociological analysis of clan and kinship relations and closely observed data on the function of magic throughout the society. In the diaries, Malinowski notes some of these same facts, but we hear much more about his constant illnesses and his (probably related) obsession with noting the details of his food and drink, his "dirty thoughts"(223), his self-performed enemas (145, 159, for example) and his reading of "trashy novels" when he doesn't feel up to working (144). Worse yet, a comparison of the two suggests the most extreme kind of cultural intolerance lurking behind the mask of the professional anthropologist. For example, in the published writings, Malinowski comes out passionately against Western assumptions that the inhabitants of primitive societies are incapable of organized labor, arguing that such assumptions reveal the inability even of Western anthropologists to see beyond their own cultural blinders:

> This error is due to the same cause which lies at the bottom of all our misconceptions about people of different cultures. If you remove a man from his social milieu, you *ipso facto* deprive him of almost all his stimuli to moral steadfastness and economic efficiency and even of interest in life. If then you measure him by moral, legal, or economic standards, also essentially foreign to him, you cannot but obtain a caricature in your estimate. ("Tribal Economics" 186).

Yet, in the diaries, we hear him railing about those same native inhabitants in a way that reveals obvious cultural blindness and prejudice:

> Wednesday, 1/21/15. . . . Went to the village hoping to photograph a few stages of the *bara*. I handed out half-*sticks* of tobacco, then watched a few dances; then took pictures—but results very poor. Not enough light for snapshots; and they would not pose long enough for time exposures.—At moments I was furious at them, particularly because after I gave them their portions of tobacco they all went away. On the whole my feelings toward the natives are decidedly tending to "*Exterminate the brutes.*" (*A Diary* 69).

Notice the clues to the writer's intended audience apparent in each passage. The published passage speaks of "all *our* misconceptions about people of different cultures," which suggests that Malinowski is imagining a Western, English-speaking audience. His choice of vocabulary, "ipso facto," "stimuli to moral steadfastness," "obtain a caricature," implies that he intends this for a well-educated audience, though he does not really use the kind of specialized anthropological jargon here that might limit his audience to professionals in his own field. Further, the logical "if . . . then" structure built into his sentences indicates that he is writing for an academic audience, that he is using evidence from his case study to build a scholarly argument. In the diary entry, the vocabulary and sentence structure are clearly more informal and give the impression of jotted notes, while untranslated terms such as *bara* imply an assumed knowledge of the language; Malinowski does not feel the need to define *bara* because he (the intended audience) already knows what it is. Similarly, he knows that "exterminate the brutes" is a line from Joseph Conrad's novel *Heart of Darkness*, so he has no reason to provide a citation. More importantly, the fact that Malinowski articulated this racist and dehumanizing sentiment toward the people he was studying and living with seems to call into question the very foundations of tolerance and shared humanity on which his professional achievements were based.

Yet if we think of the differences between these two pieces in terms of an unintended audience rather than simply as a case of blatant and shameful hypocrisy or scholarly fraudulence, it is possible to see the diaries in a slightly new light. Although Malinowski's primary audience in the diaries is clearly himself, and even if he never imagined that the diaries might be published, he was very deliberate about leaving a careful record of his own stray thoughts and impulses for future readers. In this light, the diaries read overall as the careful record of personal checks and balances kept by a man who is all too aware of how skewed the perspective of a solitary alien observer can become. For example, he clearly documents his own innate boredom at having to listen to natives describe their intricate rites and rituals rather than trying to avoid facing this failure of anthropological interest: "Tuesday 25 . . . I felt fairly well, but sweated profusely. Dinner. Ride in a *dinghy* with Ginger and Gomera'u. The latter gave me valuable information about *bwaga'u* and *Ta'ukuripokapoka*—Violent aversion to listening to him; I simply rejected inwardly all the marvelous things he had to tell me. The main ethnographic difficulty is to overcome this. I drank claret." Here he identifies the challenge of his own "aversion" to listening because he hopes to overcome this flaw, just as he notes his own tendency when ill to avoid the stresses of data collection by reading novels.

The careful observations of his diet and medication correlated to his physical condition and even his careful account of his own lustful longings also suggest an innate caution about allowing illness or emotional excess to creep up on him unawares. After all, a researcher based so far from Western medical attention that he anxiously doses himself with quinine and arsenic when ill must also be aware of the need to remain psychologically stable in this cultural isolation. The diaries allow him the outlet for these moods and desires, and arguably that free expression in turn allows him to maintain a sense of balance and professionalism. The fact that these diaries were subsequently read by an audience that Malinowski perhaps never intended or imagined becomes a problem only when these essentially private records are mistakenly read in the same context as the published writing. As the current audience for those diaries, then, we must make a particular effort to listen through our own breathing for the presence of that original audience. We must imagine the writer freely choosing to record his most private thought or bodily function, openly exposing the most professionally damning irritation with his subject matter in the effort to preserve his health, his sanity, and his professionalism. Then we might see in the diaries Malinowski the anthropologist observing and recording Malinowski the man. From the hindsight allowed by the diaries, Malinowski may have learned a great deal about the ethnographer's role; perhaps his published work was so influential because he had faced up to the darker side of field work and was able to define ethnographic professionalism with a clear awareness of its risks and challenges. In this sense, the two kinds of writing were in no way hypocritical; each addressed a subject matter in a manner appropriate for its intended audience, and each allowed the other to contain its own truth. Or did they? Can the personal truth expressed in the diaries ever be fully reconciled with the professional persona constructed in the public writings?

This example portrays in extreme form how a writer constructs a professional persona with a particular audience in mind. Most writers experience a similarly split consciousness when thoughts that might spill out easily in a conversation, an e-mail, or a journal seem inappropriate or more difficult to express within the formal structures of an academic essay. To begin with, the heightened awareness of a potential audience of professional peers and critics can lead writers to don an overly elaborate mask: unnecessarily long sentences, thesaurus-inflated word choices, risk-avoiding theses, and an equally cautious use of evidence aimed at stifling all debate. Yet, even more than Malinowski, who seemed to preserve such a strict separation between these personal and professional forums, for most writers the thoughts generated in more open-ended forums like rough drafts, journals, experimental writing and brainstorming readily cross over to enrich their professional work. In fact, the crucial achievement for an academic writer—as with any writer—is to find a way to speak a truth within the confines supplied by the audience and by the rhetorical setting, to take a risk, to have something personal at stake. The awareness of a potentially critical audience, then, becomes part of the game, not so much restricting what the writer is able to say, but supplying a set of boundaries, a kind of decorum for how it should be expressed. In the end, an awareness of those listening readers helps a writer define what "risk" is in a particular setting; they become the imagined sounding board against which a position becomes controversial, against which a particular reading becomes daring; they supply the envisioned counterarguments against which a writer develops a stronger and more complex thesis. The listener becomes the defining "other" through and against which the essay forms its own identity.

As the Malinowski examples also show, this awareness of audience inhabits every sentence and every word on the page. Audience becomes the sum total of a series of choices the writer makes about tone, diction, sentence structure, about the level of explanation we include and the things we leave out. Just as Malinowski defines terms like *kabutu* in detail for one audience and leaves out unnecessary definitions for another, just as he explains his aversion to native inhabitants at length in one forum and translates those feelings into a brief and wise reflection on how to overcome such prejudices in another forum, just as he shifts from one sentence length and structure to another, one vocabulary to another, so every writer's decisions about audience can be deduced from the choices he or she makes. Cultivating a heightened awareness of audiences—both by analyzing the audience-related choices made by other writers and by considering our own audiences—results in a greater sense of flexibility and craft, an ability to pitch an idea to particular listeners, to explain something in a way they will understand. Thinking about audience allows for a consciousness of writerly choices and their effects in the real world of actual listeners.

RELATED WORDS

Academic Thinking 1	Discipline 57
Assumptions 19	Introductions 99
Counterargument 49	Voice 187

EXERCISES

1. In a group, collect several different pieces of writing clearly intended for different audiences (academic vs. personal writing, for example, writing intended for teens or children, for men or women, a particular age group or body type, a group with a particular shared interest like golfing or pediatric medicine, etc.). For each sample, list the clues that reveal the writer's intended audience: sentence structure, tone, vocabulary, level of explanation, and so on. Have each individual in your group choose one of the samples and write a brief description of the audience implied by it, working from the clues you have listed as evidence. Then name an audience or two for whom the piece is clearly *not* intended and would be inappropriate.

2. Choose a fairly complex term or concept from one of the course readings and write several short pieces explaining that concept to three or more of the following audiences in the described rhetorical situation. In each case, choose the vocabulary and the way of speaking that would most likely appeal to that audience: (1) a diary entry or note to yourself, (2) a letter or e-mail to a friend or relative outside the class, (3) someone in the class who has read the essay but is having trouble understanding it, (4) the teacher of the class, (5) a letter to the local journal or newspaper, (6) a letter to a national journal or newspaper, (7) a letter or e-mail to a correspondent in a foreign culture, (8) a letter or e-mail to an alien visitor to the planet

3. Write a short piece aimed at a specific audience. Do not name that audience directly but plant deliberate clues that suggest or imply it. Have the other members of your group guess the intended audience.

4. Create a parody piece with a clearly apparent double audience; that is, a piece seemingly addressed to one audience but which keeps slipping into a vocabulary or a way of speaking that is completely inappropriate for that audience.

5. Read another writer's draft noting places where the intended audience is implied (by word choices, sentence structure, assumptions the writer makes) and identifying choices that seem inappropriate for that audience.

Brainstorming
How the Other Half Thinks

Brainstorm: (1) a series of sudden, violent cerebral disturbances (2) a sudden inspiration, idea, or plan: humorous term. [Collqu.] *Webster's New Universal Unabridged Dictionary*

How can one storm one's own or someone else's brain and induce a "brainstorm"? And why would one want to induce such "violent cerebral disturbances"? In addition, why would the brain need to be "stormed" rather than "asked," for example? The term *brainstorming* contains interesting riddles about one's own relation to one's brain.

Brainstorming as a technique demands that we concentrate (alone or in groups) on a term or idea and begin to write down, jot down, or shout out, thoughts that the brain yields to us in such a storming. While brainstorms can be conducted in different ways, in most brainstorms the terms, images, and ideas are at first all accepted without order or censorship, and then later they may be sorted and developed. In other words, brainstorming as a technique and thought process relies on the idea that we have thoughts that need to be suddenly called up from some other half of our brain, somewhere beyond the place that our most conscious understanding of a topic can be found. In that sense, brainstorming implies an interesting critique of more traditional linear writing and more deliberate thinking. If one storms one's brain before writing, or if several brainstormers inspire each other in a communal brainstorm, the brainstormers believe that in that induced "cerebral disturbance" or chaos one gets access to thoughts and ideas not otherwise available; perhaps because they are less conscious or perhaps because we censor them in other thinking processes as irrelevant or inappropriate or simply mysterious and astonishing. We have long accepted Freud's idea of an unconscious, and brainstorming is a way to remind ourselves that we are larger than our conscious thoughts, certainly larger than our reasonable thoughts, and thus able to surprise ourselves. As a technique then, brainstorming is indeed a method to a "madness" that would be excluded by more reasonable and deliberate ways of thinking about a paper, an argument, or a topic. It implies that those modes of thinking bar us from some other parts of our brains that are valuable and deserve attention.

In both of our experiences as writers and particularly as collaborators on this book, brainstorming works; we have spent many brainstorming sessions in creating this book. "Thesis" one of us might say holding a blank piece of paper in her hands, and then ideas flowed: problems, emotions, anecdotes, definitions, and so on. Indeed, brainstorming can appear magical precisely because it creates abundance where there was scarcity (filling a frighteningly blank page with tons of terms and ideas); it opens up topics in ways that are hidden to us if we search more consciously and deliberately. Brainstorming is productive precisely because it is unstructured.

Businesses establish think tanks because they believe in the productivity of brainstorming. The book *Rules of Thumb for Research,* its title invoking a commonsensical approach to the subject, recommends brainstorming as a time-efficient way to "find a topic you care about." It reasons.

> Brainstorming is not a waste of time. Brainstorming needs unhurried time. Yet most students are in a hurry and want to get to the library, line up sources, and start writing. To them, brainstorming sounds like delay and unneccessary work. In fact, the opposite is true: Taking time now to brainstorm will save you much more time later because you will proceed with a clear sense of the project. You will go to the library with specific questions and ideas in mind. (Silverman 6)

So what appears inefficient is efficient the authors argue. But why? Because linearity—going to the library, *lining up* sources, and going to work—can lead in the wrong direction and close down ideas precisely when one needs to open up the various directions a topic might suggest. After all, we think in images, melodies, attitudes, passions, puzzles, questions, and not just in evidence and claims. Clarity, these authors rightly suggest, comes from allowing chaos and possibilities and openness that may appear to distract but that really are part of the process itself.

And those early ideas, images, puzzles, and emotions one gathers in a first brainstorming may also reveal to us how and why we care about a topic; they may resurface as the tone, attitude, or imagery of the essay that gets born out of a brainstorming's chaotic fragments. Brainstorming as a technique reminds us that—and works because—academic thinking, no matter how reasonable and ordered it will look in its final version, is creative, messy, and often deeply passionate and personal thinking. An intellectual feat, it may well start as a "violent cerebral disturbance."

RELATED WORDS

Free-Writing 87	Voice 187
Key Terms 106	Writer's Block 195
Revision 143	

EXERCISES

1. Faced with a writing assignment, conduct a group brainstorming on the assignment. Then diagnose the responses. What questions do

these responses raise? How many different interpretations of the assignment do they imply? What energies and attitudes does the assignment engender?

2.   In a group, have each individual conduct a silent written brainstorm on a particular topic or assignment. Then pass your note sheet to the next person and analyze your colleague's notes. What strikes you as characteristic of your peer's thinking? And how could those features be used effectively in an essay?

3.   In a group, look at a student draft. After each of you have read the draft, conduct a brief brainstorm about what thoughts and emotions the draft provoked in you. Analyze your findings to determine the strongest triggers in the essay and which parts of it interested a reader or several readers most. Then discuss possibilities for revision of the essay based on your findings.

4.   Brainstorm the multiple meanings of a key term by writing down all possible counterterms and synonyms. Use these new terms to consider various directions for an essay.

5.   Brainstorm by yourself on an assignment you have been given. Keep the notes from the brainstorm and use it again when revising a later draft. Either alone or in a group, consider how you might try to incorporate at least one of its fragments—be it a certain tone, image, term, or emotional response—in your final draft.

Citation
The Rolodex of the Academic World

Citations appear to be merely the personal address book of an academic essay, giving brief information for every source a writer has quoted or has taken ideas from or has referred to in some way. In spite of the fact that citations include the minimum of information necessary for a reader to track down that source—really just a full name and an address—every academic discipline has a slightly different code for identifying their sources. Sometimes those differences are ridiculously tiny, but to writers in the discipline each part of the code is fraught with meaning. Instead of,

Jacques Derrida
Spurs
301 S. Sunnymede
Berkeley, CA 90210

a literary critic will use the particular code of his discipline, MLA style,* to notify us that he got a quote or idea from Jacques Derrida's book, *Spurs*. He might write: Derrida asks, "What, after all, is handwriting?" (127). Once we have broken into the code, we know that the number 127 does not refer the number of times Derrida made this remark or to his home address but to the page number of some source in which this quote will appear. Flipping to the end of the essay, we will find the Rolodex itself, an alphabetical list of "Works Cited" that includes all the names and addresses of all the sources referred to in that paper. Under "Derrida" we will find an entry that tells us where to find that particular source: Derrida, Jacques. *Spurs: Nietzsche's Styles*. Chicago: U of Chicago P, 1978. Always in exactly the same order with exactly the same punctuation we are given the author's name (last name first), the title of book or article, the place where the book was published, the name of the publisher, and the date of publication. The italics used for the title of this source are a further code telling us that this is a book and not an article. This appears to be a peaceable and courteous way for a writer to notify readers about where to find these sources should they want to do a little more reading—well and good.

Analogously, if an historian uses a quote or an idea from, for example, a book on prostitution in mining communities, her code, Chicago style, would start with a footnote number appearing inconspicuously in the middle of the page. She might have written something like: Research shows that eighty percent of women living in mining towns during this year were prostitutes.[2] Nonsense! we might think—where does this research come from? Tracking that number to the bottom of the page we would find the name and address of the person responsible for that research:

---

[2]Marion S. Goldman, *Gold Diggers and Silver Miners: Prostitution and Social Life on the Comstock Lode* (Ann Arbor: Univ. of Michigan Press, 1981), 144.

Here we see almost exactly the same information that would appear in the literary critic's MLA-style Rolodex put together with slightly different punctuation. In addition to this footnoted information, the historian would probably include her full Rolodex of names in a bibliography at the end of the essay. The bibliography would include not only the works she actually cited and

---

*For more information about breaking into the codes of MLA and APA style, turn to the "Works Cited" entry at the end of this book.

referred to in the article but also any works that she read or consulted as background material for the project.

Looking back through our historian's footnotes, we might also see just below the Goldman citation:

> ³Ibid., 136.
> ⁴Ibid., 130.

This code means the historian has continued to use ideas or quotes from Goldman's book two more times; "ibid." saves her the trouble of giving the same name and address every time. As long as her readers have the key to the code, this seems again like a sensible way to proceed.

Since every discipline has its code, that code tells us something about that discipline. Historians care enormously about their sources—after all, those sources are the key to documenting the past—so they want their citations right on the page. Literary critics value the direct interaction with the quote on the page, so they are usually content to list their sources for those quotations at the end of a paper. Scientists care more about the publication dates of their sources—after all, a study done in 1995 might easily supercede the findings of a study done in 1994—so their code (APA Style) gives the author's name and the date of the publication right in the body of the paper. Using that code, a scientist might say: The cloning mechanism of the RD4 molecule has proven to be the source of the problem (Ratvin, 2002).

All this suggests that the world of academic citation is a peaceful and orderly place where writers in every discipline have the proper codes for giving full, frank, and courteous information about the sources they have used. However, look just below the surface of this seemingly pleasant and mutually beneficial social contract, and the underbelly of the citation system is revealed: Scholarship is accepted or rejected on the basis of citations; a complex network of dominance and subordination is established through citations; reputations are made or sometimes left in ruins. The codes that appear to be just the nit-picking and arbitrary fussiness of "scholar squirrels," as Gore Vidal called us, allow readers to break open the entire system of interwoven ideas, conversations, schools of thought, and hierarchies of power, everything right down to the intellectual, economic, and political foundations on which academic writing is based.

To begin with the well-known but little remarked-upon core of the matter, citation systems are the copyright law of academic publishing; to publish is to establish a patent on the ideas and the particular arrangement of words in a piece. Jacques Derrida has a patent on the ideas and arrangements of words in his book *Spurs*, except for the ideas and words that were already patented by Nietzsche whom Derrida must cite. I,* along with my co-writer, have a patent on the ideas and arrangement of words in this entry except for those I cite from Derrida, Goldman, and so on. As this suggests, citations are a constant legalistic acknowl-

---

*"I" refers to Rebecca Brittenham in this case.

edgment of these patent laws, all the more strenuous because everyone involved knows how tenuous are the claims any individual can make on the ownership of knowledge, on the origination of ideas, or on the possession of a particular arrangement of words.

In many cases, these claims to ownership over the patent rights become unclear. To take an extreme example, in *Spurs*, Derrida incorporates a twenty-page analysis of one sentence found in Nietzsche's unpublished papers: "I have forgotten my umbrella." After twenty pages of analysis, who really ends up owning that sentence? Derrida himself delights in adding to this confusion:

> What if Nietzsche himself meant to say nothing, or a [sic] least not much of anything, or anything whatever? Then again, what if Nietzsche was only pretending to say something? In fact, it is even possible that it is not Nietzsche's sentence, and this notwithstanding any confident certainty that it is indeed written in his hand. What, after all, is handwriting? Is one obliged, merely because something is written in one's hand, to assume, or thus to sign it? Does one assume even one's own signature? . . . (127).

And with the factories of print erasing even the questionable evidence of hand-writing, we have little *aside* from the citation system to ensure that a particular piece of writing will be attributed to the individual who produced it. Violations of these patent laws—failing to cite one's sources—are therefore the most primal criminal acts one can commit in academia precisely because this fragile network of laws is the only thing standing between identifiable authorship and a nameless chaos of words and ideas. If an accepted, even revered scholar, is discovered to have plagiarized or falsified sources, he or she is subject to legal penalties—retraction and destruction of his or her published work, even lawsuits if actual money is involved. More crucially, that writer's reputation and career are destroyed; he or she is branded as a known traitor to a communal honor code.

Although most writers scrupulously abide by these patent laws, deciding when it is necessary to cite a source can become a grey area. When one directly quotes another writer, as I have quoted Derrida above, the need for a citation is clear. Derrida (and Nietzsche) and I are having an open interchange on the page; our distinctive ownership of particular ideas and arrangements of words is clearly demarcated with quotation marks. But what if I am merely drawing on Derrida's ideas without bringing in a direct quote? What if I vaguely paraphrase his work by saying that even a person's handwriting cannot really establish his or her ownership over a sentence? In effect, I have stolen Derrida's idea—do I need to cite him? The answer is probably yes, in this case. If I do refer directly to Derrida and quote just one of his key terms, the word "signature," I would probably use quote marks and cite him even though "signature" is a word used by many other writers in many other contexts. Yet, if I wrote an entire para-graph about Derrida's exploration of the concept of "signature," would I give the same citation fifteen times? That seems silly, so no, I would cite him the first time and then continue to just use quotation marks to remind the reader that I am using the word "signature" in the specialized sense that Derrida gives it.

To take this a step further, what if I am using this idea of handwriting in a completely different context; what if I write: Due to the growing technological expertise that goes into most forgeries, even a person's handwriting cannot fully establish his or her ownership of funds in an account. This seems clearly to have moved from the realm of Derrida's ideas into my own realm of ownership, yet it does contain the same paraphrase, which is now no longer a paraphrase of Derrida but a different idea functioning differently in a new context. Probably, in this case, I would not have a citation. But what if I had actually learned that information about the growing technological expertise of forgerers from a colleague at the office, who had mentioned it to me in conversation. Must I cite him? Yes, I really should. Or, to give another example, what if I were to write, "I have just returned from the post office to realize that I have forgotten my umbrella"? Here I have used precisely the same arrangement of words used originally by Nietzsche and then quoted by Derrida but in a completely new context—do they now belong to me? They probably do. Then what if I write, "As we all know, you can't judge a book by its cover." Here I know I am quoting hundreds of thousands of people who may have written that phrase or thought that thought, but I have no idea who originated or patented it. Clearly, I can't cite this one even if I wanted to. In each of these cases, as a writer, I make the best, the most honest (and yes, the most commonsensical) judgment I can. The code may be complex, but the goal is fairly simple: Identify for readers every idea, every word or arrangement of words that, to the best of my knowledge comes from another source. The letter of that law may become extremely muddy, but the spirit of it is reassuringly clear (and the entry on "Plagiarism" in this book may help to make it even clearer).

The academic community is probably the only place where the ownership of words and ideas is this important because words and ideas are all we have. They are the basis of our trade and, whether used in teaching or in writing, our only goods. In this sense, the subtleties of the citation codes exist to verify the quality of our scholarship and authenticate the acceptance of new scholars into the academic community. Glancing through the footnotes of an article without having read a word, historians can determine whether the writer worked in the appropriate archives and how thoroughly he or she did the research; they can tell whether the article is dealing only with primary documents and has succeeded or failed to take into account the secondary material, the work other historians have done on those documents; they can determine in fact whether or not to take the article seriously, whether or not to bother reading it at all. A literary scholar's citations can reveal the painful struggle to use a source without being overwhelmed by it, they can document a responsible understanding and analysis of a source, and they can testify to a reckless appropriation of a source to suit the writer's own purposes (see our entry on "Footnotes," for example).

Just when a reader might lose patience with all this scuffling and scrambling and get ready to dismiss it as petty nonsense, the deeper implications of the citation system become apparent. The hierarchies of disciplinary power and knowledge represented by citations can privilege one scholar over others and they can privilege some kinds of knowledge, some methods, some conclusions over others. This might even be a life or death matter. Bruno Latour and Steve Woolgar's *Laboratory Life: The Social Construction of Scientific Facts* argues that the system of citation makes possible some kinds of scientific research and completely excludes other avenues of study, in effect determining which scientific knowledge is accepted as "fact" and which never achieves that status. For example, some areas of cancer or AIDs research have been privileged over others; the study of a certain disease gains more momentum if a celebrity victim of the disease helps to mobilize public attention, while the study of other diseases can be relegated to the back burner; we hear about battles between two different teams studying the human genome project because each team knows full well that the power and additional funding accompanying their findings may outweigh the value of shared information. In this sense, citations can determine what is known in the world and how we know it, who lives and who dies, who is remembered for all time and who disappears into the infinity of the forgotten past.

RELATED WORDS

Discipline 57	Research 137
Evidence 77	Summary 159
Footnotes 81	Synthesis 172
Plagiarism 120	Works Cited 198
Quotation 130	

EXERCISES

1. List all the works from this entry that would need to be included in a "Works Cited" page. Test your results by checking them against the footnote below.*

2. Choose a book or article that you like and write a paragraph in which you (1) paraphrase the writer, (2) directly quote the writer, and (3) refer to the writer without using a quote. Decide where you do and do not need to cite, and then use the models provided by the

---

*I include here the Rolodex of works that I would need to cite for this entry. For more information on using MLA or APA style, please turn to our "Works Cited" pages at the end of this book.

WORKS CITED

Derrida, Jacques. *Spurs: Nietzsche's Styles*. Chicago: U of Chicago P, 1978.

Goldman, Marion S. *Gold Diggers and Silver Miners: Prostitution and Social Life on the Comstock Lode*. Ann Arbor: U of Michigan P, 1981.

Latour, Bruno and Steve Woolgar. *Laboratory Life: The Social Construction of Scientific Facts*. Beverly Hills: Sage Publications, 1979.

Vidal, Gore. Reply to letter of David Nielsen. *New York Review of Books* 17 December 1981: 8 pars. 7 July 2002 <http://www.nybooks.com/articles/6787>.

"Works Cited" entry at the end of this book to create a complete citation for this book or article.

3. In a group, look through the citations included in some of your course readings. For each one, identify which style guide the writer used and note his or her disciplinary background. Have each member of the group choose a different citation in the body of a text and track that citation back through the footnotes, the "Works Cited" list, and/or the Bibliography of that text. Copy the full citation out and identify each part of the code: Is this a book, a journal article, a letter, an online posting or what? Where is the author's name? What does the symbol "4.1" signify? What does each date refer to?

4. In a group, collect a number of books, articles and online materials. Using the "Works Cited" pages at the end of this book as your guide, create an MLA-style Rolodex of those sources. Then translate that Rolodex into APA or Chicago style.

Claims
Territorial Defense or Promise of Exploration?

The impulse of the essay is toward westward expansion into a new frontier. The writer heads into the new territory of a subject by staking out a series of claims and earns the right to ownership by occupying and developing each of those claims. The claim made toward the beginning of each paragraph becomes that first exploratory move, setting up a white surveyor's flag, establishing a new territory to settle. The writer then brings evidence to bear, working the claim in order to "improve" it, to establish a position there and defend the claim against all potential counterclaimants. Gradually that claim is supported, integrated into the community of other settlers, and the territory becomes settled and civilized. Then the writer can gather evidence to move on to a fresh claim a step further into the frontier and begin working the land in order to establish a position. Often one can measure the distance of these claims as the distance of a paragraph, its topic sentence establishing that white flag and its body marshaling the evidence to support and mobilize further exploration. The central claim of the essay, its thesis, becomes the sum of those paragraphs, and marks the entire territory that the essay plans to stake out, colonize, and defend.

One example of a well-known claim in academic writing is historian Frederick Jackson Turner's "frontier thesis." In 1893, Turner wrote an article in which he staked out and defended the claim that the American frontier was gone—used up. He argued that the loss of the frontier potentially meant the loss of two of the key principles of the American national character: independence and the creative democratic initiative that had been needed to establish functioning human communities in the wilderness (Milner 4). Turner's claim about the connection between the end of expansion into wilderness and the loss of these core American principles continued to inspire historians into the twentieth century; some analyzed it, some attacked it and staked out opposing claims, and some extended it by, for example, making the related claim that outer space had replaced the Western frontier (and the sense of identity) Americans had lost. As this suggests, in academic writing, one claim leads to another; scholars build from and against each other's claims.

The problem with using this language of frontier colonization and defense to describe the academic essay—aside from its stereotypically macho, gunfight-at-the-OK Corral flavor—is exactly the problem pinpointed by Turner. Especially for beginning scholars, academia appears to contain no wilderness frontiers; it is already colonized by overcivilized settlers who appear judgmental of new claims and unwilling to budge from their positions. (In fact, even the American frontier settlers were staking claims that actively ignored the existence or disregarded the rights of the Native Americans or of other colonizing groups who preceded them (Milner 198)). As a newcomer to this territory, how intimidating it might be to take on this colonizing mantle in order to begin a paragraph; how unappealing the task of gathering up the authority to stake a claim on some precolonized territory; how hard it might seem to establish and maintain one's sense of identity. The difficulty of the task imagined in this way can result in the writer positioning herself or himself only as a timid questioner or as a simple fact-stater who avoids making claims at all cost. Or it can result in the desperate claimant who hurls himself or herself headlong into this new frontier, ignoring scholars who have already written on the subject and staking out a huge territory that can never be defended in the space of an essay. To achieve a balance between these two approaches, then, it may help to think of the essay (and the frontier) less in terms of the gun-toting territorialism of movie westerns and more in terms of a Lewis-and-Clark-style expedition into the unknown.

This sense of the essay as a journey of exploration and inquiry helps to offset the colonizing mind-set. The writer is not just staking out a particular terrain but is also trying to discover what is there, to ask about the previous occupants and to learn from them. The explorer is less concerned with setting a marker in the landscape than with observing it, and it is the explorer more than the landscape who changes, becomes transformed by the journey. In this spirit, the claim becomes a promise the writer makes to attract others to accompany him or her on the journey. It is a persuasive statement aimed not at having the last word on a subject but at gathering the interest and engagement of readers. Once the initial claim has opened a door, attracted some potential interest, the rest of the paragraph works to fulfill that promise. Rather than only using evidence to defend claims from imagined attacks, the writer learns from the evidence and helps the reader discover what it has to teach. A claim is less the assertion of the writer's preexisting authority, a carefully fortressed and defensible position, and more of a risk-taking gesture that says, "Come with me, reader, this is an interesting and valuable direction to take."

An essay by historian William Cronon, "The Trouble with Wilderness," offers a useful example of the claim in all its guises: the staking out of terrain, the risk-taking gesture, and the invitation to explore and learn. Cronon's thesis (his central claim) is that the American wilderness is a purely invented and nostalgic concept, one that we use to deny the truth of the past and one that will continue to impede effective environmental policies until we recognize it as an illusion (69, 79). In itself, this seems to stake out a huge terrain since Cronon is clearly seeking to change our entire understanding of the term *wilderness*. It also seems fairly territorial since it is stepping into a landscape already heavily colonized by environmentalists, nature writers, politicians, and other historians who have all written about this topic. In both those ways, it is clearly a risk-taking gesture. Yet as Cronon sets out to support his central claim, he uses a series of smaller, more exploratory claims to further explain and develop the area he has staked out. For example, through several paragraphs he explores the link between wilderness and American identity expounded by Frederick Jackson Turner and other writers of past decades in order to make the following claim: "In just this way, wilderness came to embody the national frontier myth, standing for the wild freedom of America's past and seeming to represent a highly attractive natural alternative to the ugly artificiality of modern civilization" (78). This claim is smaller, more directly based on sources, and invites the reader to learn more about the concept of wilderness. Using these smaller claims, Cronon explores and builds on the perspectives offered by all the other writers who have staked out this subject. Step by step, he uses them to help demonstrate how "wilderness" has gradually become the antithesis of human civilizations, leading us to value "pristine" "uninhabited" nature while overlooking environmental beauty (and problems) closer to home. Whether or not we ever agree with any of his claims, the essay teaches us to think about the concept of "wilderness" in new and interesting ways and to consider current environmental policies within a larger historical perspective—to see the world around us from a slightly different slant. For this reason alone, the invitations held out by his claims were worth following.

As the Cronon example suggests, a writer may exaggerate a claim to get attention but for the most part tries to achieve some balance between the size of a claim and the evidence available to support and develop that claim. A gigantic claim that attempts to stake out the entire frontier at one gasp—"Since the beginning of time, humanity has struggled to define its relationship to nature"—might raise some polite nods of agreement, but few readers would really want the bother of a journey through such a huge and loosely established terrain. Similarly, a tightly focused claim for which there is little evidence—"Environmentalists are purposefully damaging the wilderness"—would attract few followers. Each claim tries to make a promise that the writer can reasonably fulfill in the space of a paragraph or an essay. Each claim invites the reader to take a small step into a marvelously populated frontier.

RELATED WORDS

Academic Thinking 1	Introductions 94
Argument 9	Paragraphs 114
Counterargument 49	Research 137
Discipline 57	Thesis 176
Evidence 77	Titles 180

EXERCISES

1. Identify several claims made by different writers in academic essays. Then identify five or more statements that don't appear to claim anything—statements of fact. In each case, discuss the potential controversy, the kind of debate, the need for further evidence that makes a claim different from a simple statement of fact. What are some of the methods you used to differentiate between claims and facts, and what are the grey areas—when do factual statements verge on being claims and vice versa?

2. As a group project, identify the central claim—the thesis—of three assigned essays. Create a list of techniques you might use to measure the size of each claim: How much territory has each writer staked out for him or herself? How controversial is that territory in relation to the evidence? What makes a claim too big or too small? Then, individually, write a paragraph describing the size of one writer's claims in comparison to the evidence. Write a second paragraph measuring the size of a particular claim in your own paper.

3. Using the techniques developed in exercise 2, write a paragraph about your own or another writer's draft in which you compare the size of the claims made to the amount of evidence provided. In what places could the draft use additional evidences, riskier or less risky claims?

4. Individually or in a group, choose a claim from an essay and list all the arguments you can think of to attack that claim and all the

arguments you can think of to support and defend it. Identify evidence from the essay and from your own knowledge and experience that would help to establish that claim and attract others to accept it.

5. Identify a central claim in a student essay. Then re-write the claim several times, changing its size and scope each time. Consider which of the re-written versions best fits the available evidence. Could the writer expand his or her claim by providing more evidence or by exploring in more detail the evidence he or she has provided?

Conclusions
The Horror of Ending

Alfred Hitchcock's 1963 film *The Birds* was the first Hollywood film to forgo the words "The End" on the final screen. Instead, a horror movie involving vicious and fatal attacks on humans by the ordinary birds that populate our everyday landscapes, ends with an ominous gathering of birds intently watching the protagonists' desperate attempt to flee. By refusing his viewers the reassuring closure of "The End," refusing to mark the place where horror fiction gives way to comforting reality, the filmmaker leaves us to make our way home still in the grip of that eerie dread. We find ourselves casting uneasy glances at hitherto unnoticed birds perched on the treetops or telephone poles outside our windows, so that part of the film's power, the final tribute to the filmmaker's success, is our transformed view of a once innocuous suburban domestic landscape.

The conclusions to most academic essays similarly attempt to spread the horror of unease. By leaving off the comfortable closure of narrative, refusing to wrap up all the loose ends and resolve all potential contradictions, academic writing deliberately tries to establish its power by transforming the reader's view of reality (however minutely) so that even a reader who violently rejects the essay's conclusions will never quite see that subject matter in the same way again. Further, academic writing attempts to provoke a response; each essay imagines itself in a complex network of essays that have come before and will come after. Each essayist wants to offer the last word on the subject, to carve out a claim to one small piece of intellectual territory, yet knows that the real measure of that essay's success would be—not the end

of discussion on that subject—but the continuous return of readers to question, challenge, cite, reuse that essay, to be unable to shake or argue it out of
their system.

On the one hand, in creating a concluding paragraph, then, the academic
writer seems to be in a tight spot. He or she must signal the end of this particular train of thought without calling a halt to the larger progression of thought
that the essay might inspire and without disturbing its potentially transformative effect. The neat, pat ending that resolves all potential conflict might also
stop the essay dead, while simply leaving the threads of the essay hanging in
midair will leave readers wondering what has been accomplished. In this sense,
conclusions pose a real problem. On the other hand, concluding paragraphs are
the most liberating places the writer has within the entire essay form. After all,
the essay itself is written, the evidence has been presented, there is no further
burden of proof. In fact the concluding paragraph is a moment of freedom
earned by the essay; the writer can wind the drama down, speculate about further implications, or twist the threads of the essay into one final image or
metaphor—birds ominously gathering on a telephone pole.

A moment of freedom? But what about the rules? The standard advice on
concluding the traditional college paper usually includes the following:

1. Restate your thesis, emphasizing the development that has taken place
    since your initial statement of the thesis on page 1.
2. Include your own perspective, response, impression of the subject matter.
3. Indicate the significance of your findings.

Or, to describe that advice in another way, in a conclusion the writer must
think about answering two questions for the reader: (a) What have I learned
from reading this paper? and (b) Why does it matter?

Given this play of possibilities, it is useful to examine how professional
writers occupy this "moment of liberation," by obeying or ignoring the rules,
making use of the conventions to serve their own purposes. Take for example
this paragraph by John Berger concluding an essay called "Ways of Seeing" in
which he uses images from art history to talk about how our cultural assumptions about art and history become mystified, prevent us from really discovering what is there:

> The art of the past no longer exists as it once did. Its authority is lost. In its place there
> is a language of images. What matters now is who uses that language for what purpose.
> This touches upon questions of copyright for reproduction, the ownership of art presses
> and publishers, the total policy of public art galleries and museums. As usually presented,
> these are narrow professional matters. One of the aims of this essay has been to show
> that what is really at stake is much larger. A people or a class which is cut off from its
> own past is far less free to choose and to act as a people or class than one that has been
> able to situate itself in history. This is why—and this is the only reason why—the entire
> art of the past has now become a political issue. (127)

Here Berger really obeys rules 1 and 3 by giving a developed restatement of his thesis as he argues for its further significance. He leaves his readers with a nugget of certainty about what they have learned from the essay and why it matters. He is not forced to give additional evidence; he can indicate problems of copyright and ownership without slowing down to explain or prove anything. Instead, he gathers the power of the paragraph and of the essay and rolls it toward those final two sentences—art of the past matters, this essay *matters*, because entire classes of people are being cut off from their past, being denied their freedom to choose a future. Berger is thus using the conventions, going by the rules, but is also taking full advantage of rule 2 and of the liberation from evidence and proof to sound out the warning bell, to lend passion and authority to his central claim. At the same time, he leaves us with that final, infinitely debatable and thought-provoking claim: "This is why—and this is the only reason why—the entire art of the past has now become a political issue." Like the movie audience who will never look at birds in quite the same way again, Berger's audience leaves the theater of his essay with that line resounding eerily in their heads. Is this the *only* reason why art has become political? Is the *entire* art of the past implicated? If this claim is true, what must be done now? Berger's conclusion, particularly that final claim, seems to call on its readers for further reflection, and probably for a rereading—not just of the essay, but of the art of our past and our relation to it.

RELATED WORDS

Academic Thinking 1	Paragraphs 114
Argument 9	Structure 149
Claims 38	Thesis 176
Introductions 99	Voice 187

EXERCISES

1. In a small group, read the concluding paragraphs from several academic essays and list the strategies each writer uses to end his or her essay. Discuss the effectiveness of the various strategies on your list and present them to the class, using quotes from the essays to demonstrate the strategy.

2. Choose an effective concluding paragraph and analyze the extent to which the writer follows the three rules described in this entry: Does he or she restate a thesis, build in perspective, show the significance of the paper's findings? What other things does the writer do in this conclusion? Consider the classic questions: (a) What does the writer want me to have learned from reading this essay? (b) Why does it matter?

3. Use the list of strategies you created in exercise 1 to write three completely different concluding paragraphs for your own essay or

someone else's. In each version, make an exaggerated use of one or two of those strategies.

4. Read *only* the concluding paragraph of an essay you have never read before. On the basis of that conclusion write a paragraph or make a list speculating what that essay will be about and what it will try to accomplish (its thesis and its purpose).

Coordination and Subordination
The Rule of the Sentence

When a prisoner thinks about his sentence, grammar is not the first thing on his mind. He thinks of that moment when the judge determined the course of his life for years, perhaps even forever. Once the sentence is pronounced, it is the single script of the prisoner's life; one might say that the sentence reduces the prisoner's life to a single concept or idea. Everything else he might want to do from here—go to work, fall in love, watch a baseball game—has to be coordinated with or subordinated to the sentence, accommodated within the confines of that sentence. If whatever else he wants to do does not stand in conflict to the sentence and appears of equal and independent importance, he might coordinate such an activity (for example thinking, working out, praying or reading). In most cases, though, he will probably find that it is very hard to think of a second fact about his life that is equal to his first: namely that he is sentenced to being incarcerated.

Sentences—whether grammatical or judiciary—have a unity, a pretty strict singularity; they are, by definition, expressing a single idea. And to some writers the sentence does seem to be a form of prison, with oppressive rules and regulations. Transgressions such as comma splices or run-ons, which violate the rule of the sentence, are noted by the "correction officers" as incorrect: insufficient coordination and subordination is the charge. But while the sentence is single-minded, it is not necessarily imprisoning; knowing its rule, one can play and express oneself, even play with it. Then, the sentence becomes more like the four-beat unit in a musical score or a one-family home: syncopation and guests are welcome respectively.

So, the rule of the sentence is that it contain one idea—conceptually—and that it consist fundamentally of one main clause—grammatically. It needs to have the minimum of a subject and a main verb fitted to the subject to express such a conceptual and grammatical idea: "Mr. Miller was sentenced to life in prison." This sentence—in both senses of the word—is the sentence's main idea, its main clause. Now let's assume that Mr. Miller also prays every day. How can he and we coordinate this activity with his prison sentence? We need, the rule of the sentence tells us, to signal such a coordination—to let our reader know that indeed we are coordinating the main clause of the sentence with a second one. Our choices for coordination are the linking words (coordinating conjunctions) that define a relation between the main fact in Mr. Miller's life (his prison sentence) and a second fact (his daily prayer). Those conjunctions are *and, but, yet, so, for.* The words are preceded by a comma, so as to show us that one clause has ended and another one is now linked to it. Now we can play within the rule of the sentence, piecing the two clauses together as if they were colored blocks:

1. Mr. Miller was sentenced to life in prison, and Mr. Miller prays every day.
2. Mr. Miller was sentenced to life in prison, but Mr. Miller prays every day.
3. Mr. Miller was sentenced to life in prison, yet Mr. Miller prays every day.
4. Mr. Miller was sentenced to life in prison, so Mr. Miller prays every day.
5. Mr. Miller was sentenced to life in prison, for Mr. Miller prays every day.

In each case a different story emerges of the relation between the two coordinated clauses and facts (Miller's prison sentence and his daily prayer). In case 1, we simply know that he does both. In case 2, we see that the two actions stay in contrast to each other, as if Miller is persistent in his faith in God despite the fact that he is in prison. Case 3 creates the same contrast, but it could also suggest that in spite of the restrictive surrounding and/or counter-influence of other inmates, Miller still prays. Case 4 sees the prayer as a consequence of Miller's sentence: Is he trying to persuade God to deliver him? Or does he pray out of remorse and inspired by his punishment? Case 5 tells the opposite story: I guess, Miller wanted to be in prison, and his prayers worked; or perhaps, he lives in a culture where prayer lands you in prison. The coordinating conjunction thus allows us to tell a small story in a sentence; it creates a relationship between the two distinct ideas, just as, one assumes, Miller himself would when faced with the overwhelming main idea that he is in prison for life.

So, when we neglect to use a comma before the coordinating conjunction (Mr. Miller was sentenced to life in prison but Mr. Miller prays every day), we are charged with a run-on because we have not sufficiently protected one sentence from another distinct idea. And when we leave out a coordinating conjunction (Mr. Miller was sentenced to life in prison,

Mr. Miller prays every day.), the "correction officer" charges us with a comma splice. In light of our examples, the charge actually seems rather understandable: The officer wants a story that brings the two clauses into a meaningful relation to each other. Leaving out the coordination leaves us with unanswerable and yet essential questions: Does Miller thank God that he is in prison or does he pray to God to be delivered from it? Does he pray despite or because he is in prison? Each case would make for a very different Miller and a very different God. No wonder an inquiring mind wants to know. A comma splice leaves too much of the writing, the story, to the reader. So, the rule of the sentence demands that we keep the two main ideas distinct (through the comma) and that we coordinate them through a conjunction.

What if one main clause is very closely linked to another in content, almost a repetition, illustration, or exemplification of the other? In that case, the semi-colon coordinates the two main clauses.

Mr. Miller is sentenced to prison for life; he prays every day.

Using a semicolon here makes the two sentences intimately connected; we, as readers, expect the second sentence to be an explanation of the first. Thus, the semicolon here would only make sense if Miller's sentence takes place in a culture where praying is an incarcerable offense. It also assumes that we, as readers, can make this connection ourselves. The semi-colon, or half-colon, indicates that two main clauses almost contain each other and thus do not need a more explicit link like a coordinating conjunction.

Coordination makes a story out of two independent ideas and clauses; subordination makes one idea dependent on the other. It knits a story so tightly that one of the clauses cannot stand without the other; it becomes subordinated to it. For that purpose, for telling the story of dependence rather than meaningful coexistence, grammar offers subordinating conjunctions. Like different formulas for genre fictions, these subordinating conjunctions tell us of the different dependencies: temporal (*after, before, while, once, since, until, when*), causal (*as, because, since*), consequential (*in order that, so that, that*), conditional (*if, unless*) contrasting (*even though, although, though, whereas*) local (*where*) preferential (*rather than, whether*). Added to our colored block set are many more colors and blocks that lean rather than stand. So now we can build different contraptions:

Although Mr. Miller prayed every day, he was in prison.
Although Mr. Miller was in prison, he prayed every day.
After Mr. Miller was sentenced to life in prison, he began to pray every day.
While Mr. Miller was in prison, he prayed every day.
Mr. Miller would rather pray everyday than be in prison.
And so on, and so on, and so on.

We have now an almost innumerable amount of stories to tell about Mr. Miller's two facts of life. Once one idea can be subordinated to another, the stories multiply. Subordinating conjunctions thus tell stories of intricate, unsolvable connections—just as in life, in grammar there are more opportunities for subordination than coordination. And in prison, that's even truer than anywhere else.

RELATED WORDS

Dash 53   Structure 149
Grammar 90   Subject-Verb 154
Parallelism 118   Transitions 183
Punctuation 126

EXERCISES

1. Choose a sentence in an academic essay (preferably one that seems important to the essay's argument) that includes at least one coordination or subordination. The re-write and re-read the sentence using other alternatives for the coordination or subordination. After doing so, write about the significance of the coordination or subordination the author chose.

2. Identify a comma splice in your writing and write down three different coordination possibilities for the sentence. Then rewrite the sentence again three times, subordinating one idea to the other in different ways. Choose the sentence for your final draft that comes closest to the story you want to tell.

3. Compare a paragraph of a published academic essay with a paragraph in your own writing. Count how many times each writer coordinates and subordinates; then rewrite each paragraph—the one containing less subordination and coordination into having substantially more of both, and the one having more into having substantially less. What is the effect in each case?

4. In an academic essay, circle every moment a semicolon is used. Consider in each case why the author chose the semi-colon rather than coordination or subordination or letting two sentences stand alone. Then proceed to your own draft or that of a colleague and reconsider moments when a semicolon might be the most effective choice to connect two sentences or when coordination or subordination might be more effective.

Counterargument
The Necessary Risk
of Academic Thinking

"Consider counterargument" is a frequent commentary on student papers—and one many student writers find particularly troubling. If counterargument consists of those points, objections, and questions that challenge one's own argument, doesn't it hurt an argument to consider counterargument? Is it not weakening the very point an essay wants to make? These are, of course, legitimate and real questions. Who wants to consider something that goes against one's grain, that "messes up" the argument, that makes one feel as if one needs to start anew? But, on the other hand, who wants to read something that didn't consider the counterargument? Who wants to read on when she has a constant "but" on her lips? Balancing counterargument is an art that is necessary for academic writers and their readers.

First of all, the demand for counterargument is really fundamental to the academic writing process; we cannot arrive at an interesting and complex insight if we have not looked at all angles of an issue. In other words, as we write, we need that nagging "but" that keeps us refining our points and considering the ways in which our readers might respond. If we want to move from opinion to exploration and argument, we need to consider the other side of an issue. Counterargument, in this procedural sense, is about development of a point in the first place, about inclusion of opposing readers and their view points, about establishing one's own authority, about inquiry and circumspection. It leads to the (academically) most interesting insights. It ultimately shows that the writer is imaginative, argues rather than holds opinions, considers rather than asserts, and is strong enough to face uncertainty and complication in his topic. Without considering counterargument during the writing process, a writer stays simple, vulnerable and loses authority. But what about counterargument once one has considered it in the process and arrived at a conclusion? Where and how should it function in the final, public version of an argument?

By definition, every argument one makes is, of course, a counterargument. So, argument and counterargument on the level of thesis are like conjoined twins—they are joined together, one defined by the similarity and difference of the other. If we sever them, we deprive our thesis of its nature—it being an argument, a risk, a debatable, contestable claim. Thus counterargument is absolutely necessary to argument. For example, Richard Keller Simon in his book *Trash Culture* argues that "the stories that surround us in our daily lives are very similar to the great literature of the past"(1); it is the way we look at them that makes them appear artificially different. Simon's claim is only an argument because people have argued the opposite, and Simon needs to invoke counterargument at all times to elicit the dare and meaning of his own claims. He calls for a respectful study of popular culture and provocatively suggests, for example, similarities between "*Star Wars* and *The Fairie Queen*," "*Playboy* and *The Book of the Courtier*," or "*Cosmopolitan* and the novels by Jane Austen." Fully aware of the resistance to such an argument, Simon consistently tackles counterargument. Here is one example:

> I readily admit that *Cosmopolitan* is not the same kind of literature as a Jane Austen novel, but I would argue that it is the next stage of the traditional novel form, an illustrated collage of stories about the problems faced by a young woman in courtship that is just as suited to contemporary readers as the Jane Austen novel was for the readers of the early-nineteenth-century England. (19)

Simon here uses counterargument in two ways: (1) He needs to be in dialogue with his reader, remind the reader that his claims matter and stand in opposition—but not entire opposition—to those of the readers. (2) He uses an acknowledgment of counterargument—the concession to counterargument—here to clarify his point and make it as subtle as it can be; it is not that *Cosmopolitan* and Jane Austen novels are the same, but they are historically sequential, the former replacing the latter in its cultural function. Counterargument here serves to keep the stakes high, the reader's presence alive, the resistances of readers manageable (by admitting to part of their objections), and the terms of the argument as sharp and nuanced as possible.

In a slightly different way, Rachel Adams in her book *Sideshow U.S.A.* also uses counterargument to situate and define her own project. In her introduction, presenting the view of other scholars helps her clarify and explain to her readers her own project: its argument, emphases, methodology, and evidence. Observe how she tackles the work of fellow "freakshow" scholar Susan Stewart:

> Susan Stewart writes, "[T]he spectacle exists in an outside at both its origin and ending. There is no question that there is a gap between the object and its viewer. The spectacle functions to avoid contamination: 'Stand back ladies and gentlemen, what you are about to see will shock and amaze you.' " This is a convincing description of the sideshow's intended effect: the customer is expected dutifully to absorb the spieler's monologue while gazing at the prodigious body in awestruck wonder, then making a docile exit.
>
> However, historical evidence reveals how rarely this theory was realized in practice, for sideshows are hardly spaces of restraint or decorum, and things seldom go as planned: freaks talk back, the experts lose their authority, the audience refuses to take their seats. (12–13)

Adams concludes that the "freak show itself was far more interactive than critics have acknowledged" (13); and the entire project of Adams' book is to explore and discuss this interactive disorderly character of the sideshow. By presenting Stewart's argument, Adams is able to define her own. The tone is graceful and collegial here, and yet the two points of view are starkly in contrast: After all, Adams ends up investigating and claiming precisely what for Stewart is "no question." Adams represents Stewart's point of view, even explains how she sees her coming to this conclusions. But based on evidence Adams claims that Stewart's unquestionable claim is indeed questionable and even inaccurate. Thus Stewart's work helps Adams to define and explain her own work—the precise task it fulfills and the precise claims its makes. Both Simon and Adams use counterargument to define their projects: Simon can only write in light of the opposite view—namely that high art has little in common with "trash culture." Adams' argument—less confrontational than Simon's—defines its own contribution and insight by questioning the one thing another scholar considered "no question" at all. In each case, counterargument is essential to argument.

Yet, apart from this fundamental conjoined-twin use of counterargument, at times one may encounter counterevidence that doesn't fit into one's argument without being able to fundamentally change it in our minds. What if there is evidence for a claim but also evidence for a counterclaim? In most cases this question is complicated since—as we show in our entry on "evidence"—evidence itself is never evident but consists of interpretation of data as supporting a particular claim. With that interpretation comes the possibility of competing, even contradictory, interpretations of the same data. When anthropologist Irving Rouse, in his book *The Tainos*, argues about the "sharp difference" that has been observed between "the Suzaoid and Island-Carib settlement patterns on the island of Martinique"(131) he runs into such evidentiary trouble. Interpreting the difference Rouse suggests that the Suzaoid belong to an earlier group of people, the Igneris, which "became extinct about 1450 when Caribs invaded from the mainland"(131). He thus interprets the evidence to mean that the difference between settlement patterns is a temporal one in which one culture has been replaced by another. From here, Rouse informs the reader about a debate about this evidence. He tells the reader that his conclusion is based on historical sources that document the "Island-Carib origin traditions." He comments:

> Most archeologists accept these traditions (see Allaire 1980), but a few (like Davis and Goodwin 1990) argue against them. I prefer to accept the judgment of my colleagues in ethnohistory, who tell me that the documentation of the traditions is extensive and internally consistent. I am reminded that the linguist Douglas Taylor (1939) originally questioned my use of the Igneri-to-Island-Carib sequence, which I had taken from an ethnohistorian (1935: vi), but he changed his mind after discovering the sources from which Lovén had obtained the sequence. (131)

Many academic writers would have relegated this comment to a footnote; but Rouse—who partially writes for a general audience and is interested in discussing problems of evidence—openly deals with the issue at hand. Is this

weakening his argument? He certainly admits to somewhat shaky ground—
ground that relies less on raw data than on trust in a source; this trust is an issue
of discipline (archeologist, ethnohistorians, and linguists each have a different
relation to this evidence) and an issue of patterns. Rouse tells us about the
"conversion" of linguist Douglas Taylor in an analogous case. Clearly, Rouse
admits to a possible weakness in his argument; his findings and writings become somewhat messy in light of this debate. But, in the same breath, Rouse
gains the reader's trust by scrupulously explaining his thinking about evidence;
we know we can trust his evidence elsewhere when no struggles are mentioned. He also opens up his world to us; rather than simply providing us with
neatly arranged information about the Tainos, Rouse lets us see the difficulties
and disciplinary debates about arriving at such information. Instead of conclusions we get glimpses of investigations. Indeed, Rouse uses this moment to argue a few sentences later "in my opinion, the time has come for archeologists
to join their ethnohistorical and linguistic colleagues in accepting the existence of a change in ethnic group from Igneri to Island-Carib"(131). By admitting the problem of counterinterpretations of evidence, Rouse has man-
aged to reveal a world to us in which various disciplines are trying to decipher
difficult findings and in which they are ultimately mutually depending on each
other—despite their differences.

Counterargument is an integral part of the writing process because it is
needed to develop an argument, understand the precise nature of the argument, and to consider all possible objections and complications in the process.
Counterargument in the final version of a piece of writing restores that process
for the reader; it allows the reader to see why we care about our argument and
how much we have considered complications and challenges, how the argument is an argument, and how the argument is arrived at and made. It shows
the writer to be in dialogue with other writers and readers and considering
their point of view. It exposes the very risks that make arguments arguments,
and it reveals writers as what they are: risky thinkers.

RELATED WORDS

Academic Thinking 1	Interpretation 94
Argument 9	Research 137
Claims 38	Summary 159
Evidence 77	Synthesis 172
Footnotes 81	

EXERCISES

1. Reading through some academic published essay, identify moments
   in which the writer deals with counterargument. What different ways
   does he or she employ to use counterargument for the essay? When
   finding a writer who seems to consider no counterargument of any
   kind, try to supply as much of it as you can.

2. When writing out your thesis, write out several versions of counter-argument. Then consider which one most accurately resists and thus defines your own thesis. Then write out how and why your argument overrules this counterargument.

3. When reading a student draft, note on the margin as many counter-arguments as you can; be the nagging "but." Then, in a group discuss which counterarguments should be used for development, which should be in the final version of the essay, and which are not useful for the central claim and effectiveness of the essay.

Dash
Disrupting Academic Prose

Dash *n.*: (1) Collision; a violent striking of two bodies; a smash (2) Infusion; admixture, especially in small proportion. Innocence with a *dash* of folly.—Addison (3) A rush; a short, quick movement; as to make a *dash* upon the enemy (4) A sudden check; frustration; abashment; as his hopes met with a *dash* (5) Capacity for prompt action; boldness; hence, spirit; liveliness; vivacity; showy appearance or action (6) A splash (7) The mark (—) used in printing and writing to indicate a break in a sentence, a parenthetical remark, or an omission. (*Webster's New Universal Unabridged Dictionary*)

The dash is the most dashing of punctuation marks; while other punctuation marks tend to connect, order, and hierarchize, the dash signifies breaks, collisions, and rapid shifts of pace, voice, and logic in writing. Unlike most punctuation marks, it is both ostentatious—catching our eyes when we read—and secretive—withholding connections, disrupting things, or fusing things together without mediation. Because of its bold, disruptive and dramatic nature, the dash allows writing, particularly academic writing, to move—in a way—beyond itself, to mark and transgress its own boundaries of voice, logic, and argument.

Let's look at the drama of the dash in writing. Dashes have made people famous; and some writers have made dashes famous. Consider the case of poet Emily Dickinson who, in an outspoken defiance of conventional rules of punctuation, made the dash her trademark. She forces us to think about the dashing dash, using it to open up new possibilities for both writer and reader:

They shut me up in Prose—
As when a little Girl
They put me in a Closet—
Because they liked me "still"—

Still! Could themself have peeped—
And seen my Brain—go round—
They might as wise have lodged a Bird
For Treason—in the Pound—
        J. 613 c.1862 1935 302

Dickinson uses dashes to exemplify the imprisonment she feels and escapes in her writing. Shutting her up in the rules of prose is as foolish as putting a little bird in a pound (or cage) for committing treason. She refuses to be "still," and she uses dashes to keep her writing in motion. For Dickinson, the dashes free her brain; to her, they are signs of freedom and possibility, a bold defiance of confining rules, a lively, spirited, adventurous performance that opens possibilities.

As dashes open possibilities in Dickinson's poem, they can also dramatically gather meaning and accentuate bold statements. Consider the effect of the dash in a letter by a Shoshone Indian named Washakie, who "explains, in the following 1878 message to Governor John W. Hoyt of the Wyoming territory, why he and his fellow Indians feel threatened": "Disappointment; then a deep sadness; then a grief inexpressible; then, at times, a bitterness that makes us think of the rifle, the knife, and the tomahawk, and kindles in our hearts the fires of desperation—that, sir, is the story of our experience, of our wretched lives" (*Letters of a Nation* 25–26). Washakie, like Dickinson, feels himself to be at the limit of language; he is afraid that language will not be able to express the fullness of the experience he tries to relay. Both writers struggle against a form of imprisonment: Dickinson of expression and thinking, and Washakie of being confined to a narrower and narrower strip of land and of being stripped of rights that had been granted to his people. Each writer uses the dash in dramatic ways to defy this imprisonment. The dash in Washakie's letter is the climax of the passage—halting the writing before it becomes any more threatening, giving the reader time to absorb the strength of the growing despair of the writer and the people he represents, and putting together, dramatically distilling, the meaning towards which the passage works. The dash here, then, meddles with the pace of writing, gathers all meanings together, and expresses the desperate collision of interests between the writer and reader and the writer's aggressive demand for justice. In both examples, the dashes carry the weight of each writer's struggle for his or her rights and identity—the stakes are enormous; the two instances exemplify the power of the dash, its spectacular, dashing nature.

This drama is not always appropriate for academic writing, where, after all, the writers is often trying to convey a balanced and seasoned point of view, and therefore the dash is used sparingly in most academic prose. Signifying "a break in a sentence, a parenthetical remark, or an omission," the dash is antithetical to much of academic writing and its emphasis on logical progression, coherence, and a view that takes all angles into consideration. But as such, it may reveal to us those sides of academic writing that rebel against its own rules. In other words, looking for dashes in academic writing might be a great way of reading it for its boundaries, escapes, discontents. Consider dashes in Rosalind Williams's academic essay "The Dream World of Mass Consumption." She writes at one point: "Haugmard experiments with a variety of vocabularies—aesthetic, moral, sociological, psychological—in attempting to deal with a cultural phenomenom 'as immense as it is disquieting,' too immense, certainly, to be reduced to any one terminology"(216). On first sight, the dashes here seem rather undashing, perhaps just offering an explanation of a word used in the sentence proper. They are used in a pair to mark a parenthetical remark, or aside, that the writer inserts into her sentence. And yet, when looked at more closely, this sentence, too, speaks about the limitations of language, and the dashes play a role in that argument. By listing the various vocabularies in dashes, the writer exemplifies the very immensity of the problem she speaks about, or better summarizes as one of Haugmard's concerns. Williams then uses the dashes almost as a way of expressing her sympathy for Haugmard's problem by imitating it in her own sentence structure; like him, she is concerned about the immensity of the words she wants to include in her sentence and, like him, she experiments with language—here with the dash.

And Williams's dashes, like Dickinson's, surprisingly reveal that she too feels "shut up" in the confines of (academic) prose. This becomes obvious when she uses dashes to signify omissions and breaks—those after all, really are against the rules of the game. She writes: "The vault of the Gallery of Machines had been cut up—desecrated like a 'secularized temple,' complained one admirer of the 1889 version—and overrun by a display of food products"(199). We can see how the dashes here introduce a voice less academic than Williams's own; while she describes ("cut up and overrun"), the voice she quotes between the dashes complains in strong tones about the destruction of something divine. The dashes here suggest an unexplicated fusion between Williams' academic observation and the 1889 observer's moral outrage. "During the consumer revolution borrowing was transformed into a large-scale, impersonal, rationalized system of installment purchase which made possible the acquisition of goods without ready cash—indeed a fantasy come true"(223). Here Williams once again uses the dashes to escape the narrow confines of an academic voice. The shift in language is dramatic, and yet the dash fuses the two vocabularies by putting them in the same sentence. Williams first describes the transformation in familiar academic language as a historical phenomena, only then to let that description collide with the statement after the dash. Who is speaking here, and how and why? Is it the consumer who saw this as a fantasy come true—are we, in other words, traveling in time as we did in the previous example? Or is Williams' academic description colliding with her own feelings about this transformation, a sarcastic regret? In each of the two examples, the dashes hint at an omission: Williams's own unacademic attitude towards the academic subject she is writing on. A final example:

> It is neither necessary nor possible to catalog all the dreams exploited by modern business. Although their range is as boundless as that of the human imagination, the concepts already discussed should apply to them also, in a general way. One fantasy, however, is so powerful and pervasive that it deserves special mention—the desire for sexual pleasure. (221)

In this example Williams uses the dash for "special mention," a way of mentioning that isn't easily done in more conventional, less dashing, punctuation. She carefully builds up to the climax of the thought—the mention of sexual pleasure. The sentence itself mimics the rhythm of anticipation and climactic relief. The dash halts the build up and then releases it in the most dramatic way possible. Here, too, the dash is used to signify a topic that is more dashing than all the other "dreams" and "concepts" already discussed in Williams' academic argument. There is no other dash on the five previous pages of her essay, and the next one is almost two further pages away. The drama of the dash is well-noted and well-used here. It is so crucial for this book because when reading for it and when writing with it we can see and mark the limits of conventional academic writing and thinking.

RELATED WORDS

Academic Thinking 1	Grammar 90
Coordination and Subordination 45	Punctuation 126
Discipline 57	Voice 187
Editing 63	

EXERCISES

1. List all the different uses of the dash mentioned in this entry. Then look for dashes in published writing and analyze how the dash functions in those instances. Use the definitions offered here to ask: Are there breaks in the text, omissions, or fusions? Do the dashes get us to the limits of the academic voice? How exactly? What other voices or thoughts does the dash enable?

2. In your own or another student's draft, look for dramatic moments, breaks, parenthetical remarks, and insert dashes into the writing. Then consider whether the breaks you find are (1) necessary and dramatically effective, or (2) places for revision where further explanation is possible and desirable.

3. Rewrite the excerpts of Dickinson's poem (or any other examples using dashes) by using other punctuation. What is gained and lost in the process?

Discipline
And Its Discontents

Discipline is an ambivalent term *par excellence*; most of us want to *have discipline* but not *be disciplined* by someone else. Yet, the term always inevitably implies both sides of discipline: self-control and control by others, self-willed virtue and enforcement through others. Many academics have a similarly ambivalent relation to their disciplines: They have disciplines but often also feel somewhat restricted by them.

Disciplines—English, History, Psychology, Sociology, Physics, and so on— are the single most important ordering and structuring device of academic life. If, as we pose in this book, academic life is a form of culture, then disciplines are visible subcultures, with neighborhoods, festivals, costumes, languages, newspapers, magazines, books, and peculiar habits of their own. Just walking around campus and perusing the various departments may give the lay anthropologist a first idea of a discipline. Where are buildings located in relation to each other?* How do the "dwellers" of different buildings look? What kind of posters, announcements, and flyers can be seen in different buildings? Do a little fieldwork on your campus and record your findings!

Similarly, perusing some of the subcultures' publications and comparing them to each other will give one abundant insight into the habits and traits of each discipline. For example, Figures 2 and 3 show the opening pages of two different scholarly publications, one in the field of English, the other in the field of microbiology. Even a cursory glance reveals some pretty glaring disciplinary traits.

Consider just the two titles: "Family Embraces: The Unholy Kiss and Authorial Relations in *The Wide, Wide World*" versus "Genome and Virulence Determinants of High Virulence Community-Acquired MRSA." Both titles clearly speak to insiders: For the first, one needs to know that *The Wide, Wide World* is an American novel by Susan Warner written in the middle of the nineteenth century; for the other, one needs to know that MRSA is a potentially fatal form of bacteria. But their characters are very different: The first seems to court an audience through play of words; the second aims to inform its readers about its precise content. These strategies in turn reveal different research and reading habits in the two disciplines.

---

*For this idea we are indebted to Marjorie Garber, *Academic Instincts* p. 54, where she talks about "desire lines" and how "especially noticeable [they are] on college campuses." Overall, the entry was greatly inspired by Garber's chapter on "Discipline Envy."

If reading habits are different, so are writing habits: one author versus fourteen! Obviously microbiology values collaboration more highly than English. And collaborative writing is different from writing as a single author: Note how the scientific article is structured clearly, breaking down the writing into elements (abstract, background, method, findings, interpretation) while the English article is trying to involve us in a story, starting with specific details and quotations and then the beginnings of a scholarly debate. Each writer or author-team writes within the conventions of their discipline: The science article stresses objectivity (many authors perceived and deduced this), while the English article stresses subjectivity (one author involves us in her interpretation of a story). One would hardly exaggerate when claiming that these two articles speak different languages, even have different ideas about speaking itself (when do we speak, what do we say, who speaks). So scholars are very much characterized by their disciplines, and they give their work focus by placing it in the discipline within which they have been trained.

But one does wonder whether Argersinger, for example, might not like to break her solitary routine and enjoy writing with thirteen others on Warner's novel. Or maybe she would like, at some point, to come right out with "method, findings, and interpretations"? And who knows whether Tadashi Baba wouldn't occasionally like to write something on his own, by himself, perhaps even in Japanese instead of English—the accepted and often expected scientific language for most science publications—and start off with one of his favorite poems or proverbs? Transgressions of this kind have been reported. Many scientists have turned to writing for a larger public, even to writing science fiction; the name itself shows the fantasy of mixing fiction with science and telling a story about science. And many humanities scholars have turned to more popular writing—few, however, to our knowledge to structured scientific writing. Literary scholar Joanne Dobson, for example, has taken to writing mystery novels set in English departments, and she has company in that regard as well. Many academics try to break out of their discipline; such attempts are not always greeted with approval—sometimes, they are even disciplined.

And, when looked at carefully, the campus itself often seems to bristle with less severe transgressions of order—movements between the disciplines. As Marjorie Garber points out in *Academic Instincts*, while disciplines have always insisted on—often minor—differences so as to "protect themselves against incursion and self-doubt," they have also always employed the "opposite strategy: emulation, imitation, envy"(57). The disciplines themselves, in other words, want to be distinct from each other and insist on their differences, but they also yearn for each other, something Garber calls "discipline envy." Much of this yearning for the other gets expressed and lived out in interdisciplinarity, a space that hopes to combine disciplines into a better, more interesting whole. Consider that an increasing number of majors in a college curriculum are interdisciplinary, such as women's studies, history and literature, Medieval studies, American studies; and observe the cross-listing of courses in the catalogue. Indeed, as Garber points out, the term "studies" is often used to signify interdisciplinarity, and interdisciplinarity is often considered cutting edge; yet, interdisciplinary work is always in danger of being criticized for lacking disciplinary rigor (72–79 passim). Thus disciplines often yearn to transcend themselves, even as they also eagerly patrol their borders. They are ambivalent, indeed.

RELATED WORDS

Academic Thinking 1	Syllabus 164
Assignment 14	Titles 180
Assumptions 19	Voice 187
Audience 25	

EXERCISES

1. Look at your campus map and analyze the way disciplines are organized on campus. Which disciplines are close together, which far apart, which share one building? Then visit two buildings housing different disciplines and note differences in style that you can discern: consider people, styles of offices, posters, and so on.

2. Compare and contrast two articles from different disciplines, noting differences in language, authorship, conventions, as well as evidence, footnoting, and works cited. What do these differences suggest about each discipline?

3. Compare and contrast assignments given to you in different disciplines. What are differences in the tasks you are given?

4. Look at an article written in the academic discipline you are most interested in: What meets your expectations and what surprises you? Why?

Jana L. Argersinger
Family Embraces: The Unholy Kiss and Authorial Relations in *The Wide, Wide World*

In the originally unpublished final chapter of Susan Warner's *The Wide, Wide World,* Ellen and her new husband, John Humphreys, stand together before a painting of the Madonna and child and consider its meaning. This ideal woman's beauty, John declares, exists as a mere transparency through which the viewer may perceive the light of transcendent truth, the Word of the divine Father. After briefly challenging this reading, Ellen evidently capitulates—but at the same time she tells another story about the painting directly to the reader, unheard by the ravishingly masterful husband:

> It was merely two heads, the Madonna and child, . . . yet how much! The mother's face in calm beauty bent over that of the infant as if about to give the kiss her lips were already pouting for; the expression of grave maternal dignity and love; but in the child's uplifted deep blue eyes there was a perfect heaven of affection, while the little mouth was parted, it might be either for a kiss or a smile, ready for both!

In Ellen's narrative, mother and child are poised in the moment of yearning before a kiss, and the invisible paternal presence that presides over John's reading, and incarnates itself in him, seems to dissolve into absence. This scene, in its contemplation of Ellen as storyteller, caught up in spinning a private tale of

American Literature. Volume 74. Number 2. June 2002
Copyright 2002 by Duke University Press.

family embrace, consummates a subtext that runs through the published version of the novel (1850), twining together the tropes of familial and eroticized relation to tell a story of Warner's coming-of-age as an author. That Warner permitted, and possibly sanctioned, the omission of the chapter in which the climactic expression of this subtext appears becomes part of that story.

Many readers of Warner's unexpected bestseller, from its first appearance through much of the twentieth century, have regarded it, above all, as a religious book, one that wholeheartedly embraces the values of piety, self-discipline, and (female) submission central to the revivalistic Protestantism that dominated the antebellum era. In 1852, anthologist John hailed *The Wide, Wide World* as the only novel "in which real religion, at least as understood by evangelical Christians, is exhibited with truth"; for Hart, as for legions of Warner's admiring contemporaries, the author and her text succeeded by giving passage to the Author and His Text, by turning as transparent as the painted Madonna that Warner herself proffers as possible exemplar in the novel's intended conclusion.[3] Not so for such renowned dissenters as Hawthorne and Melville, whose dismissal of what seemed to them shallow-brained scribblings rather than new pages of Holy Writ-contemptible for the commonplace piety that broke sales records in an undiscriminating marketplace—set the tone for critics in the next century. "What can be said of the intrinsic merit of the books themselves?" asks one scholar, writing in the 1940s about the "the vogue of the domestic novel" in which *The Wide, Wide World* participated. The answer he hastens to supply epitomizes the kind of judgment that. . . .

Figure 2 Scholarly Article in English

GENOME AND VIRULENCE DETERMINANTS OF HIGH VIRULENCE COMMUNITY-ACQUIRED MRSA

Summary:

Background: A new type of meticillin-resistant Staphylococcus aureus (MRSA), designated community-acquired MRSA, is becoming increasingly noticeable in the community, some strains of which cause fatal infections in otherwise healthy individuals. By contrast with hospital-acquired MRSA, community-acquired MRSA is more susceptible to non β-lactam antibiotics. We investigated the high virulence potential of certain strains of this bacterium.

Methods: We ascertained the whole genome sequence of MW2, a strain of community-acquired MRSA, by shotgun *cloning* and sequencing. MW2 caused fatal septicaemia and septic arthritis in a 16-month-old girl in North Dakota, USA, in 1998. The genome of this strain was compared with those of hospital-acquired MRSA strains, including N315 and Mu50.

Findings: Meticillin resistance gene (mecA) in MW2 was carried by a novel allelic from (type IVa) of staphylococcal cassette chromosome mec (SCCmec), by contrast with type II in N315 and Mu50. Type IVa SCCmec did not carry any of the multiple antibiotic resistance genes reported in type II SCCmec. By contrast, 19 additional virulence genes were recorded in the MW2 genome. All but two of these virulence genes were noted in four of the seven genomic islands of MW2.

Interpretation: MW2 carried a range of virulence and resistance genes that was distinct from those displayed on the chromosomes of extant S aureus strains. Most genes were carried by specific allelic forms of genomic islands in the MW2 chromosome. The combination of allelic forms of genomic islands is the genetic basis that determines the pathogenicity of medically important phenotypes of S aureus, including those of community-acquired MRSA strains.

Correspondence to: Prof Keiichi Hiramatsu (e-mail: hiram@med.juntendo.ac.jp)

Introduction

Meticillin-resistant Staphylococcus aureus (MRSA), which arose in the 1960s, typically causes infections in inpatients, who have risk factors associated with health care. In the past 5 years however, MRSA infections have been described in the general population. These infections arise in the community, and thus affected people lack traditional risk factors such as recent admittance, surgery, or long-term residence in care facilities. Community-acquired MRSA infections can cause serious and even fatal infections in otherwise healthy hosts. [1, 2]

Community-acquired MRSA typically affects children and young adults, and it causes a range of infections similar to those caused by community-acquired meticillin-susceptible S aureus (MSSA).[3] Furthermore, these infections are more likely to be susceptible to many antimicrobial classes and to have different pulsed-field gel electrophoresis subtypes than isolates that are associated with health care. There is an ominous sign that MRSA strains circulating beyond nosocomial settings are replacing community-acquired MSSA as the flora of healthy human beings in some communities.

Recently, we established the whole genome sequence of two MRSA strains, N315 and Mu50, both of which are strains associated with health care.[4] Two further hospital-acquired MRSA strains have been sequenced by others (COL, E-MRSA-16 [strain 252]; see Methods). However, the genome of any community-acquired strain with high virulence has not been analysed. In this study, we sequenced the whole genome of the community-acquired MRSA strain MW2, and aimed to investigate the genetic basis for this strain's high virulence by comparison of its genome with those of MRSA strains that are associated with health care.

Figure 3 *(continued)*

Editing
Who Is Writing What?

In its ideal form, editing might well be described as the art of true respect. Without editing there would be few final texts. Editors are to authors as producers are to screenwriters or dramatists; they bring texts into existence, first recognizing and respecting their value and then moving them from a private manuscript to a public document: making them "final," polishing them, bringing them to light, introducing them to a reader, annotating them for clarity, providing them with a context and frame. But in so doing, editors also create new meanings for a text, interpret it, bring it into existence within their own vision. As a consequence, an editor may be an author's best friend but she may also be in an adversarial relation to the author. Editor and author—dead or alive—may compete for the meaning of a text and its ownership. And while an editor can never claim ownership, he or she might well—secretly or, less often, openly—take possession of a text by interpreting it, by directing and limiting its meaning. To some degree, this process is always inevitable and always controversial. For better or worse, an editor is always more of an author than one might think.

In his introduction to *Mary Chesnut's Civil War* (a revised diary of a White Southern woman's experience of the American Civil War), the editor, historian C. Vann Woodward, reveals some of his "Editorial Problems and Policies":

> Among the reasons for undertaking this edition of Mary Chesnut's book are the excessive liberties taken by previous editors. To replace their work with a more elaborate and complete edition claiming license for erratic and unacknowledged editorial interventions, changes, and deletions would be to invite an ironic outcome of the enterprise. Some liberties will have to be claimed, but they will be taken with full notice and explanation. The general purpose will be to publish *what* the author wrote, and, insofar as appears practicable within the rules adopted, *how* she wrote it. Both the *what* and the *how* present difficulties. (liv)

Woodward's opening paragraph shows both the power and the problems an editor has. Determined to correct the wrongdoings of previous editors, he embarks on this edition to do away with their "excessive liberties" such as "erratic and unacknowledged interventions," "changes," and "deletions." He reminds us thus that had we read a previous edition of Mary Chesnut's diaries, published, for example, under the title *A Diary from Dixie* (edited by Ben Ames Williams, originally published in 1949 by Houghton Mifflin, then published by Harvard

University Press in 1980), we would have faced a strongly adulterated text in which the editor secretly and illegitimately took hold of the text and changed it. Purging the text of those liberties and restoring it to a more original, less manipulated form, he admits that he, too, had to claim "some liberties," which he promises to fully explain and acknowledge. Above all, he wants to return to the "what" and "how" of the text.

Yet, apparently this motive also propelled previous editors, including Ben Ames Williams, who writes about his 1949 edition of Chesnut's diaries:

> When I was invited to edit a new edition of the Diary, which would include passages that had been eliminated from the earlier edition, I eagerly accepted the task. According to the Introduction to an earlier edition, this Diary was first edited by Mrs. Chesnut herself. She had written it from day to day during the war, on whatever scraps of paper were available; but after the War, being an intelligent woman, she knew that the Diary should be preserved in some orderly form. So she set herself the task of transcribing the original in a series of small notebooks, and—doubtless eliding some portions as she went along—she did so.
>
> The original edition of the Diary filled some four hundred book pages. I anticipated that the complete diary would be somewhat longer; but I was not prepared for the actuality. The original edition contained about 150,000 words; the manuscript copy of the complete Diary contains nearer 400,000. (xiii–xxiv)

Williams, like Woodward, sees his job as an editor in dialogue with previous editors, including the author herself. He, like Woodward, wants to restore the text, to undo some of the editing that has been done before. So why are these editors so suspicious of other editors? Perhaps because they, more than anyone else, understand the power of an editor to alter a text; and their editing effort is, in a way, a counterediting—an attempt to undo previous editing and to provide the reader with the pure, essential version of the text. But what is that? Is there ever a text before or outside of editing? Ultimately, when we consider both editors' responses and the fact that Mrs. Chesnut herself worked over the diary several times, we can begin to see why, as Woodward put it, "both the *what* and the *how* present difficulties."

What did Mrs. Chesnut write, and *how* did she write? The facts of Mrs. Chesnut's writing, as the facts of almost all writing, are complicated. They highlight that all authors are editors, that all writing involves editing: clarifying, correcting, reassembling, cutting. Chesnut herself, as Williams notes, became her own editor when she reworked her private scraps of daily observations into a diary of "some orderly form;" at this point she must have begun to see her private writing as potentially public. Her unfinished editing now leaves a legacy to the editors to follow, or does it? Should the author as editor determine how her writing gets edited?

Woodward does not think so. "It should be remembered," he writes, "that Mary Chesnut left the last draft of her manuscript unfinished. Her proclaimed intention to 'overhaul it again—and again' remained unfulfilled at the time of her death"(liv). So Woodward is facing a document that "[lack]s the correction and polish the author might have given it." It is also, he adds, "encumbered with numerous eccentricities and idiosyncrasies of her own, many of which she probably would not, even with ample opportunity, have removed"(liv) such as "erratic capitalization, punctuation, and spelling"(liv). So he decides to take over the "overhauling."

In so doing, Woodward decides to go against what he believes to have been the editing choices of the author and to "regularize" these idiosyncrasies because "to preserve tens of thousands of oddities and errors in a formal edition out of literal regard for some standard of textual scholarship seems misguided. Such an editorial policy would be of doubtful fairness to the author and a distraction rather than a service to the reader"(lv). Thus, Woodward takes over capitalization, spelling, and punctuation of the text, editing an average of about thirty-four "errors"—errors he believes Chesnut would have never "corrected"—per type-written page and in some cases double that amount. Above and beyond that, Woodward includes some paragraphing, "silently corrects" "unintentional repetitions" or "obvious slips of the pen"(lv); furthermore, "for the sake of readability, the editor has divided the book into chapters and has given them titles"(lvi). Finally, since no title was left for the text, Woodward chooses a title—a title different from the previous edition, changing Mrs. Chesnut's diary from *A Diary from Dixie* to *Mary Chesnut's Civil War*. So Woodward responds to Chesnut's and Williams's editing with his own vision of the text, and he does take quite a few "liberties" himself in the process. An ironic outcome, after all?

Today, the two books—Williams's and Woodward's—stand side by side in the library, each an edition of Chesnut's writing. Are they different books? They have different titles, different chapters (one 23 chapters with city names as titles, the other 35 chapters with various quotations as titles), different length (one 572, the other 886 pages), and different editors. They even begin on different dates: one on February 15, 1861, an entry in which Chesnut claims that she "always kept a journal" and that "from today I will write more" (Williams 1), and the other on Februray 18, 1861, in which Chesnut notes that "I shall always regret that I had not kept a journal during the two past delightful and eventful years" (Woodward 3). These differences, on first sight, seem mind-boggling; they do show how much editing has to do with writing—with marking the boundaries and meanings of texts as well as their voices.

Consider the following two passages, entries of the same day in the two different editions:

August 4th.—Mine is a heavy, heavy heart. Of all our sorrows. Memory is the worst. Another missive from Jordan is querulous and fault-finding. Things are all wrong. But here they seem to feel that the war is over, except the President and Mr. Barnwell, and all the foreboding such as Captain Ingraham. He thinks it has only begun. (*A Diary from Dixie* 102)

August 4, 1861. A heavy, heavy heart.

"Souvent de tous nos maux, la raison est le pere."
Another missive from Jordan—querulous, faultfinding. Things are all wrong. Beauregard's Jordan who has been crossed—not the stream "in Canaan's fair and happy land, where our possessions *lie.*"
They seem to feel that the war is over here—except the president and Mr. Barnwell—above all, the foreboding friend of mine, Captain Ingraham. He thinks it hardly begun. (*Mary Chesnut's Civil War* 129)

One can clearly see the similarities between these two entries, but the differences are just as revealing. Each editor regularizes Chesnut's prose—making it grammatically correct—and each editor seems to give the entry a different flavor. Paragraphing, fonts, usage of lines, decision to translate or not, italics, all these are editing decisions that determine the final text. The second entry gives a more poetic Chesnut, a multilingual writer who plays with punctuation, different voices, paragraphs as stanzas almost. The first Chesnut is a woman writing down her personal experiences in a rather straightforward—we might say prosaic—way. Without looking at the original—and it is hard to say at this point what the original would be—we cannot quite determine where the writing by Chesnut and her editing end, and where the editing by Woodward and Williams begins. But we can see that editing on the sentence level creates voice, form, and thus ultimately content, message, a significant portion of the meaning of the text. In that sense, editors are authors even when they are not editing their own writing.

Editing, then, is a complicated and all but innocent business; it is a way of shaping an always incomplete and preliminary private manuscript into a public, finished product. In the process of this production, the text changes; its form and meaning, the how and what, are changed, determined, even created. Editing, whether done by authors or editors, involves a reimagining of the texts for the reader. Such a reimagining can be drastic involving—as Chesnut saw it—an ordering of the text for readers, an "overhauling" of the text that foregrounds the reader's needs. When her editors take over the uncompleted task, they make structural changes: creating new paragraph structures, cutting out repetitions, creating titles, even redefining when the text begins and ends. And when they correct grammatical errors, eliminate idiosyncracies, and take over punctuation, they create a voice, a character for the text that is not entirely that of the "original" author. Editing is, in that sense, hard to distinguish from writing. The "original" writing is almost just clay to be formed by various stages of editing, from large strokes of shaping the contours and inner structure of a text to the finer touches that give it a coherent, somewhat chiseled voice.

Editing academic essays is no different; here, too, both authors and editors determine the shape and voice of an essay. Academic essays, too, move from private ideas to public statements, and their shape, form, and character will be determined in the process. How can this strong chaotic idea be presented in a clear and persuasive fashion? How can a reader be oriented by paragraphs, titles, and fonts? Where does the argument begin and where does it end? Which sentences are unclear or repetitive? Which grammatical errrors should be corrected and why? Student writing, like all other academic writing, gets edited by the writer and by colleagues (in workshops, for example) and finally by the teacher—perhaps the closest parallel to the editors in Chesnut's case. Each editor participates in creating the shape and meaning of the text. With each step of editing the text becomes more public, more acceptable in a context for which it may or may not be ideally suited. Idiosyncracies, emphases, voices, thoughts, even ideas may be lost, just as others are gained. In that sense, editing, be it done by the author or another person, does significantly determine the nature and meaning of a text—it translates writing for a particular audience or context. This translation—like literal translations—may not be exactly what the author had initially in mind. Editing is a determining of meaning that sometimes becomes invisible in the final version of a text—unless made visible by the editor's introduction and comment or revealed by comparison or research. Yet, editing reveals to all of us that *what* we write is not readily apparent unless we acknowledge that others are always writing with us, producing something that hopefully remains recognizable to us. If we resist editing, we will remain silent.

RELATED WORDS

Audience 25	Punctuation 126
Coordination and Subordination 45	Revision 143
Dash 53	Voice 187
Interpretation 94	Workshop 191

EXERCISES

1. Edit a student essay—or your own draft—in the way that Woodward describes; write an introduction to the reader about the principles of your editing and highlight with a fluorescent marker where you have made editing decisions. In the margin, briefly note what kind of editing you have done: deletion, correction, rearrangement, change in punctuation, font, paragraph, title, and so on.

2. In a group have a paragraph of a student draft—or an entire draft—edited by two different persons. Then, at your next meeting, present

the group with two new versions of the edited paragraph or draft. Compare the results and discuss the possibilities in voice, argument, and shape of the paper, which the two editions suggest.

3.   Create a collected volume of student essays and write an editor's introduction explaining to your readers how the essays fit together and how they have been edited to become a whole. If your class uses an edited collection of essays, use that collection as a model.

4.   Examine the role of an editor in one assigned reading in one of your classes. Write a short essay about the editor's role—as far as you can discern it—in that text. What are his or her motivations, editing techniques, and specific editorial interventions? In what specific way do these interventions both focus and limit the meaning of the text?

5.   Create a college edition of a text you have read in a class, and write a preface to that edition. Explain to the reader how and why you have edited this text for a college audience. What makes this edition different from other editions?

6.   On your own, find a different edition to a text you are reading in a class. Compare and contrast the two editions. How do the two editions differ and what do they have in common? What is the significance of your finding?

Essay
The Etymology of the College Paper

In past centuries, writing an essay was a lighthearted, almost dashing activity, sometimes the work of a single afternoon or evening. Essays were short and required only a topic of some kind, a momentary focus or meditation on some aspect of life—"The Solitude of the Country" (Samuel Johnson), "On the Nobel Science of Self-Justification" (Maria Edgeworth), or "On the Pleasure of Hating" (William Hazlitt)—and a lively, elegant, or in some way engaging style. The writer had only to muse a little, hold forth a little, give some mild intellectual or poignant turn to the topic and, drawing the cord of significance tight, pull the whole thing to a quick end. The essay did not require laborious work with evidence and did not have to abide by a strict set of conventions including a logical pattern of organization and a stated thesis. Often the essay was seen as a way to escape some of the formal rhetorical constraints of the epic poem, the grand tragedy, the scientific treatise: it was an "assay," a trial run, a semi-frivolous gambit after a not-too weighty topic.

In the sixteenth century, Michel de Montaigne wrote about the books he happened to be reading; in the seventeenth century Francis Bacon wrote about truth and death and friends; in the eighteenth century Richard Steele wrote about love-letters; in the nineteenth century Charles Lamb wrote about having no ear for music; and in 1942 Virginia Woolf published "Streethaunting," an essay detailing the people and sights observed while walking the streets of London (a beloved topic of many previous essayists as well). "As we step out of the house on a fine evening between four and six, we shed the self our friends know us by and become part of that vast republican army of anonymous trampers, whose society is so agreeable after the solitude of one's room" (Woolf 256). These essays were exploratory; they stepped from the known into the unknown and meditated on the consequences. Because the essay was a kind of trial run, the essayist took a risk, but that risk was limited to the confines of this relatively short form. Unlike a novelist, for example, the essayist was not expected to construct a fictional world in its entirety; instead, he or she had only to establish a context shared by the reader, to sketch the groundwork of a familiar subject, a debate, a conversation in progress, and then dive into the freshly observed details of it in order to find something new, some hitherto unseen aspect.

This approach to the form, which we might call the essay-as-exploration, is still espoused by contemporary writers, such as Annie Dillard, Phillip Lopate, Joyce Carol Oates, Louise Erdrich, Edward Hoagland, and Cynthia Ozick, to name a few, with essays published in magazines like *Harpers, The New Yorker*, and *The Kenyon Review* on topics like nature or memory or visiting a prison or walking in New York City. However, this genre of essay-as-exploration has been cast into shade by the largely nineteenth- and twentieth-century phenomenon of the academic essay. In particular, the expository essay form that is the basis for the traditional college paper of today—explanatory nonfiction prose devoted to analyzing, defining, exemplifying, classifying, comparing, and contrasting a proposed subject or theme—only gained popularity after 1912 to gradually become the accepted standard for student writing at the college level (Connors 233–35). One plausible reason for this gain in popularity has been the increased specialization of academic disciplines; student writing in college is seen as an apprenticeship for the kinds of writing produced by academic and business-world professionals (scholarly articles published in the specialized journals of each field, reports, papers given at conferences, reviews, monographs).

In this sense, a "college paper" is really an academic essay in training. Calling it a "college paper" seems to emphasize the situation in which that essay is written—a college class—with all its attendant assumptions about occasion, audience, and purpose: This will be an essay written by a student in response to an assignment, the intended audience will probably be the teacher or the other members of the class, and the purpose of the essay will be to formulate and support an argument in response to the subject matter being studied in that class. Calling it a "paper" seems to emphasize the material reality of the thing, those five or ten pages neatly stapled together, the "thingness" of the thing as a product. By contrast, calling that thing an "essay" seems to emphasize the form being used, whereas calling it a "composition" might emphasize the process through which it is constructed, "composed." And perhaps the term "college paper" implies the nonvoluntary circumstances in which many of those papers are written. Yet academic essays at any level frequently respond to an assignment of some sort, formulate and support an argument about a subject matter being studied, and are written by and for others engaged in studying that subject matter. Understanding the college paper as an academic essay or an essay-as-argument, then, is to appreciate the local significance of it but also to fathom its relationship to the larger process of academic study and to the essay form in its abstract sense. The college paper is a genre with its own set of conventions—which may vary in turn from discipline to discipline and from class to class—but it is a genre with a strong underlying connection to the essay forms that proceeded it and to the published essays that are projected as its eventual outcome.

On the face of it though, the college paper, the academic essay, the essay-as-argument appears to be a very different species from the essay-as-exploration. Academic essays take months and sometimes years to write, they are created step by step through painstaking research and analysis of evidence layered into reasoned progression of thought. Take for example, an academic essay by psychologist Daniel Schacter, "Building Memories: Encoding and Retrieving the Present and the Past." It has twenty-seven endnotes supplying further information and additional sources; it includes a "selected bibliography" of over forty other works that the author has cited or consulted in the article. It brings together case studies of individuals and their phenomenally good or terribly injured memories with the work of cognitive psychologists tracing the process through which we all encode and recall memories, and with the work of artists and fiction writers who have imaginatively portrayed the function of memory. Gathering together all this material, Schacter follows through a complexly reasoned argument, signaling that chain of reasoning to his readers with sentences like this: "My central point is that the core cognitive act of visual imagery mnemonics—creating an image and linking it to a mental location—is a form of deep, elaborate encoding" (164). From this, one might say that by contrast with the lighthearted essay-as-exploration academic essays are ponderous, information-based, difficult to read; one might suppose that academic essays must be read like one swallows medication, without pleasure but knowing that one will be the better for it.

Yet Schacter's essay is not ponderous at all. He begins with the art objects in the Museum of Modern Art and the "memory ghosts" each object leaves behind in the cognitive processes of visitors, and he ends with an enlightening interpretation of the novelist Marcel Proust. He tells us the story of the professional gambler, "Bubbles P.," and the case of a fourteen-year-old with amnesia. He includes small tests that his readers can perform along the way—"tell me about last year's Thanksgiving dinner"—and helps us to understand the retrieval process involved in answering that question, not only in terms of individual cognition but within broader historical and cultural contexts as well. Reading his essay makes one think about memory, really think about it and all the processes involved in it, in an entirely new and wonderfully detailed way. Reading his essay kicks into motion those synapses in the reader's brain that could otherwise go unused for days or weeks on end—for a lifetime! It triggers that intellectual endorphin rush that comes from thinking about ideas, ideas that can be expressed abstractly but that are also applied to the specifics of examples, of evidence, ideas that are marvelous and beautiful in themselves but are also deeply relevant to the way we live our lives. Reading his essay is transforming. This is what a good academic essay, a good essay-as-argument, a good college paper can do.

The essay form functions like a small but powerful muscle that squeezes one's brain into a slightly new shape, provides a slightly new way of perceiving the world. In this, the academic essay and the essay as exploration are exactly alike. And the similarities don't end there. Like Woolf's essay about walking in London, Schacter's essay is also exploratory; it too steps from the known pathways of human cognition, probes the unknown, and meditates on the consequences. In spite of all his endnotes, all his sources, his evidence, the reasoned progression of his argument, Schacter too is taking a personal and professional risk in this essay, allowing himself to encounter the limits of what can be known and proved on the subject. In fact, one can almost trace in Schacter's essay what might have been the "trial run," the "assay," the first venture into new territory that was the origin of the essay we now see. Engrossed in the specialized work being carried out in his field, he may have glimpsed one day how he could make sense of those scientific findings within the broader contexts of art, culture, and history if he dared to step outside his own arena of specialization. Using those broader contexts, he could reach out to more readers, start a debate, join a conversation in progress, and then dive into the freshly observed details of a subject in order to uncover some hitherto unseen aspect.

RELATED WORDS

Academic Thinking 1

Argument 9

Assignment 14

Citation 32

Claims 38

Discipline 57

Footnotes 81

Quotation 130

Works Cited 198

EXERCISES

1. In a group, analyze an academic essay: What is being explored? What is being argued? What fresh slant or transformative way of seeing is being offered? What occasion or assignment, what sense of purpose, what audience does the writer seem to have in mind? Which features of this essay would also be appropriate in a college paper and which would not? Try the exercise again, this time using an academic essay by a student writer.

2. Spend an hour or two dashing off a short essay-as-exploration on a subject that interests you. Help your reader understand that topic in a slightly new way. In a group, look back over your exploratory essays and list the kinds of evidence that could be used to develop them into academic arguments.

3. Return to a draft of an academic essay you are working on. Build in a paragraph or more where you take a risk, where you reach out to your audience, tell them something new, trigger an endorphin rush.

Evaluation
How Does One Handle a Rejection
or a Bad Grade?

6:30 A.M. Monday
On most of them, you see, I want revenge. I want to make them suffer. Revenge first of all, on that guy at the publishers. I recall his letter as faithfully as I can. I can't bear to get it out from the pile.

> Dear Martin Steel,
>
>   I am afraid I'm returning The Good the Bad and the Indifferent to you. Some of us here like it a lot, but none of us (alas!) enough to publish it.
>
>   Do let us see anything else of yours,
>
>   Ronald Jones

Like your wife or your mother or your father. Just so long as it isn't a novel, short story, play or poem I'd love to see it. I mean—who does Ronald Jones think he is? What does he do on his free evenings? I can see him now—in a fetching leather bumfreezer—sitting with a few chosen friends in Charco's wine bar in Chelsea. (3)

Thus opens British writer Nigel Williams's novel *My Life Closed Twice* (1977), written as the fictional diary of writer Martin Steel; it describes the most common evaluation most writers receive: polite and often quite cursory rejection. A few cliché-ridden lines in return for years of labor, imagination, creativity! What a bargain. The response? Just as common: a form of internalized rage and hate that has seemingly nowhere to go and that cannot be gotten rid of either. Who doesn't vividly remember seething with anger and disappointment after receiving a bad grade or a short cursory rejection?

But, behold, confessed to the pages of this diary the anger has turned itself right back into novelistic imaginations: Ronald Jones, the unlikeable character, is born. And now—if we for a minute assume that there is some basis for this in his own life—we can see Williams's probable private anger over rejection channeled into the creation of his character Steel's anger, which now sits on the first page of Williams's published novel. Revenge accomplished, rejection survived, writing published after all.

It is not totally presumptive to suspect some biographical resonance here since all writers—students, novelists, scholars—know and dread rejection; and some writers even confuse all evaluation with rejection. Yet, rejection is only one form—an extreme form—of evaluation that stays foremost in our minds. Most of us, like Steel, can probably quote by heart some rejection or harsh evaluation we received. And yet, even that form, as Williams's example shows, can be used to write more and better and further. Steel vents his anger and *writes* in his diary.

Looked at more coldly, evaluation is as much part of the writing process as putting the hands on the keyboard or scribbling out notes or reading a book. It is the moment when the writer reaches a reader, the moment in which writing works as a means of communication: for better or worse. Evaluation—the assessment of value—begins often already in our own minds when we reject or go with ideas, when we do or do not take our own first drafts seriously enough to pursue them and shape them. Each revision is possible only because it is based on an evaluation: this idea is strong and needs to be developed, this thought is better put in a footnote, that paragraph really belongs to a different essay, and so on. Some people, as the cliché goes, are their own worst critics; never satisfied with their own writing, rejecting it in a sense, they may get defeated unless they find a mentor who evaluates their work differently, more generously, than they do. And there are those who love every word they write; enamored with their own production, they often need that kind critic and firm friend who can point out avenues for improvement or even speak a much needed rejection.

Why then is Williams's character so angry? Imagining Ronald Jones in the Chelsea bar, he writes:

> And who, while we are at it are "some of us"? A sandpit full of trendies, up there in Bedford Square or wherever they hang out, lounging around like the last days of the Roman Empire and sneering at Manuscripts Received? Or is it just a stupid way of saying "Me"? Ronald Fucking Jones. Probably never even *tried* to write a novel. The ultimate one-upmanship. (3)

One wonders how much of this went through Williams's mind in his own life. And perhaps revealing these thoughts ironically on paper is a way of coping with them *and* rethinking them. After all, on this first page, Martin Steel comes off as a very insecure and even immature man whose hate fantasies seem somewhat disproportionate to the letter he received. Williams shows that rejection is not a simple thing; indeed his entire novel is about Steel's obsession with a former love who rejected him. And while this added dimension of Steel's anger at rejection is only visible a few pages later, these opening lines give us ample opportunity to analyze his response to Jones's letter. Steel's fury is entirely in his head, we might say. "Like your wife or your mother or your father," writes Steel, immediately linking the rejection of his manuscript to other rejections: What is, after all, worse, more common, and more impossible to "work through" than rejection by parents and loved ones? Folded into this is the rejection of artistic work itself: "Just so long as it isn't a novel, short story, play or poem I'd love to see it." Writing is a hard thing to do; most of us will be told by others that it would be better to do something else, something more practical, marketable, conventional. Everyone knows how hard it is to survive as an artist, and so this evaluation of writing as work itself is certainly plausible if devastating for those who cannot help but write.

Steel's real fury, however, is directed at the imaginary Ronald Jones, whom he imagines drinking wine on free evenings at a trendy bar. It is a fury about power and powerlessness. There is envy and rage in Steel's tone; he clearly imagines Jones as someone from a different class (drinking wine instead of beer, one assumes, in a fashionable neighborhood rather than the local corner pub) and having free time and chosen friends. These observations could only be hateful if driven by envy. So Steel sees a difference between the poor, unfashionable, hard-working artist, and the glib, leisurely, fashionable well-off "guy at the publishers" who is part of a group of "trendies" who like "Roman Emperors" rule the world in which Steel wants to take part but whose taste he does not please. And so, dear Martin Steel, thanks but no thanks. The height of the injustice according to Steel is that "Ronald Fucking Jones," as he imagines him, "probably never even *tried* to write a novel." That is "the ultimate one-upmanship." It's just not fair.

Most of us have felt this intense sense of injustice when receiving an evaluation of our work. Why did this paper we labored over only get a C? Why does no one want to publish this article? Why does this poem get a one-line rejection slip? It is easiest, in a way, to imagine an unjust universe in which we, the victims, are given a very raw deal and the person who evaluates us is—well—a jerk. And while, of course, that may well be true in some cases, to insist on that as truth gets us nowhere and really prevents us from growing as writers. Often, when we come back to a piece a few months or years later, we can see perfectly well what that other person saw. That fury and baggage may disappear—Ronald Jones may well be just a regular guy having beer in the local pub and know what he is doing and his rejection has nothing to do with our parents or our love life. The problem with Ronald is, though, that he does not really tell Steel what he saw. He only rejects without offering Steel a way to resee his own work; so what else is there to do but hate Jones? Pure evaluation without any explanation—like a grade without comment or clue to how it was determined—is indeed hard to stomach.

Most of us are lucky enough to be part of a process in which this pure evaluation happens only—if at all—at the very end of the line. The line, when read carefully, has probably given us plenty of clues about the criteria for evaluation; and, as mentioned before, when we are honest we realize that we ourselves have evaluated our work as we went along writing it. In college writing, for example, class discussions, the assignment, workshops, or other prerequisite classes offer help in understanding the criteria for evaluation. It is those criteria that help us put the final evaluation—the grade—together with revision suggestions, with a sense of a value system rather than an arbitrary value. We need a measuring rod that we can understand and also, if we wish, reject. And our anger may blind us to the fact that such a measuring rod does and did exist.

Sometimes we are within our rights to reject a rejection, or to reevaluate an evaluation. After all a negative evaluation can be ignorant as can excessive praise; and both can be infuriatingly patronizing. So, a response to evaluation needs to be open and critical if we want to use it well; nonetheless, sometimes even fury is a great unleasher of energy and persistence that all writers need. If, coming back to a piece, we still think it is pretty darn good, we will probably submit the piece again: to another publisher, journal, or, in the case of a college paper, to a college essay competition or some other venue outside of class work. There are countless stories about writers resubmitting their work over and over (sometimes twenty or thirty times) until finally, someone, appreciates it and publishes it. The most successful books often come precisely with this biography. They may be off-the-wall, innovative, original to the point that they transcend the measuring rod with which they had been measured as insignificant or bad. Those examples should inspire us to persist; they should not blind us, however, to the importance of listening to evaluations of our work.

What a difficult balance between submission and self-assertion, between faith and blindness! No wonder most writers struggle with evaluations of their work. Many writers take a long time before they let the Ronald Jones's of the world see their work; they go to other sources: teachers, mentors, friends, peers. The workshop is one format that tries to separate evaluation from rejection and to connect it as clearly as possible to criteria and dialogue. Everybody in a workshop is a writer, and everyone's writing will be discussed, critiqued, and fundamentally supported; so, do as you want done to yourself. As Steel implies in his bitter feelings about Jones, only writers know what writers go through.

Evaluation is not an easy thing for anyone; but it might help to think about evaluation, and organize it, as an integral part of the writing process that involves an increasingly distanced reader: first oneself alone, then a trusted friend or colleague, then perhaps a workshop or classroom who is facing the same assignment, then ideally the teacher as editor and commentator on a draft, and only at the end that final (dreadful) moment of evaluation in form of a grade or rejection or acceptance slip. It is only the end of the line—and even that is just a beginning (after that there are reviews and so on). We can't be writers without evaluation, so we better make the best of it. And, of course, while rejections and bad evaluations are the rule for most writers, acceptances and positive evaluations—if rigorous and trustworthy—are the moments that counterbalance all that grief and turn it into tremendous, energizing, unforgettable joy.

RELATED WORDS

Assignment 14	Revision 143
Audience 25	Workshop 191
Editing 63	Writer's Block 195
Free-Writing 87	

EXERCISES

1. In the opening of his novel, Williams may be said to reflect ironically on his character's furious reaction to an evaluation of his work. Recall an instance where you have been furious about an evaluation such as a grade and write an ironic rendition of your response.

2. Before submitting a final draft, write out all evaluation criteria you know about from the assignment, workshops, class discussion, and prerequisite classes. Then, in a journal, write out your own honest evaluation of your paper based on those criteria. Reread them when you do receive the paper back. What are significant differences between your evaluation and the one you received from someone else?

3. Gather together and reread as many evaluations of your written college work as you can and evaluate those evaluations. Are there common concerns? Which evaluations are most helpful? How and why?

4. Rewrite an evaluation you received—and were not happy with— into a version you would have preferred to get.

5. Write a letter evaluating a draft to a colleague in your class that ex-
    emplifies the tone and content of an evaluation you find ideal.

6. List all moments of evaluation in your writing of a particular paper—
    from your own comments on yourself, to sharing with friends, to
    workshop comments on your own and other writing, to comments
    by the teacher. From there write a biography (a story of how and
    why you changed and transformed the draft into its current form) of
    this paper and mention the roles these various evaluations and evalu-
    ators played in its development.

Evidence
Discovery and Proof

As in a legal trial, a writer's use of evidence has two distinct but complemen-
tary functions: discovery and proof. In the "discovery" phase of a murder trial,
lawyers on both sides sift through evidence in order to build an interpretation:
they see what is there; they collect more evidence; they sort through, choosing
the evidence that seems most significant to the case they want to build. By law,
they are forced to disclose all the evidence they find to each other so that neither side is working from a disadvantage. In the trial phase, each side provides
an interpretation of the evidence that is as detailed and as persuasive to the
jury as possible. Similarly, in a paper, evidence provides the raw material from
which and against which the writer's ideas develop. In the "discovery phase"
the writer explores and learns from the evidence. As the writer's own argument takes shape, evidence also provides the backup, the support system
through which those ideas are convincingly presented or "proved" to a reader.
In both regards, evidence is the fundamental building material of the essay, the
clay from which the sculpture is shaped.

  Yet the writer of an essay is much freer than the trial attorney, who knows
from the outset which side of a case he or she must argue. The writer can actually use the discovery phase to discover what the evidence has to say, to play
with the evidence, unpack it, consider its possible significances. Further, the
writer is not forced to keep these two "phases" separate; the possibility of fresh
discoveries lingers throughout the process of choosing and interpreting the evidence, emerges, reemerges throughout the entire process of writing the essay.

For a writer, the act of interpretation often leads to further discovery; the process of explaining a particular piece of evidence in order to make a particular point opens up a fresh understanding of the topic.

However, the crucial activity of building an interpretation is just as important for the writer to remember as it is for the trial attorney. Evidence is not self-evident. Is a bloody glove proof of guilt? Not in itself. In fact, the bloody glove only becomes usable evidence if a series of relationships can be established between that object and the accused; the prosecutor must demonstrate point by point, link by link, that the glove was used in the crime, that the blood on the glove matches the DNA of the victim, that the accused did purchase the glove or commonly wore it, or wore one like it, or was at least capable of getting it on. In other words, the prosecutor must make a case based on the evidence; he or she cannot rely on the evidence to speak for itself. Like the piece of evidence chosen and quoted (or summarized) by a writer, the bare fact of the bloody glove means nothing until it is introduced, given an explanatory context, assigned a role, invested with significance through the interpretive activity of the lawyers for each side.

Often those interpretive contexts can give the same piece of evidence two entirely contradictory meanings. Where the prosecution will use the blood on the glove as a link in the chain proving the defendant's guilt, the defense attorney will go to some trouble to explain why there is clearly no connection between the glove and the defendant, that it was obviously left behind by the real murderer, had been lost for weeks, was stolen out of a car, was never his in the first place, doesn't even fit him—why, in short, the glove is indisputable evidence of the defendant's innocence. For a writer, those contradictory possibilities are the magic elements that add depth, complexity, and interpretive play to a reading; they allow a writer the flexibility to explore possible meanings. In fact, it is by tackling head-on the possible contradictions suggested by the evidence that a writer arrives at a thought-through position on it, a conviction that one explanation is more compelling than the others. The writer creates a compelling case by acknowledging the competing claims of the evidence and by arguing for the particular context or set of relationships that gives that evidence its most crucial, most revealing, most convincing meaning. The writer builds a story about the evidence that persuades readers to share his or her perception of it beyond the shadow of a reasonable doubt.

In an article on the widely publicized 1995 O. J. Simpson murder trial, "The Eye of Everyman: Witnessing DNA in the Simpson Trial," Sheila Jasanoff, a professor of science and public policy, argues that the prosecution lost their case because scientific evidence, particularly involving DNA, was too difficult to explain in a convincing way to the nonscientist judge and jury members. To support her argument, Jasanoff draws on evidence from the trial transcripts, from previous legal cases that set precedents involved in the trial, from newspaper coverage of the Simpson trial, from scientific studies on DNA, and from other scholarly studies. From the masses of evidence available to her, she must choose the key portions that are most relevant to her own argument and work through paraphrase, summary, direct quotation, citation of dates and facts, and endnotes to incorporate that evidence into the article. Further, to convince us, her readers, of the particular significance of the evidence she has chosen, she provides an explanatory context and an interpretation of each quote in which she calls our attention to certain features of the evidence and uses those features to persuade us that indeed this case hinged on the problem of establishing credibility for the scientific evidence.

In one section of the essay, for example, Jasanoff is trying to explain the importance of DNA evidence in contemporary legal cases. She begins with some background on the significance of blood as a symbol of guilt in our culture—using everything from Grimm's Fairy Tales to Lady Macbeth—then provides the following explanation of the difference technology has made:

> But ours is an age of scientific enchantment. Blood, along with other bodily fluids and tissues, still speaks with authority, but only through the miraculous translations wrought by science and technology. DNA typing is one such miracle, and its unprecedented power to establish the truth is reiterated almost as a refrain whenever people have occasion to talk about its use in law enforcement. Mr. Justice Orton, the British trial judge in *Regina v. Pitchfork*, the first murder case to use DNA evidence, introduced the theme of inevitability that soon became part of the technique's mystique: "The rapes and murders were of a particularly sadistic kind. And if it wasn't for DNA you might still be at large today." (718)

From there, Jasanoff goes on to cite a brief history of cases in which DNA evidence seemed to produce an inevitable conviction. However, she also slows down to analyze Justice Orton's statement, to point out how his use of the abbreviation "DNA" covers over the fallible human processes through which the blood was drawn, labeled, transported, and processed: "note, for instance, the statements above by Justice Orton . . . representing DNA as a free agent. Yet the metonymic genius of language that converts 'DNA' into a stark signifier of truth suppresses a world of social activity. Simply collecting samples can pose enormous problems of police work . . ." (718). She builds in additional evidence to demonstrate how Orton's summing up ignored the thousands of hours put in by the police to collect blood samples from young men in the vicinity of the murders and withheld the fact that the actual murderer/rapist in the case was initially overlooked because he had a reluctant friend produce a blood sample in his stead (718–19). Through the rest of Jasanoff's article, her analysis of this early case helps us to view the O. J. Simpson trial from a new perspective, helps us to see why the prosecution was so confident that the mystique of DNA evidence would win them the case and to understand why the defense was so successful in overturning that case once they were able to expose the fallibility of the individual police officers and scientists who collected and handled the blood samples. In choosing whether to include this early case in her article, then, Jasanoff had to weigh its usefulness in supporting her argument against the possibility that it would become a digression. Once she decided to include it, she had to provide enough explanatory context for us to understand the case, and she had to analyze it, interpret it, and demonstrate why it was so significant to her own argument.

As this example also suggests, the "discovery" and "proof" uses of evidence are always in subtle tension. True, the writer plunges into the body of available evidence, learns from it, develops a case based on it, but that body of evidence will always profoundly exceed the honed argument that the writer ends up making. To "prove" his or her case effectively, then, the writer ends up whittling down the mass of available evidence to the few polished gems that will best represent the point; this "phase" is all about summarizing, choosing, excluding, balancing the goals of exposition against the dangers of digression. The writing process thus demands these two opposing uses of evidence: one open-ended and exploratory, the other tightly discriminating and ruthless.

RELATED WORDS

Argument 9	Interpretation 94
Citation 32	Quotation 130
Claims 38	Summary 159
Counterargument 49	Synthesis 172
Footnotes 81	Thesis 176

EXERCISES

1. Choose one academic essay and list three or more points or claims that the writer makes. For each claim, list the kind of evidence that the writer uses to support and develop that claim. How does the writer interpret each piece of evidence and use it to make his or her point? Try this same exercise on a student-written academic essay.

2. As a group, identify a piece of evidence used in a student writer's draft then have each member of the group write a brief paragraph reinterpreting that same piece of evidence and using it to make a completely different point.

3. In a group, identify the main argument of a reading. Have half the group (the "defense") make a case in support of the writer's argument by choosing and presenting the evidence that best reveals the strengths of the piece. Have the other half of the group (the "prosecution") attack the writer's argument by choosing and presenting the evidence that most reveals the weaknesses of the piece.

4. While reading another writer's draft, mark every place where that writer uses evidence (a quotation, a statistic, an example or anecdote). In each case ask some of the following questions to help the writer use that evidence move effectively. Is this piece of evidence well-chosen? Is it relevant to the writer's argument? Does the writer provide a useful explanation of the evidence, an interpretation that

calls attention to particular features of it? Does the writer persuade us of the significance of that evidence?

5. Look at the ways in which three different writers cite and work with evidence in the assigned readings. If possible, choose readings from three different disciplines or with three strongly differing approaches. What counts as evidence in each reading (quotation, summary, statistics, charts and graphs,)? Identify one passage in which a writer introduces a pieces of evidence, analyzes it, and demonstrates its significance for his or her argument.

Footnotes*
The Autobiographies of Texts

Many people have been "guilty" of reading an essay or a book without once looking at the footnotes. Fewer can confess the opposite: that they have read the footnotes of a text without even glancing at the "text proper." Yet, this second endeavor is just as revealing about the true argument of a piece of academic writing as the first one is negligent of it. From the footnotes, we can construct the autobiography of a text: its sources and origins, its acquaintances and friends, the borders and conventions of the discipline it is written in, its enemies, its anxieties, frustrations and limitations, its moments of vanity and modesty, its moments of virtual collapse, its hopes for the future, its desires to please and include, its desires to distinguish itself, its urgent need for a foundation as well as its leaps into thin air, its wish to belong. It is in its footnotes that a text often reveals its true nature, its character, as well as traces of the troubled soul of its maker.

The endnotes to Thomas Kuhn's much anthologized essay "The Historical Structure of Scientific Discovery" may serve as an example here. Five out of nineteen endnotes give citations for sources that Kuhn used in writing his essay (e.g., endnote 12 reads "J. R. Partington, *A Short History of Chemistry*, p. 91"). These endnotes show us all the reading that went into the writing of the text; they emphasize that academic texts are invariably part of an ongoing

---

*There is no separate discussion of endnotes. Endnotes and footnotes largely serve the same functions in academic writing. Footnotes, of course, are more visible on every page; endnotes relegate the "autobiography" of the text to the end. Citation conventions, rather than authorial decisions, often decide where authors place their notes.

dialogue. Indeed, their meaning hinges on their interaction with and response to other texts, their *con*texts to which and about which they speak. In these endnotes Kuhn lets the reader in on the conversation of which his essay is a part.

The remaining fourteen notes are what is called discursive: They are behind-the-stage commentaries, reflections, and additions to his essay, which expand, characterize, and qualify his assertions in the essay itself. Let's read some of these notes without even looking at the essay itself. What do they reveal about the text to which they are attached, the author of the text, and its history and context? And do they indeed tell a story in themselves?

Kuhn's first endnote reads:

> 1. For a brilliant discussion of these points, see R. K. Merton, "Priorities in Scientific Discovery: A Chapter in the Sociology of Science," *American Sociological Review* 22 (1957): 635. Also very relevant, though it did not appear until this article had been prepared, is F. Reif, "The Competitive World of the Pure Scientist," *Science* 134 (1961): 1957.

This note actually tells us that Kuhn appears to admire Merton's "brilliant" work. The admiring tone Kuhn uses for Merton is quite different from his mention of Reif's work: that is relevant rather than brilliant, and furthermore, it comes after Kuhn's own work, not before. There seems to be an irony here since Reif's essay is about "The Competitive World of the Scientist"and Kuhn's note expresses a certain competition between Reif and Kuhn. So, in a way this note reveals both Kuhn's friends and competitors.

In the next endnote, Kuhn seems to point towards the limitations of his own essay's argument when he writes:

> 2. Not all discoveries fall so neatly as the preceding into one or the other of my two classes. For example, Anderson's work on the positron was done in complete ignorance of Dirac's theory from which new particle's existence had already been very nearly predicted. On the other hand, the immediately succeeding work by Blackett and Occhilani made full use of Dirac's theory and therefore exploited experiment more fully and constructed a more forceful case for the positron's existence than Anderson had been able to do. On this subject see N. R. Hanson, "Discovering the Positron," *British Journal for the Philosophy of Science* 12 (1961): 194; 12 (1962): 299. Hanson suggests several of the points developed here. I am much indebted to Professor Hanson for a preprint of this material.

Without understanding the details of this note we can still gather that Kuhn has simplified things in his essay to make a point: He admits to having offered a classification that is not entirely true to all the facts. In his endnote voice, outside of the clarity of his essay, he is able to reinstitute some complications that he cut from his point in the essay. Why would he do so? For one thing, his credibility is at stake; he needs to consider possible counterargument; obviously, Professor Hanson would be one person ready to offer such complicating evidence. In mentioning this simplification Kuhn shows both his expertise and his strategy as a writer to admit the limitation and insist on the classification for rhetorical purposes anyways. In so doing he is able to express his gratitude to Professor Hanson whose "preprint" he acknowledges. This remark shows him in a strong collegial relation to Hanson, who allows him to see his work before it is publically available. Hanson, Kuhn acknowledges, laid some foundations for his own points—unlike Reif who simultaneously developed his.

As Kuhn makes ample reference to the writing of others, he also uses notes to situate this particular essay in the context of his own previous work. In endnote 3 he writes:

> 3. I have adapted a less familiar example from the same viewpoint in "The Caloric Theory of Adiabatic Compression," *Isis* 49 (1958): 132. A closely similar analysis of the emergence of a new theory is included in the early pages of my essay "Energy Conservation as an Example of Simultaneous Discovery," in *Critical Problems in the History of Science*, ed. M. Clagett (Madison: University of Wisconsin Press, 1959), pp. 321–356 . . . Reference to these papers may add depth and detail to the following discussion.

Surely, this endnote encourages the reader to read more of Kuhn in order to add "depth and detail" to the discussion he notes. Another context of this essay then is Kuhn's lifework; at the same time, Kuhn, of course, establishes authority by referencing other work on the subject by himself. Thus, so far, Kuhn emerges from his notes as a well-connected, highly accomplished, and competitive scholar and thinker, who acknowledges and appreciates the work of others but is also anxious to define the borders of his own accomplishments.

While endnote 3 talked to the reader about the history of Kuhn's own work, the next note maps out the history of the conversation of which Kuhn is a part. Listen to Kuhn's narration of that history:

> 4. The still classic discussion of oxygen is A. N. Meldrum, *The Eighteenth Century Revolution in Science: The First Phase* (Calcutta, 1930), chap. 5. A more convenient and generally quite reliable discussion is included in J. B. Conant, *The Overthrow of the Phlogiston Theory: The Chemical Revolution of 1775–1789*, Harvard Case Histories in Experimental Science, case 2 (Cambridge: Harvard University Press, 1950). A recent and indispensable review which includes an account of the development of the priority controversy, is M. Daumas, *Lavoisir, theoreticien et experimentateur* (Paris, 1955), chaps. 2 and 3. H. Guerlac has added much significant detail to our knowledge of the early relations between Priestley and Lavoisir in his "Joseph Priestley's First Papers on Gases and Their Reception in France, "*Journal of the History of Medicine* 12 (1957): 1 and in his very recent monograph, *Lavoisier: The Crucial Years* (Ithaca: Cornell University, 1961). For Scheele see J. R. Partington, *A Short History of Chemistry*, 2nd ed. (London 1951), pp. 104–109.

This note—a bibliographical note which details the majors text in the debate Kuhn talks about—tells us in a nutshell the history of the conversation and how Kuhn sees that history. It also showcases his ability to summarize and characterize the entire trajectory of work on his subject in quick accomplished strokes: "still classical," "convenient and quite reliable," "recent and indispensable," "[adds] much significant detail," "very recent." We see a composite story emerging of various scientists playing roles in a common conversation, and we see a man in full command of his story.

In every conversation, there is conflict or debate. Endnote 6 tells us a bit about that:

> 6. U. Bocklund ("A Lost Letter from Scheele to Lavoisier," *Lychnos*, 1957–58, pp. 39–62) argues that Scheele communicated his discovery of oxygen to Lavoisier in a letter of September 30, 1774. Certainly the letter is important, and it clearly demonstrates that Scheele was ahead of both Priestley and Lavoisier at the time it was written. But I think the letter is not quite so candid as Bocklund supposes, and I fail to see how Lavoisier could have drawn the discovery of oxygen from it. Scheele describes the procedure for reconstituting common air, not for producing a new gas, and that, as we shall see, is almost the same information that Lavoisier received from Priestley at about the same time. In any case, there is no evidence that Lavoisier performed the sort of experiment that Scheele suggested.

Kuhn here delineates how he disagrees with Bocklund's conclusions (Lavoisier could not have drawn the discovery of oxygen from the letter Scheele sent to him) and why he disagrees (Lavoisier received the same information from Priestley, and "there is no evidence that Lavoisier performed the sort of experiment that Scheele suggested). This skillful treatment of counterargument, while showing Bocklund as an antagonist of kinds, also enhances Kuhn's credibility as a circumspect thinker.

Sometimes, footnotes need to acknowledge that a foundation of an argument is "not only" between "is" and "interpretive" but perhaps also beyond the scope of the essay. Many times endnotes tell us about impossibilities or roads not taken, the kind of things a writer has neither time, space, nor perhaps opportunity, authority, or ability to argue. Here is one of Kuhn's roads not taken:

> 16. Though the point cannot be argued here, the conditions which make the emergence of anomaly likely and those which make anomaly recognizable are to a very great extent the same. That fact may help us understand the extraordinarily large amount of simultaneous discovery in science.

Is what Kuhn talks about in this note fact or argument? It is hard to tell; since "the point cannot be argued here" we need to take one for the other. By acknowledging the shakiness of this, Kuhn actually tries to increase his credibility by implying that the point could be argued elsewhere. Similarly to the note about classifications, Kuhn lets us in on the rhetorical choices he made and had to make. Doing so, he helps us see not only what's shaky and unclear in his essay but also that he himself is the master of it and able to negotiate the gains and losses.

Without reading Kuhn's essay proper, we can thus deduce an enormous amount about Kuhn's text: the history of the conversation of which his writing is part; his reading, familiarity, and understanding of this conversation; his "chronological" rivalry with—or at least his assertion of rights against or anxiety about—Reif; his admiration of Merton; his gratitude to Professor Hanson and his work; the conscious simplifications for argument's sake; the interpretive elements of his argument; his disagreement with Bocklund; the limits of what he can prove within the confines of his essay; the role this essay plays within his life work; the rhetorical choices Kuhn makes throughout. We can also see quite a lot about Kuhn the man: his friends and rivals, his feelings about these friends and rivals, his relation to us the reader, his behavior in debates, and his strength in light of uncertainties and incompletion. Overall, the notes reveal to us ambitions, relations, uncertainties, anxieties, vanities and modesties, the essay's distinctions and affiliations—its autobiography.

Once we read the actual essay, we can readily see that the notes provide a fascinating and in some ways almost ironic subtext to the essay. Kuhn's essay argues to a large extent exactly about what his notes enact—the relation between scientists and their claims to discoveries. In the essay, Kuhn argues that it is the "nature of the scientific community" with its emphasis on "prestige" and "acquisitions" of ideas (385) that has blinded us to the fact that discovery cannot be easily "[pinpointed] in place and time" (386) but that it is rather a process that "extends over time and may often involve a number of people"(389). We want to write history by saying that x discovered y on this date and in this place, but in truth, says Kuhn, it is rarely if ever possible to make such a determination; discoveries are not made by persons but by processes involving many. We insist on the "discoverer" mostly because of our conventional ways of thinking about each person's contribution, prestige, or even ownership of ideas. The very rules of the scientific community are at stake.

How then can we read Kuhn's endnotes in light of his argument? Perhaps the simultaneity with Reif he points out is less rivalry than fodder for his claim? Or is his insistence that he was first doing the opposite? And why express gratitude to Hanson and admiration for Merton? Do those gestures contradict or enhance Kuhn's insight? Kuhn's endnotes become truly fascinating when seen in light of his argument. If they indeed stress process and cooperation, they are evidence for his claims. If they are read as delineating Kuhn's own ownership of ideas, they may well reveal Kuhn's own underlying reliance on the narrative of traditional discovery and thus put a considerable strain on his essay. As all notes, Kuhn's are simultaneously about community and about ownership; in light of his essay's argument, that makes them anxious and revealing indeed. They tell the story not only of Lavoisier, Priestley and Scheele—who are each contested candidates for being the discoverer of oxygen—but also the story of Kuhn,

Reif, and Bocklund. Thus the notes reveal what's at stake for the author and how his own life is inextricably caught up in his argument.

RELATED WORDS

Argument 9	Quotation 130
Assumptions 19	Reading 132
Citation 32	Research 137
Discipline 57	Summary 159
Evidence 77	Synthesis 172
Plagiarism 120	Works Cited 198

EXERCISES

1. Read through the footnotes or endnotes of an academic essay (in your reader, for example) and write a short "autobiography" of the text solely based on those notes. What can you gather from the footnotes about the author, the reading and research the author did, his or her colleagues and mentors, the writing of the article, the discipline it is written in, the audience it is addressed to, and so on?

2. Add footnotes to one of your essays in order to reveal its "autobiography," its sources, the ideas and experiences that influenced its writing, the class or assignment for which it was written, the input and help you might have received, the roads you did not take, and so on.

3. Read another student's essay that is without footnotes and make a list of questions you would like to see answered in footnotes. Mark also those parts of the paper that should be in footnotes rather than the main text. Discuss how you decide what is essential for the main text and what can go in footnotes.

4. "Autobiography" is just one metaphor to describe the function of footnotes. Create your own metaphors to describe an author's uses of footnotes. Bring a handout to class that teaches us through examples how you arrived at those metaphors and how they help you to understand and explain the author's use of footnotes.

5. Choose a footnote in which a writer refers to another source. Use the library or Internet to track down that source. Once you can see the larger context of the source from which your writer chose a particular passage, quote, or idea to suggest his or her relationship to the source, write a paragraph analyzing that relationship. For what purpose did the writer use the source? What can we learn about the writer and his text from his use of this source?

Free-Writing
A Rather Forced Liberation

[Free-writing exercises] are sometimes called "automatic writing," "babbling," or "jabbering" exercises. The idea is simply to write for ten minutes (later on, perhaps fifteen or twenty). Don't stop for anything. Go quickly without rushing. Never stop to look back, to cross something out, to wonder how to spell something, to wonder what word or thought to use, to think about what you are doing. If you can't think of a word or a spelling, just use a squiggle or else write, "I can't think of it." Just put down something. The easiest thing is just to put down whatever is in your mind. If you get stuck it's fine to write "I can't think of what to say, I can't think of what to say" as many times as you want; or repeat the last word you wrote over and over again; or anything else. The only requirement is that you *never* stop." (Elbow 3)

Peter Elbow's description of free-writing does make one wonder about the "freedom" of free-writing. Freedom to do what? And freedom from what? Elbow's own description wavers between freedom and coercion: "don't stop," "never look back," "go quickly without rushing," "*never* stop," are commands chaining the writers to their pens and driving them onward like a horse pulling a carriage; but the emphasis on the simple and easy, on the sense that all is "fine" stress the indulgence, the liberation that comes along with the coercion. Yes, we are free to say and think and move in whatever way we want. But we are also forced to do so, to move, to keep writing, to suspend the very idea that we are writing when we have something to say. We are forced to say, say, say, no matter what and how. That is the double nature of free-writing: whip and sugar cube, discipline and openness, method and chaos, a forced liberation.

In his essay "Student Writing in Philosophy: A Sketch of Five Techniques," Stephen Fishman comments about his teaching: "I rarely use free-writing in this pure, unalloyed form. However, in my classes, I extensively employ a hybrid called *focused free-writing*, which asks for the nonstop writing Elbow describes but about a specific subject. . . . Of all the writing-to-learn techniques, focused free-writing yielded the most immediate results for my students" (60). Free-writing is then a balancing act between channeling the mind and letting it roam; the channeling is the chaining to the pen (you must write, never stop) and, in Fishman's case, the focused topic, the roaming is the liberation from grammar, spelling, sentence structure, logic, the reader, and evaluation. In free-writing, writing becomes simply a way to move, however erratically, towards expression and even more fundamentally towards ideas themselves. But the ideas, just as in brainstorming, are nothing more than diamonds in the rough, perhaps even unrecognizable on first sight; we move to mine our mind and to discover ideas.

When first drafting this entry, I* produced the following focused free-write and sent it to Rebecca:

> Free-writing I know I should have a conflict something like free writing: babble or something smart in nay way free-writing is when you force yourself to keep writing no matter what's in your head as I do right now just that my head is racing way ahead of my thoughts and in some ways I wouldn't really need this. O no now I am hitting a blank just for a minute people ask students to do free writing no they don't ask they force them to do that nobody has ever done that to me and I haven't ever done it to any of my student but what's the idea and what's the value well it's supposed to help against writer's block and such and I can't stop even if I am sitting uncomfortably so it's supposed to help against writer's block but it is really a hard thing. It prevents the nice rhythm of the sentence the way writing halts breathes ponders so I must go on and must go on and must go on is that how Gertrude Stein wrote and I use these sentences to think about what to say next. The problem with free-writing? Is writing really a process we can teach neatly? Here is free-writing here is pre-draft etc. We know we can and yet we remain suspicisou. This is not at all going in the way that I want it to go after all I want my reader to respect me and this is much more babble than anything it prevents me from thinking almost since I feel like I am on a rope, like one that hangs between two tenement houses and is full of laundry and then I get pulled back to the window if you know what I mean, I can't stop yet, anyway my thinking is like one thin line, totally one-dimensional and flat even though of course I am making an argument about free-writing at the same time but the student who must write on something else must have a very hard time because form and content don't work together I don't know I can't really see this working but I only know when I go back and see the long trail of thoughts that I have produced in that way Is this all about production making us sort of writing machines I wonder I wonder still am wondering trying top figure out how I could pursue that thought without stopping to write or moving on to something else doesn't one want to stay with a thing instead of being on this endless trainride always hurrying on waving to people at different stations hardly seeing them not much more than colroed dots I can't go on much longer should I? Who can read this? Yet I feel if we want to discuss free writing there cannot be a better way to this than to discuss this itself 'showing instead of telling' all teachers believe in that and particularly all essayists and so what is this showing and is there gonna be more if I go on? I just don't know and get more and more fascinated with this thing not wanting to stop because I hope more will come you know how it is when one writes and one writes things one never even thought of I don't know whether that's going to be happening now at all what more can I say about free-writing Writing is scary and this is not it is tiring but not scary only in the sense that one wonders whether anything can come off this. . . . Here the free-write ended.

What came of this exercise? Looking back, I see that the entry is full of anxieties about doing a free-write, teaching free-writing, and imagining a reader at

---

*The "I" here refers to Hildegard Hoeller

the same time. But there is also dramatic movement from anxiety to elation, a progression in which my thinking and writing slowly adjust. First, I am thinking ahead ("my head is racing way ahead of my thoughts"). Then I want to stop and pursue an idea but find myself moving on too quickly ("it prevents me from thinking"). Finally, by the end, I am actually doing the free-write, using writing as thinking ("I get more and more fascinated with this thing not wanting to stop because I hope more will come"). Like a horse—I imagine—that finds itself falling in step with the carriage it draws and running no matter where, happy to explore wherever the journey will drive it. In the end, the anxieties have been replaced with a form of tired exhilaration ("Writing is scary and this is not it is tiring but not scary only in the sense that one wonders whether anything can come off this"). The final fear left in the end is that of doubting the method itself.

This free-write was my first, but not my last. Free-writing has become part of my writing process; I use it as a form of magic: What will I say? And why? And will something worthwhile emerge? In this case, the entry you now read is the answer to that question. Free-writing is a paradoxical mixture of freedom and coercion, anxiety and elation. It may not work for everyone but it is worth a try; it dramatically illustrates that writing is not primarily an expression of ideas but just as much a process of discovering and even generating them.

RELATED WORDS

Assignment 14	Revision 143
Audience 25	Writer's Block 195
Brainstorming 30	

EXERCISES

1. Do a focused free-write. For example, when faced with an assignment, determine a key term or central topic and free-write on it for ten minutes. Then do the same with a different aspect of the assignment. For elements of assignments, see our entry on "Assignment."

2. When faced with an assignment, in a group of three or so, have each member determine a focus for a free-write and conduct the free-write; the "leader" should time the event and make sure that everyone writes. Then, after doing three of those, discuss the results. What are main ideas, expressions, attitudes, terms that were generated?

3. Based on exercises 1 or 2, analyze the most useful things emerging from the free-write and develop those further in your writing or thinking process. This development may include another free-write assignment on a key term or question that you or someone else generated in the first free-writing.

4. When reading an assigned essay, free-write after each paragraph for a limited amount of time—three minutes, for example. As a group, assemble the free-writes to generate a larger response to the essay.

5. Use exercise 4 for a student draft and then analyze the response to formulate a letter that helps the writer with a revision of the essay.

6. Free-write for five minutes on an assignment given to you. Analyze your free-write either by rereading it carefully individually or by discussing it in a group; based on your analysis, generate both questions about and approaches to the assignment.

Grammar
The Magic of a Writer's Craft

In her essay, "Why I Write," acclaimed novelist, essayist, and screenwriter Joan Didion says "Grammar is a piano I play by ear, since I seem to have been out of school the year the rules were mentioned. All I know about grammar is its infinite power. To shift the structure of a sentence alters the meaning of that sentence, as definitely and inflexibly as the position of a camera alters the meaning of the object photographed. Many people know about camera angles now, but not so many know about sentences" (7). As Didion suggests here, grammar is not just an arrangement of words and punctuation marks that conveys a pre-formulated idea from the writer's head to the page. The way one sets up the sentence, the lens one chooses, the twist or turn one gives it, will shape and deliver that idea in a particular way, from a particular slant that is as individual as a handprint. In fact, while current uses of "grammar" frequently limit its meaning to the rules of usage, in previous centuries it was defined as "the art of speaking and writing a language correctly," and in the Middle Ages it was considered "synonymous with learning in general [including] magic and astrology" (OED, "Grammar," 1). Thus, "grammar," understood in the broader sense that Didion implies, is the amazingly fluid and flexible intersection of language, perspective, and meaning—the essence of a writer's craft.

Considered in this way, grammar seems like a kind of magic still, a sinuous set of relations invisibly binding words into communicative acts. Yet that magical sense of the open-endedness of language, of the infinite possible directions in which a sentence or a paragraph might go, can also seem overwhelming. For some writers there is sheer brutality in the number of choices and the amount of responsibility involved in writing a five-page essay; after all, creating one simple sentence involves a thousand decisions about what might be included or left out. When there are so many infinitesimal choices, so many hundreds of thousands of possible arrangements of words available to writers in a given instance, no wonder we sometimes flee in exhaustion to cliches, simple sentences, and familiar constructions or bulldoze on without contemplating a fraction of those possibilities in order to get something written. Alternatively, grammar can seem like the absence of choice. Just as many movie and television viewers don't particularly notice the camera angles, the close-ups or long shots, and the editing unless they begin to study film or make films, the choices involved in developing complex sentences, paragraphs, and essays can seem invisible, mysterious. Language in this case appears to be a transparent or unwieldy medium simply conveying or refusing to convey its burden of meaning. Grammar becomes the detailed system of rules that guard the entry into language—something to push through in order to get ideas into language—and writing can feel like the loss of control over ideas as they get pressed through the medium of language and before they get onto the page.

Yet most of the news about grammar is encouraging. Just as a viewer gains sophistication in recognizing camera angles by watching films and taking careful note of the details of focus and camera placement, most writers, like Didion, learn grammar primarily through immersion, through reading, paying close attention to the moves other writers make, and then trying those moves out for themselves. When people say they don't know grammar, they usually only mean that they haven't picked up the terminology and rules of grammar: punctuation usage, subjects and verbs, subordination and coordination, parallelism, and the like. Native speakers of a language who are unfamiliar with this terminology can still write and speak in highly functional if not error-free sentences. From there, learning the grammar of academic writing involves a similar process of adjusting one's ear to the language, noting the words, the pauses, the inflections. This process can certainly be enhanced by learning the rules and the terminology but knowing the rules cannot replace the benefits of simply reading closely and listening to the words on the page—of building a larger repertoire of notes to play.

In this process of adapting to the grammar of academic writing, it may help to remember that every culture has its own system of internal rules which usually appear mysterious to those outside that culture, and yet appear perfectly natural to those within it. In "Communication in a Global Village," Dean Barnlund, a professor of Education and Communications, points out that every culture has these internalized "rulebooks of meaning":

It is not too surprising that many cultures refer to themselves as "The People," relegating all other human beings to a subhuman form of life. To the person who drinks blood, the eating of meat is repulsive. Someone who conveys respect by standing is upset by someone who conveys it by sitting down; both may regard kneeling as absurd. Burying the dead may prompt tears in one society, smiles in another, and dancing in a third. If spitting on the street makes sense to some, it will appear bizarre that others carry their spit in their pocket; neither may quite appreciate someone who spits to express gratitude. (51–52)

If we stop to look at Barnlund's use of language here, we might notice that the first sentence contains the most abstract thought expressed in the passage. All the sentences after that are merely examples illustrating and providing evidence for that first sentence; one example piled on another, sentence after sentence, clause after clause. In two cases, Barnlund emphasizes the cumulative effects by using a semi-colon to paste two examples from contrasting cultures right up against each other. Going back to Didion's camera angle metaphor, we could say that the first sentence is the wide angle shot that establishes the main idea being expressed in the passage. The sentences that follow are a series of close-ups showing all the individual instances that help to characterize, explain and support this main idea. Further, in presenting his ideas in this way, with these kinds of sentence structures, Barnlund is operating completely within the "rulebooks of meaning" commonly used in his academic culture, crafting meaning within the conventions of academic writing. Imagine for example that he had phrased his first sentence as follows: "Many cultures refer to themselves as 'The People' and view all others as subhumans—no big surprise!" These slight shifts in word choice, sentence structure, and punctuation are enough to transform the tone and effect of the sentence making it sound less like an abstract, intellectual thought and more like a knee-jerk reaction.

As the form and substance of the Barnlund example suggest, every culture has its grammar, the meaningful set of structures through which it functions, and academia is no different. And, although those conventions are primarily used to foster shared communication of ideas, they can sometimes be used as the ideological tools of that culture, determining success and status, controlling who belongs and who does not. Grammar is in this sense both a larger cultural "rulebook of meaning" and a set of rules that police that culture. Academic culture and literate culture in general define themselves using both those senses of grammar: both the common codes, conventions, assumptions, contexts, audiences, purposes that help us to communicate and the rules by which we measure whether or not a person is educated. As Roger Sale points out, the rules of grammar operating in Shakespeare's time were much less rigid than they are now, partly because relatively few people in the fifteenth and sixteenth centuries were literate. "Only when literacy became the norm, open to people from all levels of society, from different regions with differing dialects, did people began worrying about standardizing English and identifying rules of correct usage" (24). This sense of historical context offers a useful reminder that grammar's "rulebooks" of meaning develop and change just as languages and cultures change. The pressure to fix those rules in place stems partly from a cultural anxiety about defining and policing what it means to be "educated," and partly from a more positive desire to maintain and cultivate effective communication.

Writers learn to work within both those functions: We deal with the awareness that we will be judged on the basis of correct or incorrect usage, and we take advantage of the system by using its rules to communicate well. Similarly, within academic culture, learning the conventions will help a writer succeed, and using those conventions can also open up a world of meaning, an awareness of how paragraphs and sentences can function to convey, shape, and develop what that writer wants to say. In fact, because of their meaning-making capacity, we should view the grammar of academic writing as a treasure trove of fresh choices, of new ways to structure a sentence and new ways to see the world, and we should study academic writing as a tutorial for setting up camera angles that we hitherto never dreamed of.

RELATED WORDS

Academic Thinking 1	Metaphor 110
Claims 38	Paragraphs 114
Coordination and Subordination 45	Parallelism 8
Dash 53	Punctuation 126
Editing 63	Subject-Verb 154

EXERCISES

1. Adopting Didion's metaphor, think of sentence structure as a series of camera angles. In an academic essay identify sentences that seem to be "wide-angle shots" and sentences that seem to be "close-ups." Where is the writer stepping back to give you the larger context, the abstract concept, the big claim, where is he or she zooming in to give examples, do a close analysis and what kinds of sentence structures does he or she use in each case? Write a paragraph in which you discuss two or three sample sentences, using quotes to illustrate the camera angles and explaining where you see them.

2. Test Didion's claim that changing the grammar of a sentence will inevitably change its meaning by rewriting a sentence several different ways. In each case, vary the sentence structure, the punctuation, or the word choice noting if and how the meaning of the sentence shifts as well.

3. Write a paragraph in which you create your own metaphor to replace or add to Didion's idea about camera angles. Invent your own way of describing some different kinds of sentence structures, and use quotes from your own writing or from an assigned reading to illustrate.

4. In a group, look through a grammar handbook and choose one spe-
    cific aspect of usage that has always puzzled or confused at least one
    person in your group (such as the difference between "that" and
    "which," semi-colon usage, or the problem with dangling modifiers,
    for example). List all the rules involving that aspect of usage and
    work them over until you have explained each one in a way that is
    clear and understandable to everyone in the group. Then find exam-
    ples of sentences in which a professional writer in one of your as-
    signed essays is practicing the usage you studied (when and why that
    writer uses semi-colons for example or how he or she avoids—we
    hope—dangling modifiers). Next, find examples of that same usage
    in your own writing and identify the reason for each usage.

5. In a group, look through a grammar handbook and find five of the
    most common usage errors (the grammatical equivalent of drinking
    blood or spitting on the floor in our culture). Have each member of
    the group write a grammar handbook entry, explaining one of the
    errors in his or her own words, giving one or two examples from his
    or her own writing or invented examples of the error, and discussing
    how to correct it. (These can be compiled into a handbook for a
    class or accumulated as a personal handbook that you can add to over
    time as you encounter new kinds of sentence structures and come up
    with new questions about grammar).

6. Draw on the members of your class who speak a second language to
    help the class list some of the "rulebooks" of grammar or culture
    (English and/or other languages and cultures) that, for a newcomer,
    seem to have *no* reasonable basis, are puzzling, surprising, and/or dif-
    ficult to learn. As a class, create a second list describing some of the
    "rulebooks" of academic culture that also seem to have *no* reasonable
    basis, are puzzling, surprising, and/or difficult to learn.

Interpretation
When a Banana Is Not Just a Banana

While the role of the United Nations interpreter who goes to work each day
and translates on the spot the speech of one diplomat into the language of another seems perfectly understandable, the job of interpretion in academic writ-

ing seems a little less straightforward. What kind of job is it? Who would pay us for doing such a job? Why is it necessary? The United Nations translator is negotiating the difference between two languages, expressing or explaining the thoughts of one person in the language of another. One need only compare the function of these highly trained individuals and their complex understanding of linguistic and political nuances with the crude output of a computerized language translator to appreciate the extent to which they are truly cultural mediators. Since each language brings with it a cultural network of assumptions, contexts, and implications that make the words meaningful, the interpreter must translate the actual words while imaginatively recasting that cultural network of meaning into the context of another language. Imagine translating the idiom, "it's time to face the music," from English into another language, for example.

What does it mean, then, to act as an interpreter within one's own language? On the one hand, the work is completely analogous to that of the United Nations' translator. In academic culture, the interpreter's job is to explain one person's ideas in a way that is understandable and meaningful to the interpreter's own readers. This often involves a negotiation between the perception, vocabulary, and purpose of the original writer and the interpreter's own viewpoint, word choices, and "take" on what the writer is saying. In this sense, the interpreter creates a balance between the role of translator—summarizing, explaining, and staying faithful to the intentions and ideas of the original writer—and the role of creator—one who overrides the intention of the original writer in order to build in her or his own perspective and make his or her own point. In academic writing, the interpreter explains an art object, a cultural phenomenon, or a piece of writing, in order to create from the original the interpreter's own artwork, the interpreter's own meaning. That art of interpretation often develops from summary through analysis to a moment of lift-off when the interpreter demonstrates his or her own perspective and motivation in using the original text. In order to convince their own readers of the validity and power of their art, good interpreters will carefully preserve some balance between that summary and analysis of the original writer and their own interpretive motivations, so that one never completely overwhelms the other.

In "Learning from the Banana," for example, literary and cultural critic, Susan Willis develops a fresh interpretation of a novel by William Faulkner by working initially from a careful summary of Faulkner's novel:

The novel depicts a backward sharecropping family. It tells of the death of Addie Bundren (the mother) and her family's hapless ten-day-long journey from their Mississippi farm to Jefferson where she will be buried. Hauled through flood, fire and hot summer sun, the mother in her coffin is the novel's central figure, whose scope widens to embrace her immediate family members, piled into a mule-drawn buckboard and accompanying her to her grave. (587)

From this careful, condensed description of the setting, characters, and plot of the novel, Willis begins her interpretation of it by inviting us to view the plot from a fresh perspective:

> Reading the family's journey from countryside to provincial metropolis as a historical metaphor allows us to see the plight of a single family as a figure for the migration of this country's agricultural work force to the cities. The family's migration is a geographic metaphor describing demographic change. (587)

Here we see Willis's own vocabulary and approach clearly coming into play. Faulkner did not use phrases like "the migration of this country's agricultural work force," but he did portray a family migrating from farm to city. Willis invites us to stand back a little from the details of the novel to see that it represents the larger demographic changes occurring in this period and the historical development of "sharecropping," of displaced farmers moving from place to place in order to find work.

From this distanced perspective, Willis then focuses in on a close analysis of one sentence from the novel where one character asks a child "Wouldn't you rather have bananas?" From a detailed analysis of this one sentence, its meaning within the story—where "bananas" become the substitute for all that the family has lost or cannot afford to buy—and the larger implications of its meaning beyond the story, Willis develops her own interpretation of the novel. In her interpretive artwork, the novel and the scene involving bananas become the basis for a historical and sociological consideration of twentieth-century international commodity culture, and the resulting supermarkets with their abundance of goods including Third-World imports like bananas that replace the produce of local farmers:

> The Bundren family, perched in their buckboard and eating their way through a bag of bananas, defines an economics whose components include their own demise as producers and reintegration as consumers. From Chilean peaches and nectarines, which have become acceptable wintertime equivalents for our own more readily available pears and apples, right down to the ordinary banana, the Third World is no longer perceived as the distant supplier of *exotic* commodities, but is instead a cornucopia spilling out a steady supply of ordinary foodstuffs for North America's supermarkets. (591)

Beginning from Faulkner's novel, Willis thus builds an interpretive artwork of her own, an article that goes far beyond Faulkner's novel and has its own set of purposes. Through summary and analysis she works with the meanings that are there in the text or implied by it; through interpretation she imports the text into a meaning-making context of her own.

Much of academic writing depends in some way on the act of interpretation, but interpretation is also the means through which we understand ourselves and our culture at large. For example, when two people face each other and extend their right hands in a brief clasp, only interpretation can tell us that this is a handshake, a ritual of greeting not to be mistaken for "holding hands," when two people stand side by side and clasp hands for a more extended period. Yet only people who are familiar with this cultural ritual would be able to read its meaning. Further, within this system of familiar cultural codes, we can often deduce by the duration and nature of the handshake (the two-handed clasp vs. the "high five," for instance) and the surrounding context clues whether this is the first meeting of strangers, the renewal of an old friendship, a minister comforting a mourning spouse, the reluctant truce between enemies, or two business people concluding a deal. The meeting of lips can, depending on context clues, signify the briefest social encounter or grounds for divorce. Differences in cultural background, perspective, even individual character will result in slightly different interpretations of the same event.

Anthropologist Clifford Geertz examines these differences in interpretation as one of the main challenges facing ethnographers when they go to observe a foreign culture. As he points out, it becomes easy to misinterpret situations or rituals if the ethnographer reads them through his or her own set of cultural assumptions. In explaining this challenge, Geertz uses the terms "thick" and "thin" description to describe the difference between *interpreting* a situation or ritual and merely observing it. For example, stripped of all interpretation, the "thin description" of what we call a "wink" is just a "rapid contraction of one eyelid" (*Interpretation* 6). It could mean anything or nothing: it could be a brief muscle spasm, a twitch; it could signify a speck of dust caught in the winker's eye. If anthropologists hope to interpret that wink correctly, they must learn about the culture and about the particular situation in which that wink occurs: it could be a complex signal to an intended viewer signifying a shared joke, or the winker's ridicule of an oblivious third party, or an elaborate parody of a wink, or even the rehearsal of a parody wink in the mirror (*Interpretation* 7). Interpretation, then, is the process by which we take into account (or build in) all the context clues that lend that contraction of the right eyelid a particular meaning. Without interpretation, that contraction of the eyelid is just raw data; it could mean anything or nothing.

Similarly in academic writing, the interpreter must not only use evidence to support her perception of that data, she must provide a persuasive explanatory context that makes that data meaningful. In the Susan Willis example discussed previously, Willis must not only demonstrate that she has read and understood Faulkner's novel, she must also build in the new historical and sociological contexts from which she wants to view the novel and convince us that her reading is appropriate and meaningful. Without the interpretation, we would end up with just a "thin description" of Faulkner's novel. However, as readers we are not willing to accept an interpretation that seems too far-fetched. Since Willis wants to convince us that supermarkets and bananas are that important for understanding the broader meaning of Faulkner's novel, she must not only provide supporting evidence (from Faulkner, from the history of Third-World imports), but must also translate that data, give it a context that will be meaningful and convincing to her audience. In fact, functioning explicitly like a Geertzian anthropologist, she pauses to explain exactly what bananas would have meant to the Bundren family in the context of their time and place: "For Faulkner's sharecroppers, the bananas represent luxury consumption, not the commonplace everyday-in-the-lunchbox fruits they have become for us. Instead, they are the exotic, the tropical, the equivalent of kiwis and cactus apples in our supermarkets today" (591). Here we see Willis beginning to build a "thick description," an interpretation of the evidence that helps us translate between our own understanding of bananas and the meaning they would have had in the sharecropper setting of Faulkner's novel. In doing so, she makes available a fresh view of Faulkner's novel and of the historical era it represents by translating both within the interpretive culture of her own article.

RELATED WORDS

Academic Thinking 1	Quotation 130
Argument 9	Reading 132
Evidence 77	Summary 159
Metaphor 110	Synthesis 172

EXERCISES

1. In a group, find several examples in which writers quote or summarize and then interpret another source. For each example, pinpoint the moment of lift-off, the moment where the writer begins to actively interpret the source. Look in particular for places where each writer builds in a fresh perspective or context that helps you to understand the source in a new way.

2. Create a deliberately "thin" description of a gesture or of some aspect of cultural interaction, stripped as much of possible of all its meaningful coding, explanation, and context clues. Then create a "thick" interpretation of that same gesture or interaction, filling in all the interpretive layers of coding and context that give it a particular meaning.

3. Choose a paragraph from an academic essay and paraphrase it, keeping to the role of the faithful translator by painstakingly and responsibly explaining the original reading. Then deliberately create an interpretation of the paragraph that is completely far-fetched. See how much evidence from the essay and how much explanatory context you can build in to make your far-fetched interpretation as convincing as possible. Compare the results with those of other members of your group and consider which interpretations seem most persuasive and why.

4. In a group, choose a passage from an assigned reading that seems complex enough to need interpretive explanation. Have each member of the group write an explanation of the passage adding an example from his or her own knowledge and experience. Then take turns verbally interpreting the passage for the rest of your group, with each member of the group adding a fresh perspective on the material. Rewrite your interpretation of the passage using the group's ideas to help develop and deepen your understanding.

5. Choose a moment in a student draft where the writer introduces and interprets a piece of evidence. Is the writer providing enough explanatory context for that evidence, using summary and analysis to help you to understand what it meant within the original source? Is the writer providing a fresh interpretive context, a new way of understanding that evidence? Wherever possible, suggest ways in which the writer could translate more or push that interpretation even further.

Introductions
The Risk of Beginning

The introductory paragraph of an essay is as simple, as rule-bound, as complex, and as unpredictable as introducing oneself to a stranger at a party. The formula for the latter is simple enough: two individuals exchange names and attempt to establish enough common ground to find a topic of conversation in which they both can engage and that will last until one or the other can make the excuse of finding a drink or moving on to another person. Often one invokes the names of the party's host in an effort to find some mutual acquaintances who will lead to that common ground: "So, how do you know Ella Blank?" The only real risk is of making or getting a bad first impression, which might entail spending the rest of the evening avoiding or being avoided by the new acquaintance—yet that relatively small danger is enough to induce heart-pounding, palm-sweating anxiety in all but the most socially assured. And of course, if some common ground is established, this introduction could be the beginning of a lasting friendship or lead to a transformative encounter; at the very least, it could result in ten minutes of entertaining chat.

Similarly, the formula for the introduction to a college paper is simple enough. Student writers in particular are often told that the elements to include in that opening paragraph are:

1. some general thoughts or an example that establishes a common ground between the writer and the potential reader or "hooks" the reader in some way;

2. a formal introduction of the key players in the essay, which might involve defining the key terms to be used in the essay and/or identifying the main sources on which the essay is based including their titles and the authors' full names—the essay's equivalent of "Ella Blank"—including an indication of how each source might contribute to the discussion;

3. a declaration of the main topic, issue, question, or problem that the writer and the reader will be pursuing in the essay (commonly known as a thesis statement, which most often appears as the last sentence in the opening paragraph).

Yet, as this formula suggests, while the reader is very much in the position of the casual cocktail-party guest, the writer has much more at stake. The writer is determined to hook the reader in that opening paragraph, is bent on establishing enough interest and common ground to ensure the reader's commitment to the rest of the essay. Further, the writer has already decided on the topic under consideration and is deliberately maneuvering the reader toward that one topic out of all the others he or she might have chosen. In fact, that opening encounter created by that first paragraph is a high drama of writerly seduction. Suddenly, the writer is there on the page, accosting the reader who has innocently turned to that first page, setting the tone of the encounter, starting a train of thought in motion and indicating its direction. The writer tries to be engaging, authoritative, possibly witty or intriguing. The opening paragraph creates a scene of excitement that the reader wants to join: it introduces a significant conflict, asks a crucial question, poses an important problem, promises the reader a worthwhile encounter. And behind this attractive facade the writer is busy plotting the direction of the essay, setting up the expectations that he or she already knows the essay will fulfill.

All this sounds like quite a burden. And in truth, the advice writers often get to write the introductory paragraph last, once they really do know where the essay is headed, is perfectly sound. There is no need to begin writing an essay at the beginning—far easier to jump directly in, analyze a source, pursue a question, tell the truth about a topic and see where it leads. Or, if a draft without an introductory paragraph feels too much like a headless trunk rushing gorily around with no brain and no direction, a writer can actually use the formula listed here to create a kind of skeleton introduction, one that sets up a relationship to the assignment and predicts a likely direction the paper might take. Once the essay has been written and revised, the writer then has the luxury of going back to that boney outline of a head to ask, "what kind of flesh should I give this?" Arguably, this is a moment of luxury since the real work, which is the writing of the essay body, is done, or nearly done. The writer has no burden of proof in an introduction; instead, that opening paragraph takes the plunge of a first encounter, risks an opening remark, conjures up the being, the voice who will speak in that essay, offers the reader a topic to consider, a problem to solve, and a sense of direction.

The following introduction by feminist political theorist Joanne H. Wright corresponds fairly well to the formula described previously. Her essay, "Going Against the Grain: Hobbes's Case for Original Maternal Dominion," appeared in the *Journal of Women's History* and was therefore intended for an audience of other professionals in her field, historians and serious students of history. This helps to explain why her first sentence does not even bother to introduce English seventeenth-century philosopher and political theorist Thomas Hobbes by his full name—she can safely assume that everyone in her intended audience will know exactly who Hobbes is:

> In the *Leviathan*, Hobbes developed an enigmatic and politically contentious theory of the nature of gender relations. His depiction of women as independent contractors in the state of nature, contractors even with the children they bear, stood in radical opposition to prevailing understandings of gender and motherhood in seventeenth-century England. His vision contrasted even with the women who battled for religious freedom during the Interregnum, those who challenged gender hierarchies on issues of faith and conscience but left the political theory of patriarchalism essentially untouched. Before leaving women behind altogether, Hobbes effectively disrupted gender norms, opening a space in which gender relations are dramatically—if briefly—reconceived. Because Hobbes went against the grain in his conception of gender relations his work provides a provocative window into the operation of gender and the relationship between gender and political discourse in seventeenth-century England. (123)

In a way, Wright establishes a "common ground" with her audience by assuming quite a bit about what they already know; that Hobbes' book, *Leviathan,* was in general about social contracts and not about gender relations, that the "Interregnum" was the period from 1653–1658 during which Oliver Cromwell and parliamentary authority replaced the monarchy. In fact, she "hooks" her readers by dispensing with the preliminary chit-chat and cutting right to her thesis, which in turn seems like one possible model for many college essays, since it is often true that everyone in the class has read the same materials. In terms of "key players," her audience knows immediately that she will be working with the part of Hobbes that *does* deal with gender relations and, as the thesis in the last sentence clearly states, she will be using Hobbes to help her readers get a better understanding of gender relations and politics in this period. As it turns out, she actually reserves one of her "key players" for the second paragraph since her essay is largely a response to the work of feminist political theorist Carole Pateman, but the resulting opening is solid and businesslike. This is not creative risk-taking, not an attention-grabbing or mind-bending opener, but it is a workmanlike and reasonably effective introductory paragraph.

On the other hand, even the briefest survey of essays by academic writers will show them playing all kinds of games with these rules, abandoning some elements of the formula and reinventing others. Sometimes they will devote the entire first paragraph to some personal or impersonal anecdote and reserve any overt statements about their topic until paragraph two, or leave their readers surfing the waves of the body paragraphs carried along by a tone of authority and supporting transitions but without a clear sense of what the thesis is to be. Sometimes they will identify a key source, but often they will leave aside those references until the later work of evidence-building begins in the essay. For example, "The Experience of Policy" by social worker Lynda Workman begins, "I sit quietly at my desk, aware and yet unaware of my surroundings" and goes on to describe her office, the walls, filing cabinets, the books and most of all the forms, "rows of forms, all different for different purposes: to record information, to record statistics, to declare witnessed truths" (749). Unlike Wright's, this opening works to situate the speaker within specific surroundings, invites the reader to visualize an encounter, and sets a mood for the essay. As it turns out, the innumerable forms that fill the office in this scene also set the stage for the central problems involved in implementing social service policies that the entire essay will explore. Thus, as with most effective opening paragraphs, the seeds of the entire essay are embedded there, masked within a seemingly casual description.

Sometimes an effective opening seems to spring open, inviting the reader to continue, sometimes it appears tightly curled, posing a riddle that only reading the essay can solve. Often a good introduction begins with a sound, a voice like a magician speaking itself into life. For example, the opening paragraph of art historian John Berger's essay, "Ways of Seeing" is exactly two lines long: "Seeing comes before words. The child looks and recognizes before it can speak" (50). This seems at first to abandon all rules, to speak elliptically without a thesis or an identifiable direction and without posing a problem. Instead, the first thing we hear is that magician's voice, a voice so thoughtful, so reflective that one's pulses seem to slow. Suddenly, in those two sentences, there is all the time in the world to ponder, to look at the paragraph like a child ready to take in its possible meaning. Seeing comes before words? But how do we, how does a child make sense of what it sees before it has the words to categorize or distinguish one object from another? We are faced with a riddle, and the quiet authority of the essayist's voice invites us to continue, to participate in developing the riddle's solution.

Where Berger begins with the drama of the voice itself, other writers choose to foreground the debate that the essay will explore. For instance, political scientist Anne Norton's "The Signs of Shopping" introduces us to an ongoing debate in full swing, but does not tell us her own thesis, her own position in that debate:*

> The mall has been the subject of innumerable debates. Created out of the modernist impulse for planning and the centralization of public activity, the mall has become the distinguishing sign of suburban decentralization, springing up in unplanned profusion. Intended to restore something of the lost unity of city life to the suburbs, the mall has come to export styles and strategies to stores at the urban center. Deplored by modernists, it is regarded with affection only by their postmodern foes. Ruled more by their content than by their creators' avowed intent, the once sleek futurist shells have taken on a certain aura of postmodern playfulness and popular glitz. (62–63)

Here the opening sentence works as a hook, not only because her intended readers know what "the mall" is, but also because the sentence itself is short and succinct. We then get a brief historical view and an introduction to some of the key issues and players in this particular debate. We have a fairly good sense that we will hear more from modernists, who regret the shape and direction their ideal "public centers" have taken, and we will hear more from postmodernists who are fascinated by multiple uses and surface glitter of the malls themselves. However, we are not quite sure where Norton herself stands in this debate, or what she will be arguing in this piece. Is she a postmodernist setting up the modernists to provide herself with a counterargument? Will she place herself somewhere in the middle of this debate? A thesis would help us to know where Norton fits into the picture she has sketched, but in the meantime the debate itself poses a problem: How will Norton or we decide between these two conflicting positions?

By contrast, literary and cultural critic Susan Willis immediately announces the thesis of her essay, "Disney World: Public Use/Private State" and then leaps into a series of examples:

> At Disney World, the erasure of spontaneity is so great that spontaneity itself has been programmed. On the "Jungle Cruise" khaki-clad tour guides teasingly engage the visitors with their banter, whose apparent spontaneity has been carefully scripted and painstakingly rehearsed. Nothing is left to the imagination or the unforseen. Even the paths and walkways represent the programmed assimilation of the spontaneous. According to published reports, there were no established walkways laid down for the opening-day crowds at Disneyland. Rather, the Disney Imagineers waited to see where people would walk, then paved over their spontaneous footpaths to make prescribed routes. (744)

Here, the hook is less in the opening sentence (which intrigues but is also hard to absorb) and more in the punchy examples that help to unpack the thesis—how can we pass up the chance to read about "Jungle Cruise" khaki-clad tour

---

*Although this piece is actually a selection from Norton's book, *The Republic of Signs,* it appears in its excerpted "essay" form in *Signs of Life.* The fact that it was selected from a longer piece may explain its lack of a thesis.

guides! Willis leaves us in no doubt about what she plans to argue and where she stands on the issue; we get the immediate sense that programmed spontaneity is a problem for Willis, that Disney World fools us into thinking our experiences are unplanned, and that the question of whether or not this leaves any room for real individuality will be a major concern of this essay. What Willis leaves less clearly defined is the other side of the debate, something that will no doubt emerge through the counterevidence presented in her essay, and which may be hinted at in the last example of this paragraph: After all, if Disney allowed the first crowds to create spontaneous walkways, perhaps they are only catering to and supporting individuality and spontaneity.

Perhaps because many writers, unlike Willis, do tend to begin with a broader effort to establish common ground and then narrow a topic down to the very specific thesis they plan to argue (as Wright does, for example), a standard and classically abused opening begins from the hugely general, from the establishing of common ground with a thousand unknown readers, and proceeds to a blow-by-blow organizational statement describing every move the essayist plans to make. Often described as the funnel shape or the up-ended triangle, this kind of opening seemingly begins like a satellite camera with a view of the universe, then focuses on the planet earth, on America, on the state of Texas, on the town of Waco, then closes in through the rooftops into the bedroom of Roger and Sylvia and zooms in for a close-up just as they are beginning an argument about the dirty red socks on the floor. In its least effective manifestations, this formula really does try to encompass the universe and in the process loses its grip on the reader: "Since the beginning of time . . . ." or "These readings are both similar and different" or a truism like "As the saying goes, you can't judge a book by its cover." Missing a sense of drama or the possibility of real debate, the reader turns away, moves on to the next promising encounter.

Which brings us to the core truth of introductory paragraphs: They must take a risk. They must pose a real question that the essay will struggle to answer, set up a meaningful debate that may be impossible to resolve, attack a significant issue that the essay will explore from a fresh perspective. If the writer is embarking on a risk-free and completely predictable venture, if the essay begins with a foregone conclusion, why in the world would we want to go along? If the writer takes a risk right up front, sets out on an unpredictable adventure with courage, determination, and "Jungle Cruise" guides, how tempting it is to join in.

RELATED WORDS

Assignment 14	Essay 68
Audience 25	Key Terms 106
Claims 38	Thesis 176
Conclusions 42	Titles 180
Discipline 57	Voice 187

EXERCISES

1. Working in a group, analyze one or more introductory paragraphs from the assigned readings. Describe several of the strategies each writer uses. What problem or debate does he or she pose? Which parts of the "formula" does he or she seem leave out? Try the same exercise using one or more drafts from the writers in your group.

2. Choose one of the introductory paragraphs you have analyzed in exercise 1. Write a paragraph of your own describing the voice created in this opening, the audience it seems to imagine, the direction it suggests the essay will take, and the problem or debate that it invites the reader to help explore. How much of a risk is the writer taking in this introduction?

3. Choose an introductory paragraph from an essay you have not yet read. List all the expectations it sets up: What will this essay be about? What are its key terms? What is the writer's thesis? What sort of person does the writer seem to be? Does the introduction make you want to read further along in the essay? Why or why not?

4. Working from a paper draft of your own, write a completely formulaic opening paragraph, one that does the absolute minimum in setting your reader up to read the paper. Then write an over-the-top opening, one that abandons the rules, takes a huge risk, and/or makes promises that the essay couldn't possibly fulfill. Finally, write an opening balanced somewhere between these two, one that sets up a thesis, involves your reader in the topic of the essay and tempts him or her to continue reading.

5. Choose the introductory paragraph you admire the most from any essay you have read. Write an introductory paragraph for your own paper in which you mimic or parody the voice, the ingredients, even the sentence structures used in that opening.

6. In a group, compare the introductory paragraphs from your drafts. Identify the strategies each writer has used and note places where the additional strategies discussed in this entry might be helpful. What promises does each introduction make, and are those promises fulfilled in the essay? What risks does each writer take? To what extent does each writer create an opening that draws you in?

Key Terms
The Main Characters of Essays

> I propose to examine two distinct models for the exhibition of works of art, one cen-
> tered on what I shall call resonance and the other on wonder. By *resonance* I mean the
> power of the displayed object to reach out beyond its formal boundaries to a larger
> world, to evoke in the viewer the complex, dynamic cultural forces from which it has
> emerged and for which it may be taken by a viewer to stand. By *wonder* I mean the
> power of the displayed object to stop the viewer in his or her tracks, to convey an ar-
> resting sense of uniqueness, to evoke an exalted attention. (Stephen Greenblatt, "Reso-
> nance and Wonder" 42)

This opening paragraph of Stephen Greenblatt's essay "Resonance and
Wonder" highlights and celebrates a fundamental fact of all essays: They are
foremost about words. Essays need key terms; or, to put it differently, terms are
the keys to essays. Greenblatt italicizes the keys to his essay in order to stress
that they are not self-understood words but *his terms* as he defines them for his
essay and as they become interesting in relation to each other. If we can think
of the essay as a play or a novel for a moment, then we can think of its key
terms as characters. In his introduction then, Greenblatt simply introduces his
two main characters, resonance and wonder.

From there the essay proceeds, just as a play or novel would, by tracing
the growth of these main characters, by developing them, by making their
meaning and relevance clearer and clearer, and by examining their increasingly complex relation to each other. In each paragraph one or both terms
reappear, and with each appearance—just as in a play or novel—we learn
more about them. The best way to read Greenblatt's essay then—and a great
way to read all essays—is to focus on those key terms and examine how their
meaning and relationship to each other develops throughout the essay. Consider the following two body paragraphs—separated by ellipses—as two scenes
in which the key terms appear:

> But the inhibition of viewing in the State Jewish Museum is paradoxically bound up with
> its resonance. This resonance depends not upon visual stimulation but upon a felt inten-
> sity of names, and behind the names, as the very term *resonance* suggests, of voices: the
> voices of those who chanted, studied, muttered their prayers, wept, and then were for-
> ever silenced. And mingled with these voices are others—of those Jews in 1389 who
> were murdered in the Old-New Synagogue where they were seeking refuge, of the great
> sixteenth-century Kabbalist Jehuda ben Bezalel (who is known as Rabbi Loew and who is

fabled to have created the golem), and of the twentieth century's ironic Kabbalist from Prague, Franz Kafka. (47)

. . .

My immediate thought was that the whole Coca-Cola stand could be shipped to New York and put on display in the Museum of Modern Art. It is that kind of impulse that moves us away <u>from resonance and toward wonder.</u> For MOMA is one of the great contemporary places not for the hearing of intertwining voices, not for historical memory, not for ethnographic thickness, but for intense, indeed enchanted looking. Looking may be called enchanted when the act of attention draws a circle around itself from which everything but the object is excluded, when intensity of regard blocks out all circumambient images, stills all murmuring voices. To be sure, the viewer may have purchased a catalogue, read an inscription on the wall, or switched on a cassette player, but in the moment of <u>wonder</u> all of this apparatus seems mere static. (49 [emphasis ours, italics Greenblatt's])

Both paragraphs serve to develop the characters or meanings of the two key terms. The opening paragraph told us that resonance has to do with the cultural context within which an object speaks while wonder is about the awe an object inspires. In these two body paragraphs, Greenblatt develops these definitions further. Using the literal relation of resonance to hearing ("re-sounding")—rather than viewing—Greenblatt is able to understand and explain the strong impact of the State Jewish Museum despite its lack of visually interesting objects; it is the voices of those "jews murdered in 1389" that we can hear so forcefully precisely because we do not see anything spectacular. And in the second paragraph, which moves us explicitly from resonance to wonder, he uses a very different example, the Coca-Cola stand, to give *wonder* a character distinct from *resonance*. What indeed could be more different than an exhibition and memory of a horrible murder than a Coca-Cola stand? Moving from one to the other, Greenblatt exhibits perfect memory of his earlier paragraphs, including the one quoted here, when he lists again all the things wonder is *not,* that is, all the things—"intertwining voices, historical memory, ethnographic thickness"—he has slowly developed to be the characteristics of resonance. Greenblatt thus expands on this difference in the terms by linking resonance to voices and hearing and wonder to sights and looking. He reminds us that we both hear (listen, read) and see (view) in a museum and that those two activities are different, perhaps even in conflict.

The key terms, and the contrasts that define them, become the core of his essay, and they are used here not only as growing characters but also as tools to review, to orient, to summarize, and to move along. By the end of the essay, they have become "household names" for us; we have seen the terms applied and growing throughout his essay, one paragraph at a time. And we have begun to understand that they stand in opposition in museum exhibits: that one is chosen at the expense of the other as in the examples of the resonant State Jewish Museum which has no visual appeal and the visually appealing Coca-Cola stand at MOMA which has no resonance, no "historical memory," no "voices," no "thickness." It is at this moment, in a classic essayistic move, that

Greenblatt somewhat dissolves the opposition he set up in the opening paragraph, transforming his terms from opposite to complements and thus giving his key terms their final exit:

> But is a triumph of one over the other necessary? For the purposes of this paper, I have obviously exaggerated the extent to which these are alternative models for museums: in fact, almost every exhibition worth viewing has elements of both. I think that the impact of most exhibitions is likely to be enhanced if there is a strong initial appeal to <u>wonder</u>, a <u>wonder</u> that then leads to the desire for <u>resonance</u>, for it is generally easier in our culture to pass from <u>wonder</u> to <u>resonance</u> than from <u>resonance</u> to <u>wonder</u>. In either case, the goal—difficult but not utopian—should be to press beyond the limits of the models, cross boundaries, create strong hybrids. For both the poetics and the politics of representation are most completely fulfilled in the experience of <u>wonderful</u> <u>resonance</u> and <u>resonant</u> <u>wonder</u>. (54 [emphasis added])

"Wonderful resonance and resonant wonder" are the "utopian goal" that museums should strive for: poetics and politics, past and present, viewing and hearing. Greenblatt admits to us in the end that the opposition between his key terms was a rhetorical move, a way of teaching us; and all teaching, probably, involves initial exaggeration. But once the lesson is learned, we need to move on, toward a more complex understanding of the world and toward a solution of the conflict he presents. We can do so once we have a firm grasp on those terms Greenblatt gives us (resonance and wonder); it is only then that we can even begin to understand that resonant wonder and wonderful resonance may well be the solution to the conflict between resonance and wonder.

"Resonance and Wonder" is a beautiful, perhaps even exceptional, key term essay because its content, development, and structure center so totally on these two terms. Greenblatt's elegantly choreographed piece teaches us how writers care about words, how writing is about words, and how words live through writing. The writer gives birth to his key terms—even though the words *resonance* and *wonder* already existed of course—tells their story, and gives them to us to keep. It is easy to see how these words will shape our next experience in a museum; and it is easy to see how they could reappear in one of our own essays, undoubtedly gaining new life and meaning there, just as characters in novels and people in life, for that matter, grow with each new situation they encounter and each experience they have.

Academic thinking relies on such a growing vocabulary as much as essays rely on key terms. Disciplines share their own set of key terms, and academic writers often become famous for coining such a key term, such as anthropologists Mary Louise Pratt for "contact zone," Victor Turner for "liminality," or Thomas Kuhn for "paradigm shift." Most influential thinkers are credited and remembered that way: Freud and the "Oedipus Complex," Darwin and "Evolution," or even the Republican party and "trickle-down economics." "Coining" a term and being "credited" for it are apt metaphors since developed key terms become a form of currency within and beyond an essay: within because they function as the means through which writers handle, connect, and give value and meaning to the things they write about; and beyond because they become the property, even brand name, of authors and define their value. Key terms, one might conclude, are one of the keys to academic writing and success.

┌─ **RELATED WORDS** ─────────────────────────────────┐

Argument 9   Metaphor 110

Brainstorming 30   Paragraphs 114

Discipline 57   Structure 149

Essay 68   Thesis 176

Free-Writing 87   Titles 180

Inroductions 99

└───┘

EXERCISES

1. In an academic essay, circle what appear to be key terms. In a discussion, determine what you think are the key terms of the essay. Assemble a list of definitions that emerge from all the places where it is used. In a group, consider the following questions: How are the terms used? How do their definitions vary and develop? What structure of the essay emerges as a result? Individually or as a group, write down what you think the plot of the essay is, based on the use of key terms.

2. Using a draft written by a student, write down what you think are the key terms of the essay and then consider how they are and could be used and defined throughout. Try to incorporate at least one of them in each topic sentence and write an outline of the paper which describes how the key terms are used in each paragraph.

3. Pick a key term from an assignment or essay, and brainstorm or freewrite first on associations with the term and then various opposites of the term to determine what the central tension of an essay might be. For example, the term *love* gains completely different meanings when it is opposed to sex, friendship, hate, money, and so on. Determine a pairing—such as resonance and wonder—and, imitating Greenblatt, write an opening paragraph of your essay that defines the terms and their relation to each other.

4. Check a key term—of your own or someone else's essay—in the *Oxford English Dictionary* (OED) and consider the differences between the way the term is defined in the dictionary and the way it is used in the essay. Then use some of the definitions, quotations, and history of the term to develop your use and understanding of the key terms in the draft. If dealing with your own draft, incorporate some of the OED's definition into your essay; if reading someone else's essay, use the OED definitions to write a response to the essay. For models consult our entries on the "Dash," "Assignment," and "Syllabus."

5. Using an academic essay or book, assemble an entry on one key term that resembles an *OED* entry; for example, quote the term wherever used and deduce various definitions of the word. Use page numbers (instead of dates) as a form of chronology.

Metaphor
Its Wonders and Dangers

The metaphor—rather than its less radical cousin the simile*—is the hinge between rationality and irrationality, between writing and painting. It is, as poet Robert Frost says it, "a momentary stay against confusion"(394). Momentary because metaphors come to us as if out of the blue, a sudden gift of insight shaping itself into words, and momentary also because they ultimately do not stand up to persistent scrutiny. Of course the metaphor is not a hinge! What am I thinking? One is a small metal object, the other an abstract rhetorical concept. Metaphors, "[figures] of speech that imply a comparison between two unlike entities" (*Encyclopedia Britannica*), offer translations from one realm to another.

We expect metaphors in poetry; we relish the images and the meanings a metaphor can capture there. Emily Dickinson writes: "A Dying Tiger— moaned for Drink—/I hunted all the Sand—/I caught the Dripping of a Rock/and bore it in my Hand—" (275). The "I" of the poem and the "tiger" are implicitly compared here even though they are clearly unlike entities. The poem does not say: I am like a tiger; it simply fuses the tiger and the "I." As a result, each line carries many meanings: we envision the speaker like a tiger, but we also see a tiger thirstily roaming the sand for water until a hand bears the water. The metaphor allows us to see two things at once, merging them into each other and translating human behavior into animal behavior and vice versa. This is an almost eerie play with our reality. The encyclopedia comments: "The metaphor makes a qualitative leap from a reasonable, perhaps prosaic comparison, to an identification or fusion of two objects, to make one new entity partaking of the characteristics of both. Many critics regard the making of metaphors as a system of thought ante-

---

*We call it less radical because it *likens* rather than *equates* two dissimilar things. In other words, it lets us know of the conceptual leap it makes.

dating or bypassing logic" (*Encyclopedia Britannica*). We can easily see how Dickinson's Tiger/I bypasses all logic and expands our world of seeing, saying, and understanding.

This bypassing of logic may account for the fact that metaphors are rarer in academic writing than in poetry. Much of academic writing is supposed to state its point in a clear and logical fashion and to give evidence; so we do not expect either play or multiple meanings. Yet, academic thinking, too, needs and uses metaphors: sometimes to structure an entire essay or illustrate a major concept, but sometimes also just to clarify a smaller point. Consider Paolo Freire's often cited and anthologized essay "The 'Banking' Concept of Education" as an example of both of these uses. Freire begins his essay by describing what he considers to be the typical "narrative" situation of education in which the teacher talks and the student listens. This first metaphor (that existing education is narration) encapsulates the problem Freire addresses. "The contents," he writes, "tend in the process of being narrated to become lifeless and petrified. Education is suffering from narration sickness" (207). Freire here uses several metaphors to reveal his critique (and assumptions) about education; "lifeless, petrified, and sick" are metaphors used to suggest that education is diseased, even dead, when it should be a lively, pulsing, and healthy organism.

But these metaphors are only used to lead up to the central metaphor of the essay: the banking concept. After describing the teacher–student relationship a bit further, he concludes:

> Narration (with the teacher as narrator) leads the students to memorize mechanically the narrated content. Worse yet, it turns them into "containers," into "receptacles" to be "filled" by the teacher. The more completely he fills the receptacles, the better a teacher he is. The more meekly the receptacles permit themselves to be filled, the better students they are.
>
> Education thus becomes an act of depositing, in which the students are the depositories and the teacher is the depositor. . . . This is the "banking" concept of education, in which the scope of action allowed to the students extends only as far as receiving, filing, and storing the deposits. (207–08)

Freire thus has arrived at his central metaphor, the banking concept, through several smaller and more temporary metaphorical steps (indicated through quotation marks around the metaphorical terms "receptacles" and "banking"), each one capturing and clarifying his ideas about education and each one preparing us for his central metaphor. He first equates students with "containers" and "receptacles." This gets him to the metaphor of "filling the student," or "depositing" content during education. The term "depositing"—itself a metaphor for putting money in an account—leads him to equating education with banking. The banking concept is more powerful than the metaphor of the "receptacle" (the warm-up band if you wish) because it is even less neutral: It carries the political echoes Freire wants. Through his metaphors we have traveled from a living, active body to the cold, passive, institutional image of a depository in a bank. We know, by his metaphors, that something living has died in the process, and that larger "interests" have replaced it.

It is this implication of the metaphor that Freire relies on; after all, he suggests that such education is an education that indeed serves the interests of the ruling class, that is literally oppressive. His metaphor thus helps him to create the political implications that fuel his thinking and that allow him to pose an alternative pedagogy of dialogue and process as a revolutionary antidote against "banks" and all they stand for and protect. Freire's extended metaphor has taken hold of its readers and has become almost a household word. Is it able to survive its own longevity—its life beyond the essay—without revealing its own limitations or losing its life, becoming petrified itself?

Sometimes extended metaphorical thinking can be harmful, argues Susan Sontag in *Illness as Metaphor* (1978). Extended metaphors might be mistaken for truths and thus lead to wrong judgments. Sontag specifically examines the metaphorical ways in which people have seen consumption in the nineteenth century and cancer in the twentieth. She shows that tuberculosis—or consumption—in the nineteenth century was described as an illness that expressed passion and character (an excess really of both, or a repression of both); the consequence of such metaphorical thinking was a false etiology (a false conception of the origins of the illness), which lay blame and responsibility on the patient. Similarly, she argues, cancer became metaphorized in the 1970s as a result of a cancerous personality, as if particular people expressed themselves through cancer. In either case, the metaphorical way of thinking about disease blamed (or credited) the patient for the disease. Such thinking obviously helped the healthy to distance themselves from the horrors of disease by making it understandable and ultimately moral. Nothing, after all, is scarier than facing the fact that illnesses strike all of us randomly, without meaning.

Sontag uses a quick, temporary metaphor herself to make us rethink this position: "Illness is the night-side of life," she writes, "a more onerous citizenship. Everyone who is born holds dual citizenship, in the kingdom of the well and in the kingdom of the sick. Although we all prefer to use only the good passport, sooner or later each of us is obliged, at least for a spell, to identify ourselves as citizens of that other place"(3–4). Sontag uses the metaphor of the "dual citizenship" to implicate all of us—of course, we all know that we are ill sometimes, but when we are not, we like to forget about the ill, push them away as if they are living in a different country (hospital, nursing homes, mental institutions, etc.). Sontag's metaphor counters that tendency and captures two important points: One, we are all ill at some point, and second we all have rights and duties—we are citizens. Her book is devoted to reestablishing these rights and duties and to "liberating" the ill from the regime of those metaphors that deprive them of their rights and that spread "stereotypes of national character" (3–4). Sontag does not hold on to that metaphor beyond the introduction. It is only there to draw us in and to remind us of our fundamental, inescapable, involvement in the subject and the natural rights patients (we) should have and to liberate us from metaphorical thinking that deprives us of these natural rights.

So, would Sontag also want to liberate us from Freire's metaphor of the "banking concept of education"? Freire himself uses the metaphor explicitly in the name of political liberation. The implication of Freire's metaphor is that banks—just as the banking kind of education—are inevitably bad; he implies that narrating education is used to defend the rights of the oppressor (banks and money interests). In some ways, Freire's argument about education is feeding the reader metaphorical content—making us a receptacle for the metaphorical meaning and making our like or dislike of narrated education contingent with our like and dislike of banks and a particular economic order. That perhaps is itself a form of "banking," a feeding of an ideological connection between form (narration and listening) and content (the interests of the rich and the bank). And isn't Freire's essay, particularly in this use of the metaphor narrating to us and assuming that we listen? The metaphor in Freire is by no means playful—nothing like Dickinson's fusion of the tiger and "I" which leaves us suspended between realities. Rather it carries with it implications that are almost contradicting its overt message.

The wonder of the metaphor is its alchemical quality—beyond reason it fuses two unlike objects and clarifies and expands their character through the fusion. But held on too hard and too long, it also reveals its dangers and limitations. Some metaphors are good enough for a sentence, some for an entire essay, and very few should exist very much beyond that.

RELATED WORDS

Assumptions 19	Key Terms 106
Brainstorming 30	Reading 132
Dash 53	Titles 180

EXERCISES

1. In an academic essay (whether written by a published author or a student or an entry in this book) highlight all uses of metaphors you can identify. Then analyze the author's use of metaphors: Which ones are momentary? Which ones are held onto for a paragraph? Which ones for the entire essay? If you cannot find metaphors, proceed to exercise 2.

2. Deliberately insert metaphors in an academic essay. Where might they work? Try to introduce a metaphor for a quick illustration, another for the focus of a paragraph, and discuss whether one could be used for the whole essay.

3. Write up an analysis of a piece of academic writing in the way you have discussed it in class but with the difference that you use metaphors for all insights: The quotes are crutches (or friends) in this

essay, the ideas jump like frogs or dance like a well-trained ballet troop, the voice seduces, the key terms are signposts, and so on.

4.   Metaphors are teaching tools. Prepare a lesson on one aspect of academic writing (paragraph, quotation, etc.) that relies on a metaphor or metaphors for illustration. For example, this paragraph is a tangled web, this one a balloon and so on.

5.   Rewrite a paragraph from this book that uses metaphors by eliminating the metaphor. What is the effect?

Paragraphs
The Unfolding Drama

Think of the paragraph as a scene in television drama. Each paragraph or scene furthers the action of the drama by one step. It introduces only the minimum number of characters and elements needed to establish a context, to create a particular turn in the plot, to reveal or develop a crucial aspect of character, to make or extend a particular point. Imagine, then, a docudrama we will call, "For Better or Worse." The lead character, Jolene, is in the doctor's office discovering that she has a sexually transmitted disease (cut to commercial). Now, she is in her parked car, stained medical cotton still taped to her arm, watching children with their mothers in a sunny playground; her reactions establish her own desire for this role and produce further anguish about her condition; weepily, she starts the car and begins to drive (cut to commercial). Arriving home in the car, she paces tensely, awaiting the arrival of her husband; he arrives, she breaks the news, and in his guilt he reveals his infidelity (cut to commercial). The length of each scene may vary depending on the complexity and scope of the point being established, but both are reasonably predictable (strictly so on television) because a well-paced drama calculates the approximate length of our attention span, our scope of comprehension, the emotional pitch we can bear (cut to Jolene's mother on the phone providing some comfort and much comic relief with her voluble abuse of the husband). Viewers can follow one significant move in a chain of events up to a certain level of complexity. Once we have grasped that crucial turn or discovery, we are ready to follow the drama to the next paragraph. Tax our attention or comprehension with too long or too involved a scene, and we are less likely to follow the action; interrupt our concentration with too many short scenes, too many choppy edits, and we are less likely to stay engaged. Fail to sufficiently signal how we get from one scene to the next, and we are lost.

In academic writing, most paragraphs begin with a topic sentence that announces the main point of that paragraph, include evidence that will support and develop that point, and end with an analysis demonstrating the significance of that evidence and connecting the paragraph to the writer's thesis. Although writers devise infinite variations on these three elements—topic sentence, evidence, significance—they supply the basic structure for most body paragraphs. Take for example, a paragraph from the middle of novelist and public intellectual Susan Sontag's nonfiction study of photography, "In Plato's Cave." Sontag's thesis is that photographic images—like those shadows Plato described flickering on the walls of the cave—should never be mistaken for reality, for wisdom, or for ethical or political knowledge; at the same time she wants to warn us that photography will always present the illusion that it is all those things and more. In the following paragraph, she uses the example of tourists' snapshots to develop her thesis:

> A way of certifying experience, taking photographs is also a way of refusing it—by limiting experience to a search for the photogenic, by converting experience into an image, a souvenir. Travel becomes a strategy for accumulating photographs. The very activity of taking pictures is soothing, and assuages general feelings of disorientation that are likely to be exacerbated by travel. Most tourists feel compelled to put the camera between themselves and whatever is remarkable that they encounter. Unsure of other responses, they take a picture. This gives shape to experience: stop, take a photograph, and move on. The method especially appeals to people handicapped by a ruthless work ethic—Germans, Japanese, and Americans. Using a camera appeases the anxiety which the work-driven feel about not working when they are on vacation and supposed to be having fun. They have something to do that is like a friendly imitation of work: they can take pictures. (467)

From the first sentence we know that this paragraph is going to explore the issue of how taking photographs is a way of refusing or limiting an actual experience. In addition to simply announcing the subject matter of the paragraph—people take pictures when traveling—notice how an effective topic sentence makes a claim about that subject matter that the paragraph will have to support and develop—by taking pictures people are shutting out the actual experience. Many readers are likely to disagree with that claim, so Sontag must provide evidence to convince us of its validity and to show us what she means by it. As evidence, Sontag gives us the example of tourists who use photography in ways that prevent them from engaging with the new scenes and experiences they encounter. Many academic writers would supply a more specific quote or summary of a source to back up this claim, but Sontag can get away with this looser example because she is writing for a less specific public audience. What is the significance of her evidence, what has she learned from it, and how does it connect to and develop her thesis? Although we might have to dig a little to answer those questions, clearly the example of the tourists has helped Sontag extend her initial claim: Taking photographs is a way of refusing experience but it is *also* a way to fool yourself into thinking that you are having some experiences and even getting some work done. In this sense, the evidence ties directly into Sontag's thesis and simultaneously helps to develop it by one notch. As a whole then, just like the scene in the docudrama, this paragraph contains one move in Sontag's overall argument; it is just long enough and complex enough to focus our full attention, allow us to grasp her main point, teach us one thing, and get us ready for the next scene.

A good body paragraph contains this autonomous life. It functions as a whole to make a particular point and to move the thesis along by one more stage. Yet that same paragraph is deeply integrated into the rest of the essay. To take the "body" metaphor seriously, paragraphs are the sinuous limbs of an essay; each one incorporates a muscular tension between its autonomous identity—a head, a neck, an arm, a hand—and its identity as part of the whole. In fact, ripping a body paragraph from the middle of a work as I have done here, helps to emphasize the torn-away tendrils connecting this particular paragraph to the paragraphs that come before and after it. By turning back for a moment to that first sentence in Sontag's paragraph, we can even deduce from those tendril clues to how this paragraph connects to the previous one. While this paragraph shows us how photography refuses experience, the previous paragraph sets up the positive side, shows us how photography certifies experience and gives us evidence that we were there. What will the next paragraph be about? Will it demonstrate other ways in which people use the camera to limit their experience? Will it build from the work ethic that drives people to "work at" taking pictures? We can answer that question with one look at the topic sentence of Sontag's next paragraph: "People robbed of their past seem to make the most fervent picture takers, at home and abroad" (467). Clearly, Sontag is planning to build on her point about why some national groups take more pictures than others, perhaps tell us how these people use photographs to fill in the past they feel they have lost.

The need for signaling such paragraph transitions may be even more crucial in an essay like this than in a docudrama. After all, if "For Better or Worse" suddenly introduces a car chase scene using characters we don't recognize, we would proceed in the faith that at some point we will be told how that scene connects to the rest of the plot and affects Jolene's life. Most readers would be much less willing to follow an equivalent break in the paragraph structure of scholarly prose partly because, for better or worse, the genre of the documentary inspires more faith in predictability than the genre of the academic essay. As the entry in this book on "Transitions" also emphasizes, those links from paragraph to paragraph are not only keeping the reader's attention, they are also the component parts of one continuous argument, and they must push along with a steady momentum to keep that argument going and growing. Just by looking at the topic sentences of an essay, one can deduce the central argument of that essay, see how it moves from point to point, understand how it is organized. One strength of Sontag's writing is that each of her paragraphs keeps a powerful tension between the part, the *immediate* claim of each paragraph ("people robbed of their past make the most fervent picture takers," for example), and the larger central claim or argument of the essay as a whole (photographs give us the false illusion that we are experiencing life). In fact, one of Sontag's key rhetorical strategies involves maintaining that tension with particular care partly because her claims often lack sufficient supporting evidence. Thus, the drama of her essay will not be in the evidence or analysis provided by any one paragraph; it will happen in the velocity of the action, the combined power of all those paragraphs moving in sequence, clubbing us with heady claim piled on heady claim, all racing toward an energetic, complex, and persuasive whole.

RELATED WORDS

Claims 38	Parallelism 118
Essay 68	Structure 149
Evidence 77	Thesis 176
Key Terms 106	Transitions 183

EXERCISES

1. In a group, choose body paragraphs from five different essays (or five paragraphs from one essay). Identify how many of your samples include the three basic elements: topic sentence, evidence, significance. What variations, replacements or additional elements do writers build in? Then write (or rewrite from a draft) a paragraph of your own that contains these three basic elements.

2. Choose an essay you haven't read that seems to have strong topic sentences. List the topic sentences on a separate sheet of paper and deduce the writer's main argument from that list.

3. In a group, choose one particularly strong and one particularly weak paragraph from the assigned readings. Analyze both paragraphs and make a list of the criteria that make them effective or not, including quotations from the paragraphs.

4. In a colleague's draft, choose a sequence of paragraphs, identify the topic sentence, evidence, and significance for each one, and underline all the connective sentences, words, and phrases that help to signal how the action is proceeding from one paragraph to the next. Where are those signals the strongest? Where are you in danger of becoming lost or confused?

5. Cut an essay into separate paragraphs, give the parts to other class members, and have them reassemble the paper on the basis of the transitional clues provided in the essay. When those clues are missing, use your readers' suggestions to revise the essay.

Parallelism
Grammar and Equality

Parallelism is a similarity of grammatical form for similar elements of meaning within a sentence or among sentences. (Aaron 124)

Frederick Douglass's "Narrative of the Life of Frederick Douglass, an American Slave" (1845) provides a textbook case for the beauty and power of successful parallel structures; in his road from illiterate slave to literate free American, Douglass made parallel sentences an integral part of his literacy. His parallelisms occur in two different forms, which dominate the writing in his narrative: lists of three parallel elements, and opposition of two parallel elements. For example, he writes of the injustices of slavery in general and of the slave overseer Gore in particular:

> To be accused was to be convicted, and to be convicted was to be punished; the one always following the other with immutable certainty. To escape punishment was to escape accusation; and few slaves had the fortune to do either, under the overseership of Mr. Gore. He was just proud enough to demand the most debasing homage of the slave, and quite servile enough to crouch, himself, at the feet of the master. He was ambitious enough to be contented with nothing short of the highest rank of overseers, and persevering enough to reach the height of his ambition. He was cruel enough to inflict the severest punishment, artful enough to descend to the lowest trickery, and obdurate enough to be insensible to the voice of a reproving conscience. (*Heath Anthology* 1833)

Douglass's prose is exceedingly orderly in this passage, carefully observing the rules of parallelisms. He balances elements with the precise parallelism grammar handbooks describe: for example, "To be accused was to be convicted" is paralleled by "to be convicted was to be punished"; or "ambitious enough to be contented with nothing short of the highest rank of overseers" is paralleled by "persevering enough to reach the height of his ambition." The parallelism almost works like a form of poetry, a structural rhyme if you wish, in which the structures are exactly the same but some of the words are different. The difference of the words is highlighted by the sameness of the clauses.

But Douglass's orderly sentences, their parallelism, are only exposing the absurdities and horrors of slavery. Because of the parallelisms, we cannot help but see the nonsensicalness of the slave master's logic: Accusation, conviction, and punishment follow each other without thought or reflection. Thus, the parallel structures Douglass uses here exemplify the rigid order, the mechanical way, in which slavery punished all slaves. Within the confines of the sentence structures, as within the confines of the terrorist rule of plantation slavery, there is no hope for deviation or mercy. In his sentence structures, Douglass encodes the inhumanity of the plantation logic. But they also express his systematic, analytical understanding of slavery. The parallelisms contain his fury and showcase him as a skilled, somewhat distanced, and very structural almost academic thinker.*

In 1848, Douglass, now an escaped slave, writes and publishes a letter to his former master Captain Thomas Auld, in which he explains to his master "the grounds upon which I have justified myself in running away." In the middle of the letter, Douglass uses powerful parallelisms to do so:

> The morality of the act I dispose of as follows: I am myself; you are yourself; we are two distinct persons, equal persons. What you are, I am. You are a man, and so am I. God created both, and made us separate beings. I am not by nature bond to you, or you to me. Nature does not make your existence depend upon me, or mine depend upon yours. I cannot walk upon your legs, or you upon mine. I cannot breathe for you, or you for me; I must breathe for myself, and you for yourself. (*Letters of a Nation* 96)

Whereas in the previous example, Douglass uses parallelisms to mock the absurd order of slavery, in this passage he uses parallelisms to assert the fundamental equality between his former master and himself. In the carefully balanced sentences of this passage ("I am myself; you are yourself"), Douglass forcefully redefines his relation to his master as one of parallel but equal value. Thus, he claims parallelism as a fundamental American grammar of equality.

This grammar of equality—the posing of equal ideas, the balancing of various elements, the structure it expresses, and its analytical quality—makes it an important tool in academic writing as well. Just as in Douglass's life, in grammar also, parallelism rebels against subordination and hierarchy in the name of balance and equality. Academic writing, just as Douglass's account, uses parallelism to give order to ideas, to balance thoughts and insight, to create equality in a list, and to weigh things fairly against each other. For example, describing the various positions academics have taken towards anthropologist Marcel Mauss, James Clifford writes in *The Predicament of Culture:* "Some recall Mauss as a loyal Durkheimian. Others see a forerunner of structuralism. Some see primarily an anthropologist, others a historian. . . . Some stress Mauss's iconoclasm, others his coherent socialist-humanist vision. Some see a brilliant armchair theorist. Others remember a sharp empirical observer" (125). He concludes: "The different versions of Mauss are not irreconcilable, but they do not quite add up"(125). Clifford uses parallelism here to give each view an equal role, and to show that they all coexist, none more important than the other. He almost makes poetry out of what could be just a chaotic list of various opinions; he structures them by given them parallel, equal lives. He, like

---

*There were concerns about Douglass's skilled rhetoric; some wanted Douglass to write in a less finished style so as to protect the "authenticity" of the voice in the slave narrative.

Douglass, offers order without subordination; he, like Douglass, uses grammar to express equality.

RELATED WORDS

Coordination and Subordination 45   Subject–Verb 154
Grammar 90   Voice 187

EXERCISES

1. Find parallel structures in an assigned reading and examine their function. What order is being established by them, and what equivalences are expressed by them?

2. In a compare/contrast essay, write a list of elements that are similar and different in the two things you compare. Then use parallelisms such as Douglass's to put into sentences those similarities and differences.

3. In a student draft, find equivalences—two ideas that are compared, two sentences that speak directly to each other—and express them in parallelisms.

4. In an outline for an argument list three or four reasons for your point of view. Then rewrite this list by using for each reason a parallel structure—the same sentence structure just with different words capturing the different points you want to make. For example, list four reasons to use parallelisms in your writing, and express those reasons in parallelisms.

Plagiarism
The Politics of Common Good and Private Property

He was a big, hulking man, with reddish hair and freckled face, evidently of the laboring class, though not successful, judging by the vague grime and poverty of his appearance. For a moment he made as if he would open the window; then he changed his mind and went to the door instead. He did not knock, but walked straight in. ("Mrs. Adis" 321)

He was a big, black man with pale brown eyes in which there was an odd mixture of fear and amazement. The light showed streaks of gray soil on his heavy, sweating face and great hands, and on his torn clothes. In his woolly hair clung bits of dried leaves and dead grass. He made a gesture as if to tap on the window, but turned away to the door instead. Without knocking he opened it and went in. ("Sanctuary" 15)

> "I'm in trouble." His hands were shaking a little.
> "What you done?"
> "I shot a man, Mrs. Adis." (321)

> "Ah's in trouble, Mis' Poole," the man explained, his voice shaking, his fingers twitching.
> "W' at you done done now?"
> "Shot a man, Mis' Poole." (15)

When Nella Larsen published her story "Sanctuary" in the *Forum* in January of 1930, she was at the height and abruptly at the end of her career. Larsen had successfully published several novels and had been the first African-American woman to receive a Guggenheim fellowship. But when readers noticed the similarities between her story and Sheila Kaye-Smith's story "Mrs. Adis" published in the *Century Magazine* in January of 1922—similarities both in specific details and in plot line—a scandal ensued from which Larsen never recovered. "Literary Dirt," wrote Harold Jackman to Countee Cullen on January 27, 1930, "Nella Larsen Imes has a story in *Forum* for this month called *Sanctuary*. It has been found out—at least Sidney Peterson was the first to my knowledge to discover this—that it is an exact blue print of a story by Sheila Kaye-Smith called *Mrs. Adis* which is in a book called *Joanna Goodens Marries and Other Stories*. The only difference is that Nella has made a racial story out of hers, but the procedure is the same as Kaye-Smith's, and Anne and Sidney have found out that the dialogue in some places is almost identical. If you can get ahold of the *Forum* and the Smith book do so and compare them. But isn't that a terrible thing. It remains to be seen whether the *Forum* people will find this out" (Davis 348). They did, publishing a reader's letter which, as some others, pointed their attention to the similarities; the editors investigated and allowed Larsen to respond to the charges.

In the April 1930 edition of the *Forum*, the editors published a defense of Larsen, telling their readers that they had examined Larsen's drafts and concluded that an "extraordinary coincidence"—such as the one when the incandescent lamp had been invented simultaneously by two different people—must have taken place. They also published an explanation by Larsen, in which she "[tells] exactly how [she] came by the material out of which [she] wrote 'Sanctuary.'" She writes:

> The story is one that was told to me by an old Negro woman who, in my nursing days, was an inmate of Lincoln Hospital, East 141st Street, New York City. Her name was Christophe or Christopher. That was something during the years from 1912–1915. All the doctors and executives in this institution were white. All the nurses were Negroes. As in any other hospital, all infractions of rules and instances of neglect of duty were

reported to and dealt with by the superintendent of nurses, who was white. It used to distress the old folk—Mrs. Christopher in particular—that we Negro nurses often had to tell things about each other to the white people. Her oft-repeated convictions were that if the Negro race would only stick together, we might get somewhere some day, and that what the white folks didn't know about us wouldn't hurt us.

All this used to amuse me until she told some of us about the death of her husband, who, she said, had been killed by a young Negro, and the killer had come to her for hiding without knowing whom he had killed. When the officers of the law arrived and she learned about her man, she still shielded the slayer, because, she told us, she intended to deal with him herself afterwards without any interference from "white folks."

For some fifteen years I believed this story absolutely and entertained a kind of admiring pity for the old woman. But lately, in talking it over with Negroes, I find that the tale is so old and so well known that it is almost folklore. It has many variations: sometimes it is a woman's brother, husband, son, lover, preacher, beloved master, or even her father, mother, sister, or daughter who is killed. A Negro sociologist tells me that there are literally hundreds of these stories. Anyone could have written it up at any time. (41)

So these are the facts of the case as far as we have them; nowhere, in letters, archival materials, or other sources, do we come closer to the truth. There is no confession, only the documents above. How can we judge? Is this plagiarism? Or is Larsen's defense believeable? On what grounds do we make such a determination? Those questions we leave up to the reader.

But Larsen's case—the actual stories, the editor's procedure, and Larsen's response—sheds interesting light on the issue of plagiarism itself. Whether truthful or not, Larsen's defense questions the idea of plagiarism itself. After all, when she explains that the story was actually part of black folklore, existing in hundreds of versions, she defers the origin of the story indefinitely (beyond even the moment Mrs. Christopher tells it to her between 1912 and 1915); she also refuses the concept that it could have any private ownership since "anyone could have written it up at anytime." This explanation challenges the very paradigm within which Larsen has been accused—moving her story out of a white written culture into a black oral culture, where ownership and originality are not relevant concepts. Indeed, she herself in the course of this explanation revises her understanding of authenticity, authorship, and origin when she begins to see her mistake in seeing the story as Mrs. Christopher's personal story, the telling and origin of which can be placed in time and space and author. She learns how to read the story not as "absolute" truth but as folklore, part of a racial commonwealth or common good that belongs to all black people and that has been shaped and reshaped hundreds of time. It is there for anyone to write down. Larsen's explanation of the production of her story then shifts her work into a context in which arguments about plagiarism become meaningless, inappropriate, even scientifically proven—through the confirmation of the Negro sociologist—to be naïve misreadings of the story and of black literary production in general.

Whether one believes that Larsen heard the story in this way or not, she does have a point about plagiarism. Plagiarism assumes a form of originality and ownership that is historically—and Larsen suggests here also racially and culturally—specific. In the introduction to his book *Stolen Words: Forays into the Origins and Ravages of Plagiarism,* Thomas Mallon traces the historical moment in which plagiarism becomes a serious crime. First, plagiarism—the stealing of someone else's ideas and expressions—presumes that originality is a prime quality of written expression. In the history of writing that is a relatively new idea. After all, for most of literary history "the guiding spirits of the literary dead were deliberately conjured, a time before ancestor worship gave way to that form of youth-enthrallment known as originality"(3). And "originality—not just innocence of plagiarism but the making of something really and truly new—set itself down as a cardinal literary virtue sometime in the middle of the eighteenth century"(Mallon 24). The virtues of imitation and emulation were replaced by that of originality and innovation. The reasons for this shift, were, according to Mallon, not so much abstract but rather very concrete. "One thing is clear: plagiarism didn't become a truly sore point with writers until they thought of writing as their trade"(3–4). And that change was created by a machine. "It was printing, of course," he writes, "that changed everything, putting troubadours out of business. . . . The Writer, a new professional, was invented by a machine. Suddenly his capital and identity were at stake" (4). Thus a new world developed of ownership and competition with a good deal of "feuding and possessiveness"(4). When Nella Larsen defends herself by placing her story within an oral folkloric tradition, she reveals these precise historical foundations of plagiarism. She also distances herself implicitly from a white print culture, which claims writing as private property, and relocates herself within a black oral culture in which accusations of plagiarism are simply not relevant because the stories are common good.

Transposing this problem to contemporary college writing, we can see that things haven't gotten easier nor have the rules about plagiarism eased up. On the contrary, just as plagiarism arguably ruined Larsen's careers, plagiarism can expel students from school and go on their permanent record, threatening and even ending their careers. Plagiarism is the cardinal crime in academia; scholars are writers by trade, and their ideas need to be protected in a competitive environment in which original ideas determine salaries and tenure decisions. And students are writers by trade in which personal insight determines grades and access to jobs and graduate schools. So, here too, "capital and identity [are] at stake" (Mallon 4).

And yet, academic life is a mixture of an oral and a print culture. While writing papers follows the rules of print culture and private ownership, the classroom and the professional conference are oral traditions designed for the free exchange of ideas; they create as a group effort common ideas to be shared. And exams often test the students' ability to retell the common story of the course. So where do we draw the line? When is an idea free and when not? The Internet—as a new technology—offers a further formidable challenge to the distinction between oral and print culture. It offers endless wamounts of sources often without authors' names and an unprecedented accessibility. Why then is plagiarism the cardinal crime in academic life and how can it be avoided?

Looking at Larsen's story in relation to Kaye-Smith's reveals one important aspect of plagiarism: plagiarism is the theft of ideas *and* words—not just words. Larsen changes many (even most) words in her version—assuming she did indeed plagiarize—but the idea belongs to Kaye-Smith's since she published her story first. But what is the idea of the story? Larsen colors Kaye-Smith's words turning the story into a story about race rather than class; all of Larsen's "plagiarism" is indeed an act of creation and imagination—just not enough of it. Indeed, Larsen had long played with the idea of coloring a white story, and not knowing her true motives, it might well be that she is doing just that in this story. But is that enough to exonerate her? Plagiarism then defines the boundaries between originality and imitation in ways that are not always clear-cut. Where does creation begin? Where does theft begin? After all, just as fiction writers often learn by imitation, academics learn by summary and synthesis as well as by absorbing lectures, taking notes, and representing knowledge. Indeed, much of academic work is just that: representing knowledge gained and written up by others.* Neil Hertz concludes in a study about academic discourse and plagiarism that "the enforcement of legitimate boundaries is a gesture of scapegoating which reveals and projects repressed anxiety about the authority of the dominant position and its relation to the originality and authenticity of its own discourse"(quoted in Randall, 538–39). In other words, plagiarism is a capital sin in academic life because its prohibition protects a very difficult tenuous line. It draws a boundary between the communal and individual aspects of academic production—a boundary that allows for individual ownership of ideas within a communal effort of development of knowledge. A difficult task, indeed!

Yet, in this difficulty also lies the solution—not for the fiction writer but for the student and scholar. Many academic conventions ensure that we have a way of acknowledging what we have read, who has influenced us, where we have gotten our ideas and knowledge (see our entries on "Citation," "Quotation," "Footnotes"). The academic plagiarist fails to see that these acknowledgments are already a large part of his own accomplishment. Academic authority is predicated on the work of others—it is our response to others. If we steal from others we steal from ourselves, avoiding the dialogue that makes it possible for us to exist as academic thinkers. And our own response to other academic sources is what comprises our originality: our individual being on the page. As academics

---

*It is interesting to note that there are—just as Larsen implies—cultural differences in that regard. For example, student work in German universities emphasizes summary and synthesis much more than American universities do. American academic life—perhaps reflecting America's more youth-oriented culture—stresses originality more than European university life, which stays closer to its medieval roots.

we paradoxically need others to be ourselves; those who steal by denying these others erase themselves regardless of whether they get caught or not.

RELATED WORDS

Citation 32	Quotation 130
Claims 38	Summary 159
Counterargument 49	Synthesis 172
Footnotes 81	Work Cited 198

EXERCISES

1. Based on the facts as you see them here, write an argument that either convicts or exonerates Larsen from plagiarism. What definition of plagiarism is your argument based on?

2. As a class, develop a definition and a series of rules about plagiarism and acknowledgments. When, for example, should a thought presented in class by a student be cited or quoted and when does it freely belong to the group?

3. In a draft of yours, acknowledge as many sources as possible using citation, quotation, and footnotes.

4. Write three paragraphs in which you use a source: one as a deliberate plagiarism, one with some acknowledgment of the source, and one with fully detailed acknowledgment. Compare the effects of the three paragraphs.

5. Deliberately cut together a paragraph plagiarizing from Internet sources. Then produce a paragraph giving full acknowledgment to all the Internet sources used. Compare the results.

Punctuation
An Art Within Reason

Punctuation is a reasoned art. Reasoned because, unlike English grammar as a whole, which is wayward and given to infinite exceptions and irregularities, punctuation is relatively straightforward and finite. There are less than ten punctuation marks worth worrying about, and each one has predictable and logical functions that one can find listed in any grammar handbook. For instance, there are really only four or five main reasons for using a comma, and, when in doubt, a writer can consult that list of five to check on the reason for using a comma in any particular situation. If there is no good reason for the comma, voila, no comma. In fact, all the complexities of punctuating a sentence stem from the fabulously infinite combinations and patterns of growth that the structure of a single sentence can contain, and punctuation is the most dependable part of that flexible and unpredictable development. It is the code, the series of signals, that help us break into the mysterious meaning of sentences. Since the rules of punctuation stand firm even when the vocabulary and structure of a sentence ascend into abstract difficulty, they become the reliable set of beacons to follow, especially in academic writing where greater complexity of sentence structure often evolves as part of the complexity of ideas being expressed.

Take for example the following paragraph in an essay by feminist theorist, Rita Felski exploring the function of autobiographical, "confessional" writing:

> The term "confession" has occasionally acquired slightly dismissive overtones in recent years. No such connotation is intended here; I use "confession" simply to specify a type of autobiographical writing which signals its intention to foreground the most personal and intimate details of the author's life. Francis Hart writes: " 'Confession' is personal history that seeks to communicate or express the essential nature, the truth of the self." Like consciousness-raising, the confessional text makes public that which has been private, typically claiming to avoid filtering mechanisms of objectivity and detachment in its pursuit of the truth of subjective experience. (83)

If we consider the punctuation in the paragraph as a series of signposts, a road map helping us to follow the ideas being expressed, the value of such reliable signaling becomes clear. Felski's goal in this paragraph is to define the central term of her essay, "On Confession," clearly and fully so that she can refer to it and build on it throughout the entire essay. Notice how she uses quotation marks to set off the term "confession" in the first two sentences, to drag it in our minds from the realm of vague familiarity and give it a sharpened, newly configured meaning. In the third sentence, those quotation marks play a related role in identifying a citation; they work with the colon to set off the words that Francis Hart wrote as his own and not Felski's. Notice too how the semicolon after "here" in the second sentence functions to join two independent clauses, each of which could stand alone as a sentence but which are so intertwined in meaning that they can work as a combined unit. By connecting them with a semicolon rather than separating them into two sentences, Felski juxtaposes her definition of "confession" against its opposite, against the dismissive connotation of the word that she rejects.

Because the rules of punctuation are relatively straightforward, it seems natural to assume as well that writers' choices involving periods, colons, semicolons, commas, and so on are fairly limited—that a writer simply sticks as much as possible to the "right" punctuation for a given sentence and avoids the "wrong" punctuation. On the contrary, writers' decisions about punctuation are as numerous and various as the choices they make about the content of their sentences. For instance, in the passage quoted, Felski could have said, "The term 'confession' has occasionally acquired slightly dismissive overtones in recent years, but no such connotation is intended here. I use 'confession' simply to specify a type of autobiographical writing which. . . ." Notice how this alternative has the advantage of neatly packaging the entire problem of "dismissive overtones" in a separate sentence. Instead, she chose to emphasize her rejection of the dismissive connotation by using it to begin a sentence and to call our attention to her own heroic reclaiming of the term by hitching the rejection phrase to her nonjudgmental definition of the term. Experienced writers frequently choose punctuation with these kinds of rhetorical effects in mind, but, even when the choices are not deliberate or conscious, writers are deeply influenced by the situation, the type of writing, the intended audience, the subject matter, and by individual habits and preferences that can make punctuation usage as characteristic as a handprint.

A contrasting example from a "confessional" journal entry by poet May Sarton helps to dramatize the differences these choices can make.

The reasons for depression are not so interesting as the way one handles it, simply to stay alive. This morning I woke at four and lay awake for an hour or so in a bad state. It is raining again. I got up finally and went about the daily chores, waiting for the sense of doom to lift—and what did it was watering the house plants. Suddenly joy came back because I was fulfilling a simple need, a living one. Dusting never has this effect (and that may be why I am such a poor housekeeper!), but feeding the cats when they are hungry, giving Punch clean water, makes me suddenly feel calm and happy. (99)

Here, Sarton relies primarily on commas and on simpler sentence constructions to describe her experience of depression, so that her use of the dash in
the fourth sentence is particularly striking among this plainer company. The
overall simplicity combined with the dash and the use of parentheses in the
sixth sentence serve to remind us that this is an informal situation, a piece of
journal writing seemingly directed to no audience beyond the author herself.
In fact, Sarton's dreamy accumulation of comma-linked clauses suggests a lack
of planning, more of a musing, exploratory approach to her topic that calls attention to Felski's sparing use of commas, to the more formal situation implied
by Felski's style, and to the more reasoned, analytical approach she brings to
her topic. Yet Sarton's choice of the dash (rather than a comma or a sentence
break) is extremely effective in allowing the last half of the fourth sentence to
escape, to lift free from the predictable confines of the sentence structure just as
it describes the lifting of her mood. The use of parentheses and the exclamation point are also intriguing in this light because they hint at Sarton's recogni-
tion of an eventual audience beyond herself; the exclamation point especially
seems to function like a wink, inviting that audience to share the joke about
her housekeeping.

These elements of choice then, the arena of play a writer has within a
fairly rule-bound set of forms, elevates punctuation to an art within reason. By
caging the infinite variety of choices made possible by the sentence within
highly structured and recognizable codes of meaning, punctuation marks help
the writer find control within freedom and freedom within control. For readers too, studying a writer's punctuation profile becomes a key tool of analysis, a
way of detecting how that writer thinks, breathes, sounds, a way of identifying
the characteristic elements of his or her style. Instead of imagining a writer's
punctuation profile as a silhouette filled in by the words of the sentence, it becomes clear that the punctuation and the content of the sentence inhabit each
other; together, they shape the writer's meaning.

┌─ **RELATED WORDS** ─────────────────────────────────┐

Audience 25	Grammar 90
Coordination and Subordination 45	Parallelism 118
Dash 53	Subject-Verb 154
Editing 63	Voice 187

└──┘

EXERCISES

1. In a group, choose two pieces of writing from disparate sources (for
    example from a scientific vs. a humanities discipline, from an e-mail vs.
    a formal letter, or from two academic essays that seem very different in

approach or tone). Circle every punctuation mark used by both writers and count up how many times each writer uses specific marks such as the comma, the semicolon, the period, and so on. Discuss how these punctuation marks become clues about the situation in which the writing was produced, the implied audience, the mood, personality, or style of the writer, perhaps even details about the writer's gender, age, educational background, interests, and habits. Then, working individually, write a punctuation profile describing what you have deduced about the writer and the essay based on the punctuation.

2. As a group project, look up the comma (or another frequently used punctuation mark) in three different grammar handbooks. List the various rules of usage supplied for that punctuation mark and discuss the differences in how the three grammar books present that mark. Write a description of that punctuation mark and its main functions. What kind of character profile would a heavy use of this mark suggest? What if a writer tended to use this mark much more heavily according to one rule (to set off modifying phrases like Sarton, for example) than another (to set off introductory elements like Felski, for example)?

3. Using an academic essay, circle the punctuation marks on one full page, and use those marks to write a punctuation profile of the writer. What can you deduce about style, voice, intention, sense of audience, and so on based on that writer's use of punctuation? Write a descriptive punctuation profile of the writer. Perform the same analysis using your own paper. Write a descriptive punctuation profile of yourself as a writer.

4. As a group project choose an academic essay and look at the writer's use of a particular punctuation mark (such as the comma or the semicolon). Using a grammar handbook, identify the rules of usage and the reasons behind the writer's use of that mark throughout one or two pages of the essay. Then move to a draft of your own paper, circle every occurrence of that mark on one page of your paper and identify the rule of usage and the reasons behind every use of that mark.

5. Choose a paragraph from a student draft and rewrite it only or primarily by changing, adding, or deleting punctuation marks. Try to make the revised paragraph as different as possible from the original.

Quotation
Show Me How You Quote and I Tell You Who You Are

In academic writing, as in life, listening and responding are the spice of life. We reveal our characters not only by what we say but also by how we listen, respond, and bring out or stifle the other. Strong academic writing presents an alchemy of voices. The way in which writers quote, listen to quotes, respond to quotes, embed their own ideas within a conversation reveals their character. Do they combat the quote or delight in its company? Do they tend to bring out the richness or the limitations of a quote? Whom do they enrich and whom do they reduce? Do they quote to assemble a network of friends and patrons in their writing? Or do they tend to quote to dismiss the quotes and make space for their own voice? Do they quote so excessively that we cannot hear them anymore? Or do they quote so little that we cannot see the context, evidence, or illustration of their claims, cannot see them really at all as part of an academic community? Quotations then are essential for academic writing; and looking at how someone quotes is an extremely illuminating form of analysis. It moves us from figuring out what we read to understanding who we are reading; and ultimately, the latter is an important part of the former.

Consider Tzvetan Todorov's book *The Conquest of America* as an example. Todorov is trying to understand the larger problem of our relation to others—those that we perceive as radically different—by looking at Columbus's encounter with those people he labeled Indians. "This book," he writes, "will be an attempt to understand what happened in that year [1492], and during the century that followed, through the readings of several texts, whose authors will be my characters"(5). Todorov here affirms that understanding means reading, and that his sources are like characters; he sees writing as a choreography of voices and understanding a subject as engaging in a dialogue with those voices. So, listen to his way of listening in the opening paragraph of his chapter "Columbus and the Indians":

Columbus speaks about the men he sees only because they too, after all, constitute a part of the landscape. His allusions to the inhabitants of the islands always occur amid his notations concerning nature, somewhere between birds and trees. "In the interior of the lands, there are many mines of metal and countless inhabitants" ("Letter to Santangel," February-March 1493). "Hitherto, things had gone better and better for him, in that he had discovered so many lands as well as woods, plants, fruits and flowers as well as the

> people" ("Journal," 25/11/1492). "The roots of this place are as thick as a man's legs, and all the people, he says, were strong and brave" (16/18/1492): we readily see how the inhabitants are introduced, by means of comparison necessary to describe the roots. "Here, they observed that the married women wore clouts of cotton, but the wenches nothing, save for a few who were already eighteen years old. There were also dogs, mastiffs, and terriers. They found as well a man who had in his nose a gold stud the size of half a *castellano*" (17/19/1492): this allusion to the dogs among the remarks on the women and the men indicates nicely the scale on which the latter will be assessed. (34)

Todorov makes Columbus into a character, as he says; but in the act of doing so he truly shows us a bit of his own character as well. Quoting to expose Columbus's character, he palpably reveals his own in the process. He frames Columbus and his quotes, drawing us, the readers into his way of seeing. He clearly wants us (note his use of "we") to see Columbus as he sees him; but his own character, as it becomes visible here, might also make us feel some sympathy for Columbus. Perhaps we might wonder whether our own writings could survive Todorov's form of scrutiny—his passionate, quick-tempered and somewhat slanted way of listening. Is he brilliantly incisive here or rudely jumping to conclusions? Is he revealing or distorting Columbus's views? The drama of this passage then is twofold: On the one hand, it is between Todorov and Columbus, on the other hand, it is also between Todorov and us. Todorov clearly tries to persuade us that Columbus's way of seeing others is dehumanizing; but perhaps, we might wonder, is Todorov's way of reading Columbus dehumanizing as well? While he appears to let the quotes speak for themselves, he clearly also frames them and follows them up with a colon after which he offers his own interpretation as if it was nothing more than a translation: This means that, the colon states. Thus, we feel Todorov's urgent and edgy engagement in his topic and book—a book he dedicates to a "Mayan woman devoured by dogs." His way of responding to Columbus's voice betrays at least as much about himself as about his source. Not only his book, but also his dealings with Columbus, are about the relation of the self to the other.

How we quote reveals to a degree who we are; it casts us in relation to the character of a source. Are we more or less combative, objective, knowledgeable, witty, sensitive than the source to which we respond? How we respond, in turn, is determined by our temperament as well as by what we do, whom we know, whom we choose as friends, or whom we have as enemies. We listen and respond differently inside and outside the office, in a love letter or in an academic lecture, inside one or another discipline. Indeed, disciplines themselves come with styles of quotations; some disciplines strive for objectivity, others for strong and creative interpretation. So, Todorov will be more acceptable amongst literary critics than amongst historians. His metaphor of talking about his source as a character rather than a primary document already reveals that he wants to read creatively and not for facts. Quotation then reveals both the rhythms of our personality and the context of our speaking position; it reveals who we are on the page.

┌─ **RELATED WORDS** ─────────────────────────────────┐
└───┘

EXERCISES

1. In one or more pieces of academic writing (published or student writing, writing in different disciplines) analyze moments of quotation by revealing the relationship between the author and the quoted writer: Identify different kinds of strategies writers use to quote and respond to sources. What kind of "character" do different strategies of quotation reveal?

2. Imitate or parody Todorov's way of quoting and responding by using passages from an assigned text.

3. After doing exercises 1 and 2, as a class assemble a handbook entry on dos and don'ts of academic quotations. What, in your mind, are good guidelines for academic quoting?

4. Drastically rewrite the character of your paper by changing its way of quoting and responding.

Reading
As Revelation

In Mary Shelley's novel *Frankenstein*, the Creature, who has been assembled from a motley collection of stolen human parts and then endowed with ungodly life, proves his claim to true humanity by learning to read. We know too that in literate societies the fundamental act of learning to read marks the transition from childhood dependence to adult communication. Alberto Manguel's *A History of Reading* discusses how children become socialized in a broader sense as they learn to read and are read to; they become "acquainted with a common past" and gradually become part of the "communal memory" of their culture and of humanity (71). And yet, with that access to an adult communal memory comes a perceived danger in the subversive power of knowledge on the inexperienced mind, so that in the nineteenth century, for instance, novels were often forbidden reading for young women for fear of the corrupting worldly (i.e., sexual) knowledge they might transmit. Novelist Edith Wharton describes the thrill of gaining free access to her parents' library (where she was allowed to read everything but the novels, for which she had to get special permission): "Oh, the rapture of my first explorations in that dear dear library! . . . I can *feel* the rough shaggy surface of the Turkey rug on which I used to lie stretched by the hour, my chin in my hands, poring over one precious volume after the other and forming fantastic conceptions of life from the heterogeneous wisdom thus absorbed" (14).

This experience of immersion in a book, where time and space disappear and the rug (or the sofa) becomes a magic carpet to a more exotic and delightful place, may be the core pleasure to which readers of all ages and at all stages return. Add in the subversive thrill of forbidden knowledge gained through reading, and we can understand why the act of reading has been celebrated by writers, artists, and movie makers through time. A painting by Pierre Auguste Renoir, "Camille Monet Reading" from 1873, shows a woman propped up against the cushions of a sofa, mouth slightly parted gazing with rapt, slack-jawed intensity at the soft-backed yellow novel she holds in both hands. A movie by French director Michael DeVille, *La Lectrice* [*The Reader*], portrays the eroticism of the reading act in scene after scene showing a young woman reading. The camera close-ups trained lovingly on each creamy flecked page and the unmistakably crisp sound of each page turning are rendered with sheer tactile precision so that, watching, we vicariously feel the texture of the book against our fingers even as we experience the pleasure of the listener.

These scenes of immersed pleasure are both disrupted and transformed in reading academic texts. I* say disrupted because reading analytically involves a pose of focused alertness—pen in hand, ready to pounce—that is somewhat antithetical to Wharton's pose of slack absorption, elbows buried in the Turkish carpet, mind freely transported to a near-dream state. Following the steps of a reasoned argument, taking notes, stopping to question a complexly detailed point, turning back to test one claim against another—all these activities conflict with the delicious abandonment of self, the oblivion made possible by reading a light novel. I say transformed because reading analytically effects a different kind of immersion: into a *culture* of books rather than in a single book, into the "communal memory" of scholars and thinkers through time. This gradual immersion through the reading of many books and articles does not involve the same abandonment of self but does offer its own form of transcendence. In "States of Reading," Sven Birkerts describes reading, "realized . . . *immersed*" reading as

---

*Here the "I" refers to Rebecca Brittenham

a "transformation of consciousness" that is "*not* a continuation of the daily by other means. It is not simply another thing one does, like gathering up the laundry, pondering a recipe, checking the tire pressure, or even talking to a friend on the telephone. Reading is a change of state of a very particular sort" (102). He argues that by accepting the focused "meaning structure" provided by a novel we are transported from the looser, more diffuse sense in which we ordinarily experience the world, the passage of time, to a sharply defined world and time in which everything has an "intellectual and aesthetic purpose" (104). This description, whether involving a novel or an essay, gets at the key pleasure of reading analytically; once engaged, the intellectual content of the piece becomes the machinery of transport to a world created between writer and reader, a world full of conflicts, perhaps, but one based on the full participation of both sides. Once the reader has taken part (even momentarily) in that world, its meaning structures will be endlessly available as a slightly (or sometimes entirely) transformed way of understanding the subject matter.

Which leads us to the most fundamental and interesting difference about reading academic writing as opposed to reading a light novel: It rarely works in a straight line or at a single gulp. Reading an academic essay is all about endlessly returning to understand more, to unpack previous examples, to compare one part of an essay to another; it is all about delaying the psychological urgency to "get" the point immediately and instead allowing for gradual absorption and play. In fact, in an academic context, first readings are just a general inquiry, an opening of the refrigerator door to take a survey of its contents before deciding where to focus. The first reading is an almost random sampling of the contents of an essay, during which we adjust to the writer's voice, gauge the time it will take to move through a paragraph or two, feel out our level of interest. If it is a complex essay, the first reading may be all about a deliberate suspension of anxiety, a deferral of the need to understand the thing at one blow. Luckily, the academic essay, even more than the novel, is a fairly predictable genre. The writer's thesis will likely appear somewhere in the first paragraph or the first page and reappear in some form toward the end of the essay. The topic sentences (i.e., the first sentence of each paragraph) will tend to signal or announce the main point the writer is planning to explore in that paragraph. In Birkerts' essay, for example, his opening paragraph tells us straight out that the essay will explore people's changing experiences of reading over the years. This is not exactly a thesis, but it is a direction—we know where the essay is headed. The topic sentences of the first two paragraphs signal that he has immediately embarked on giving us that history: "We know from historians, for example that before the seventh century there were few who read silently" and "After Menocchio's day [the sixteenth century], with the proliferation of mechanically produced books and the general democratization of education, reading not only spread more rapidly . . ." (72–73), and so on. With these brief but pungent cues, we have a sense of Birkerts giving his history of reading, moving rapidly along at a pace of several centuries per paragraph, headed . . . where? No doubt the subsequent paragraphs will tell us.

From this safety net of semi-predictability, an academic essay could go anywhere, and could at any moment become unpredictably difficult to follow. Thus, every rereading can be a targeted foray, each one planning and implementing a deliberately limited engagement. Didn't understand a thing? No problem—we go back to that one place where the hazy blur started to swim into focus, copy a sentence or two out, and write about it, translate it into understandable terms. We talk about it. Then we can go back to test whether the things we have written and said seem meaningful in the context of that one paragraph, to see if the sense we have made of one part brings even a sentence more of the surrounding text into focus. We can isolate one of Birkerts' body paragraphs to see how he presents one minor point. What kind of evidence is he using, and how does he want us to view that evidence? We can ignore the body of the text for the moment and look only at the footnotes for clues—what kind of sources is he citing? We can read through the essay looking for key terms, terms that are carefully defined and reused in the reading. Or we can ignore the key terms for the moment and look just at the examples. With Birkerts, for instance, we might just look at one or two of the stories he tells about different kinds of reading through the ages. Later we can work from these examples to identify and unpack his key terms and figure out his main argument. Can't follow the main line of argument? We can make a paragraph by paragraph outline, identifying the main point of each paragraph, tracing the writer's train of thought from one moment to the next. We can compare the opening paragraph to the closing paragraph just to see where the writer promises to take us and how that is different from where he or she ends up. We can read a passage out loud just to hear the writer speak; we can use our own examples to explain what the writer is saying; we can discuss the essay with other people. Best of all, we can let the reading propel us into writing and let the writing tell us about what we have read.

In academic settings, reading is writing and writing is reading. Both of these meaning-making activities work together to create that experience of intellectual lift-off and belonging, that momentary reorganization of a complex and ill-defined world into a beautiful, sense-making pattern which occurs somewhere in a smart book and in a smart paper. Because the amount we put into a reading determines the amount we get out, the pleasure of oblivion loses out to the pleasure of analysis. The desire to simply fall into the transformative matrix of the thing read becomes instead a more cautious and wily encounter; we begin to test an essay's meaning structures as we read, to think about how we might use it to modify what is already known and understood, to ask, "How could I use this Birkerts fellow to express my own ideas about where academic reading fits into the immersion idea?" We begin to write and interpret as we read. The subversive danger of knowledge feared by Wharton's parents is realized in the academic's complete seduction by the pleasure of accumulating and of making knowledge.

EXERCISES

1. Try a series of rereading forays. Pick up an academic essay that you haven't read, put down your pen and simply skim it, looking for random ideas, checking out the length of paragraphs, testing out a sentence here or there. Put down the essay and make a note about what you can recall. Pick up the essay, read the introductory paragraph carefully, read each of the topic sentences, and read the conclusion. Put it down and make a note about what you can recall. The third time, choose two body paragraphs that appeal to you and read them carefully, making notes. Write about how those two paragraphs could possibly connect to the introduction. Then pick up the essay and try reading it from beginning to end this time underlining or making marginal notes as you go, identifying important or interesting ideas, key terms, and puzzling moments that would be worth going back to. Use your notes from all these forays to write a short description of your experiences as an academic reader. Which strategies seemed to work the best for you? Where did you encounter the most difficulty?

2. Read the first two paragraphs of an essay carefully and then write five to ten questions you would hope to have answered by the time you get to the end of that essay.

3. Read through an essay and then write three questions that might help a reader pay particular attention to three different points the writer makes in different parts of the essay. Assign your questions to another reader in the class.

4. Once you have read and discussed an essay, create an outline of it by identifying the main point of each paragraph on a separate sheet of paper. Compare and discuss your outline with other members of a group and work together to identify the writer's main argument.

5. In a group, identify the key terms of an essay that you have read and discussed. Work together to (a) find definitions for one of those terms in the essay, (b) explain the term in your own words, (c) find an example in the essay that helps to explain the term, and (d) give examples from your own knowledge and experience that help to explain the term.

6. Choose a passage from the beginning of an essay and one from the end of the same essay. Write a separate description and explanation of each of those passages. Then write a paragraph analyzing how the writer got from one to the other, how the two passages connect.

Research
Not on the Trail of the Assassins

In dozens of Hollywood films we have watched the researcher slogging away in the vast recesses of a law library, poring over clippings in a newspaper archive, or plowing through the dusty files of a county records office. We have seen Julia Roberts in *The Pelican Brief* and in *Erin Brockovitch* or Kevin Costner and his team in *JFK* hunched over books and files in determined pursuit of the key piece of evidence that will send the perp to jail or the one legal precedent that will help to win the case. Although these scenes take place in a movie minute or two, the shifts in lighting that play over the patiently bent head and the altered positions of the researcher tell us that numerous hours or days have passed before the key items are uncovered. Of course, in the movies the researcher eventually does find that crucial source, at which point she or he slams shut the book (or the filing cabinet) and runs from the library with the crucial bit of evidence in hand, usually pursued by assassins.

Partly because of these images, we tend to think of research as the uncovering of a trail of clues leading to a predetermined end. We focus on the hunt itself and we fetishize the imagined results of that hunt—a search does not seem successful unless it results in the perfect set of sources. This common fiction of research as high-pressure fact collecting tends to obscure the intrinsic connections between the research and writing processes; it overlooks the fact that—for producing academic essays if not for convicting felons—research is an open-ended journey of exploration as much about creative construction as it is about source collecting. Research writing in most academic settings actually involves much more varied (and familiar) processes of written inquiry: brainstorming, reading and rereading, developing key search terms, generating ideas, envisioning the kinds of sources that might contribute to the topic, forging imaginative connections between sources, sketching out ideas, diving into preliminary drafts, developing a position, evaluating the sources collected on the basis of those early drafts, analyzing them, synthesizing them, rewriting, re-thinking, outlining, estimating the kinds of sources still needed to support each changing phase of a paper, and so on. Considered in this light, every academic essay is to some degree an example of "researched" writing. Studying any academic essay helps to demonstrate this inherent connection between research and writing, between source collection and the thesis-driven interpretive synthesis of those sources.

An examination of "The Triumph of Tinkering," by psychologist and sociologist of science Sherry Turkle, reveals that the topic and perhaps even the main argument of her essay were probably developed before Turkle ever began her search for outside sources. The essay contrasts two disparate styles of computer programming, the "universal" method widely taught to computer science students in the 1970s and 1980s and the "bricolage" style developed by later programmers, many of them women. Turkle spends time in the essay developing definitions and descriptions of her two key terms. The universal method involves very clear-cut organizational steps; the programmer would create a "master plan," a tight structure of subprogramming tasks needed to create a particular program, and then would accomplish each of those separate tasks in order (554). In contrast, the bricolage method involves more free associative jumping between the various subprogramming tasks, a pulling together of disparate elements in a looser organizational format that allows each piece of coding to develop in relation to the others. For a time, the "soft" style of bricolage was considered to be an inferior approach rather than a style; it was seen as "a stage in a progression to a superior form," so that early programmers had to learn to force their thinking into the universal style or "fake" that approach in order to continue in the field (559). Turkle's main argument in the piece is that these two approaches really are styles, different methods of problem solving that have everything to do with the programmer's character and interests, and even gender. She points out that early prejudices against the bricolage approach were hard on students who didn't fit the mold, but they were also detrimental to the growth of the field, which has benefitted from a more open-ended, inclusive culture.

In compiling supporting evidence for this argument, Turkle, in true bricolage fashion, draws together sources as disparate as student poetry, the work of Swiss psychologist Jean Piaget, anthropologist Lévi Strauss, mathematician Edsger W. Dijkstra, feminist psychologist Carol Gilligan, sociologist Evelyn Fox Keller, geneticist Barbara McClintock, and the painter Francis Bacon. She does not draw on the sources one might have predicted, that is, books and articles about programming written by other experts in her field, though it is likely that she read enough of that material to know that her own work was original. It becomes clear that the important factor in her "research" was not that hunt for the perfect article on computer programming and gender or on programming styles and human psychology. Instead, beginning from a particular problem she had observed involving computer programming styles, she pulled together a set of highly disparate readings that helped her to think about the gender issues and the psychological and sociological implications relating to that problem. The original part of her article is less the argument itself than the style of research; by drawing all these disparate sources together and allowing each element to reveal something new about the others, she demonstrates that computer programming is not an objectively removed "hard" science but a complex human culture involving different psychological styles and sociological implications.

Although Turkle's approach helps to emphasize research as a process of inquiry that far exceeds the actual collecting of sources, clearly research methods will vary from writer to writer, from discipline to discipline, and from topic to topic. Deducing the research from a finished piece also tells us little about the possible pitfalls of topic development, of collecting, evaluating, and working with sources: the uncertainty, the seemingly arbitrary decisions, the missing or delayed sources, the dead-ends, the hours spent in libraries with seemingly nothing to show for it. The research odyssey undertaken by a student writer, Kristi Schmidt, offers a closer look at actual experiences involved in the inquiry process.* The paper, "The Shared Power of End-of-Life Decisions" was written in the final weeks of a first-year English composition course.

Schmidt began her research journey in response to an assignment that specified using five or more sources to develop a topic based on the assigned course readings and stemming from previous writing completed during the semester. This was helpful because it meant that she could start with material that was already familiar, though of course it limited the number of directions her research could take. One of the course readings was an essay on doctor/patient relationships by physician Howard Brody and another, Dean Barnlund's "Communication in a Global Village," dealt with problems of cross-cultural communication in political and business contexts. In a previous paper, Schmidt had synthesized the ideas of these two writers in order to explore problems of doctor/patient communication. For her research paper, she decided to both narrow and develop this topic by zeroing in on the issue of doctor/patient communication during end-of-life decisions. Thus, when she sat down to plan her actual source-collecting, she already had a fairly well-defined topic and she had two secondary sources, but as yet she had no thesis and no primary sources showing actual examples of doctors and families making decisions about prolonging life for terminally ill or dying patients.

Schmidt knew about some of the issues families face in making these decisions—which was partly why she chose this topic—but she needed more information on the medical professions' perspective, and she decided to start the collection process there. A reference librarian guided her to two specialized medical encyclopedias, which outlined some of the issues and provided a list of

---

*This research description works from drafts of the paper and from close observation of many students' research experiences. In that sense it is a composite portrait showing some typical directions the inquiry process can take and is not meant to be an accurate portrayal of Schmidt's particular experiences.

sources. Again with the librarian's help, she began some computer searches, quickly learning to value the databases accessed through the college library like "Ebscohost" and "Lexis-Nexis," which resulted in journal articles or magazine and newspaper accounts. She also tried a series of Internet searches that turned up hundreds of links, many of which turned out to be people's home-pages, businesses selling medical technology, or other blind alleys. However, by pursing some of the links ending in "org" and "edu" rather than "com," she found some useful background information in one or two legitimate Websites run by patient-advocacy organizations. She was beginning to understand the difference between her primary sources, the case studies that provided direct evidence of patient/doctor communication, and her secondary sources like the Barnlund and Brody essays, in which the authors stepped back to analyze or offer commentary. At this point, though, she was feeling a little overwhelmed by the sheer mass of material out there and anxious about her deadline. She had gained some skill in evaluating the reliability of the sources she was finding—determining whether they were scholarly or generalized, looking for lengthier, researched pieces rather than one-page snippets, checking for bibliographies, cross-checking the names of authors and organizations—but she was having trouble determining which sources would be useful for her paper and which would not.

Wisely, she put the data collecting aside for a day and sat down to define a research question—a problem that the paper would explore—and to come up with some key terms that would help her do a more specialized search. The research question could stem from her earlier work on Barnlund and Brody. She started by asking "How important is communication in helping patients and doctors work together to make end-of-life decisions?" but her workshop group thought that the answer to this question was too obviously "very important." Instead, she decided to pose the more open-ended question, "What can doctors and patients do to improve communication on end-of-life decisions?" With the group's help and by quickly rereading the Barnlund and Brody essays, she came up with a list of search terms and phrases such as "physician patient relations," "terminal illness and communication," "end-of-life and ethics," "medical ethics and euthanasia," "right to die" that might lead to productive searches on some of the scholarly databases available through the college library. She began a draft sketching out some of her ideas about the topic and listing some of the possible directions it could go.

After some initial frustration about promising leads that turned out to be too technical, too far off the topic, or lacking verifiable citation information, Schmidt discovered one interesting article based on a case study involving end-of-life decisions. While she did not end up using that particular article, she found in its bibliography a journal called *Annals of Internal Medicine* which proved to be a gold mine of sources, including both primary case studies of physicians' experiences with dying patients and secondary articles analyzing particular end-of-life issues. None of these articles focused exactly on the issue of communication, but many described situations that clearly involved problems of communication. She also collected a few articles about doctor/patient communication that did not deal specifically with end-of-life issues, so she felt she might be able to pull together (bricolage-fashion) these two different kinds of sources in order to make some interesting points. She returned to her draft with these new sources and began to play around with ways to connect them to the key terms she had taken from Barnlund and Brody. Then she tried to create an outline of the paper by grouping the various sources together; from this she realized that some were less interesting than others or lacked enough information on the communication issue to be useful for her project. However, skimming through one of those articles she came across a reference to a well-known case in which the parents of Karen Ann Quinlan, a young woman whose illness had left her comatose and seemingly dependent on respirators and feeding tubes, sued for their daughter's "right to die" (Schmidt 2). After tracking down some lengthy news coverage of the case, Schmidt felt sure she could use this as one of the central examples in her paper. Through the college library's online catalogue, Schmidt also discovered and ordered several books that sounded promising, and, although two were not what she expected and one was not delivered in time, she ended up with one that she was almost sure she could use.

At this point, Schmidt had fifteen or more possible sources, and she felt fairly confident that at least five of those would work for the paper. After reading through the most promising articles and taking some notes, she wrote a more detailed draft in which she analyzed some of the sources to demonstrate how the communication issue affected each case. From this draft she sketched out a preliminary outline. The paper would begin with Barnlund and Brody, who she had already written about and whose work would help her set up the issue of doctor/patient communication. Then she would analyze four or five case studies involving end-of-life decisions using Barnlund and Brody to help show why particular communication problems existed with each one and what the doctors and patients had done to address those problems. Finally, she would use some of the other secondary articles to piece together a solution or series of potential solutions to the problem. After rearranging her draft and beginning to add some of the examples sketched out in the outline, however, Schmidt realized she was trying to cover too much material. She felt anxious about getting the material to fit together and, with the deadline looming, she still hadn't developed a strong thesis, a sense of what she herself wanted to argue.

Her workshop group suggested that she drop Barnlund and the focus on communication—a suggestion that she rejected because she felt that his ideas about communication were central to her point. They also suggested that she get rid of some of the case studies and focus on the ones that best illustrated similar issues, which she did. From revising the draft and then, with a reader's help, creating a more detailed post-draft outline, she also realized that she was beginning to find a thesis, which in turn helped her to choose which evidence would be most useful in supporting and developing her argument. A last-minute, extremely targeted search also turned up an article that would help support the argument she was now making. Although she ended up revisiting the search engines a few more times to retrieve one source that she had initially discarded and to check on several citations for which she had incomplete information, another draft or two of the paper brought her to the end of this research odyssey and to a successful end to the semester.

As this writer's trajectory suggests, a researched academic essay can be largely an extension of the same reading and writing processes that go into an essay based on assigned class readings. In fact, during the research inquiry, the writer is merely broadening his or her source base, ideally beginning from the concepts and materials presented in class rather than starting from completely fresh ground. Similarly, the actual collection and evaluation of sources is primarily driven and shaped by the writing, by the development of ideas, by rereading and the production of drafts. The real challenges lie less in hunting down the perfect sources than in studying the sources at hand, developing a perspective and a set of tools for analyzing them, forging connections between them, finding something to say about them that matters.

RELATED WORDS

Argument 9	Plagiarism 120
Assignment 14	Quotation 130
Citation 32	Reading 132
Claims 38	Structure 149
Counterargument 42	Summary 159
Evidence 77	Synthesis 172
Footnotes 81	Thesis 176
Key Terms 106	

EXERCISES

1. Choose a topic that you know something about or that you plan to use for an actual research paper. Following Turkle's example, create a list of disparate sources that you might combine in order to show some new dimension to this topic—something you read in another class, a newspaper article, magazine, or novel you read, an experience you have had. Then create a list of search terms you might use in order to do further research on this topic using computer databases.

2. As you do the research for a paper, keep a record of your "research odyssey," describing the steps you take, the dead-ends you hit, the time you spend, and so on. Note when you are creating or developing a topic and when you are actually collecting sources, what you find, and how you evaluate what you find. Note when you are read-

ing through sources, when you are writing, when you are collecting additional sources, when you discuss your topic with others. Keep a record of how much of this process is solitary and how much involves other people. Then write a paper telling the story of your research journey, describing the various stages in the process, and analyzing your own style of research writing. In the paper identify the research problem, issue, or question you pursued, the key sources you found, and what slant you would take on the issue or problem were you to write the paper.

3. In a group, choose an academic essay that has multiple citations, identify whether each source is primary or secondary and say why. Then identify the primary and secondary sources in a student draft and suggest which kinds of sources the writer might add and why.

4. Working in a group, choose an academic essay and deduce the research process that helped to create it. What general topic might the writer have started out with? What search terms might the writer have used in hunting for sources? What are the main sources that the writer is drawing on and what does each one contribute to the topic? Of all the sources cited, is there one that the writer may have considered to be the "perfect" source? Write a paragraph describing the writer's approach: In what ways is it similar to or different from the universal style and/or the bricolage style? Is there another metaphor that helps to describe it?

Revision
A Writer's Survival Guide

Revision is writing's liberation. Drafts mark the unfolding of a writer's thoughts over time. Just as a film camera can note the passing of a day by revealing tiny adjustments of light and shadow or specks of accumulated dust or by showing entrances and exits of people, dogs, or flying objects, the differences between drafts can be subtle shadings of light and shadow, the adjustment of words and phrasing, the slight alteration of a mood or thought. Yet the differences between drafts can also be as huge as the room exploding, the camera flying off the wall—a revolution in thought. The draft marks the spot where a writer got tired or rushed to be done; it exists there as a substantial memory waiting to be revisited, carried forward, transformed.

Drafting is the ultimate luxury, letting the writing take its course without fear or favor, plunging into risk, talking through a lame idea or garbling a smart one, all with the comfort of knowing that everything can be changed, erased, or reconstructed. Yet too often, under the pressures of time and the anxiety of production, we don't allow ourselves that luxury. We leap too quickly into the editing phase, honing one sentence or worrying over a paragraph before allowing a thought to spill out or grow, deleting or writing over old files without ever pausing to print out a version and test with fresh eyes the coherence of our own thoughts from paragraph to paragraph and page to page. Drafts allow us to remember the choices we made as writers, to recognize our accomplishments, to see the risks we took as well as the opportunities we left behind.

Adrienne Rich argues that "Re-vision—the act of looking back, of seeing with fresh eyes, of entering an old text from a new critical direction—is for women more than a chapter in cultural history: it is an act of survival. Until we can understand the assumptions in which we are drenched we cannot know ourselves" (604). I* do not think Rich overstates the case when she says that revision is a matter of survival; understanding the past in order to recognize the hold it has on one's thinking, expectations, and perceived limitations seems a crucial matter for women or men. For a long time, as a beginning writer, I was afraid that drafting would weaken the pristine force of my ideas, that I would lose that initial freshness, or worse yet, that some early draft containing the essential nugget, the well-phrased thought, or the crucial response would get discarded. Since I was not always able to tell what was "good" or "bad" in my own writing, I was afraid that in the process of revising I might actually be making things worse. When I handed in a paper for a course, I wasn't sure whether it was a work of genius or a piece of garbage but I was sure it was one or the other—an "A" or an "F"—but nothing in between. Although at the time I did not realize that I was investing in my survival as a writer, I gradually began to realize that by saving drafts I could have it both ways; I could always work backward to resurrect some discarded thought or paragraph. Because of this, drafting became a palpable relief, a way to delay the anxiety of seemingly arbitrary choices.

At that point, near the end of my second year in college, I went through a phase of hoarding every draft, every discarded note and phrase. Sometimes I never looked back at the earlier versions, but often I could look back and realize that the revision was better—a million times better—than that scratchy early version. Or at times, comparing two different versions of a sentence or paragraph made concretely evident the two directions an essay could go—it became a way to understand the choices I was making about audience, argument, or voice. When computers replaced typewriters, I was so dazzled by the

---

*The "I" here refers to Rebecca Brittenham.

pleasures of endlessly editing on the screen that I had to force myself to print out a draft, sit down with it in a clean, well-lighted place, and really consider what thoughts had made it to the page. Looking back at these drafts, I could allow myself a hindsighted view of that history of decisions, indecision, thoughts discarded, thoughts evolved. Instead of making a blank slate of myself as a writer every time I handed in a paper and started on a new assignment, I became capable of more realistic assessments of what I had accomplished and what needed to be done. I began to assemble the collage of myself as a writer, adding, changing perspective, shifting infinitesimally over time.

For example, in the first draft of an entry on "Revision" for this book, I wrote:

Why I Write*

In answer to the question, "Why do you write," novelist Margaret Atwood once said: "There's the blank page, and the thing that obsesses you. There's the story that wants to take you over and there's your resistance to it. There's your longing to get out of this, this servitude, to play hooky, to do anything else: wash the laundry, see a movie. There are words and their inertias, their biases, their insufficiencies, their glories" (156). Of all the truths she gets at in that short passage, the most resonant for me is contained in the last sentence. There are words: words to make you sick with boredom, like "advantageous management practices"; words to have fun with, like "that addlepated, roly-poly fathead" and "the mouth feel of fat"; words to get drunk on like "uxorious," "evanescent," and "gallimaufry," and words that make you wonder, like "hugger-mugger," "mingy," and "defenestrate." There are words that give clumping, paltry expression to the thought, and words that sing out a marvelous realization, or layer in an unintended subtlety.

Yet, while all this activity involving words describes the truth of writing in academia just as it describes the truth of writing novels, much of Atwood's description is completely wrong for academic writing. Where is the thing "obsessing you"? Where is the "story" taking control of your mind and emotions, driving you to speak? Writing a paper for a class or an article for a scholarly journal involves rationality, organization and craft, not passion or obsession. It involves compromise, working within the demands of the assignment or the journal's formal requirements; it involves the pressure of deadlines, the need to communicate clearly, concisely, and directly, to demonstrate one's mastery of expected knowledge or skills.

At this point in the entry, I suddenly felt envious of Margaret Atwood getting up every morning to write marvelous novels about school-girl cruelties and science-fiction sex. By contrast, I felt depressed about the project of academic writing and unable to continue the entry. I decided to make a cup of coffee, and play a game of toss and retrieve with the cat. When I returned to the computer twenty minutes later with my coffee and a dish of M & Ms, I reread what I had

---

*In using this theme from Margaret Atwood, I am following in a long line of distinguished thefts; Joan Didion in her essay "Why I Write" mentions stealing the idea from George Orwell, who no doubt stole it from someone else. See the entry on "Plagiarism."

written and decided to parody my earlier depression, to exaggerate that contrast between the novelist and the academic. My second version went like this:

Why I Write

As a writer in academia, I am an automaton of the system. I write to the formula provided and seek only to fulfill its directives. I have literally nothing of my own to say. Because of this, I can only hope to restate what has already been said in a slightly new way. Writing in this fashion makes me so concretely anxious that I would do almost anything to escape the imprisonment of the pen, the computer keyboard. I would use a Q-tip to remove microscopic dust particles from my computer screen. I would sort M & Ms into distinct color squadrons, red captains, yellow sergeants, brown privates, blue honor guards, all marching to watery extinction in my mouth. I would read and reread almost anything in the hopes of finding some ideas to get me going. A telephone call, the newspaper delivery, the mail all become events of great interest because they are momentary avenues of escape.

I would do almost anything to escape and yet I stay. Because I stay, I begin to realize that this description, while accurate, does not tell the whole truth. To begin with, there is the tactile pleasure of my fingers on the keyboard, the subtle clicking record of my thoughts. Then there is that moment when the trapped mind moves of its own accord, engages, the delicious synchronicity of mind and words at work. An unforseen complexity appears on the screen—how am I to solve it? The contradiction posed is insurmountable—where should I position myself? Where do I stand? An hour has passed, the mail has come, the phone is ringing, and I do not care because now I am in delirious pursuit of the thought that matters most at this moment, riding the words barebacked, shocked at the words appearing on the screen, recognizing for a moment the truth that had escaped me. And if that truth escapes me still, there is the pleasure of craft. I can hem and haw, I can puzzle and consider. I can make a big splash, a huge declaration, assert my control. I can worry and tug and bedevil the evidence until it reveals its secrets. I might stumble upon a clear and powerful thesis that announces where I have been heading all this time and what I was hoping to accomplish. I can slide to a conclusion and let the exhilaration of finishing wash over me.

After trying to answer that question, "Why do you write," eight different ways, novelist Margaret Atwood makes a ninth and final attempt: "There's the blank page, and the thing that obsesses you. There's the story that wants to take you over and there's your resistance to it. There's your longing to get out of this, this servitude, to play hooky, to do anything else: wash the laundry, see a movie. There are words and their inertias, their biases, their insufficiencies, their glories. There are the risks you take and your loss of nerve, and the help that comes when you're least expecting it. There's the laborious revision, the scrawled-over, crumpled-up pages that drift across the floor like spilled litter. There's the one sentence you know you will save" (156). I would argue that the fiction-writing labor she describes is almost equally true of the labor of academic writing. While the "story" driving a piece of academic prose may not be immediately discernible, that urge toward narration, toward communicating a meaningful progression of thought somehow is still there. The painfulness of "servitude" is certainly still there, servitude to the assignment, the form, the discipline of writing itself. And yet "servitude" does not really capture the relation of the writer to the form; it also becomes a kind of game—how can the confines of this form be used to say something, to accomplish something interesting? And there are certainly also the words: words to make you sick with boredom, like "advantageous management practices" but also words that are plump and fun, like "the mouth feel of fat" and "that addlepated, roly-poly nincompoop." There are words strong enough to get drunk on like "uxorious," "evanescent," and "mingy," and there are words to keep you guessing, like "hugger-mugger," "gallimaufry," and "defenestrate." There are words that give clumping, paltry expression to the thought, and words that sing out a marvelous realization, or layer in an unintended subtlety.

And the thing that obsesses you? There is the obsession of thought, different perhaps from the passion of novelistic creation or self-expression, but nonetheless gripping, nonetheless cruel in its ability to play you from heights of pleasurable articulation to the stale drudgery of the task at hand, from discovery to loss and back.

Somewhere in the middle of writing this version, I started to enjoy myself, to remember the places of creativity to be found among the conventions of academic writing, the pleasure of rescuing words like "hugger-mugger" from the earlier draft. However, I wasn't sure where to go from there, which of the two versions to use as my starting point for the revised entry. I showed the two versions to a friend who has become a trusted reader. She said, "Since the entry is on revision, I think you need to include both versions, but right now they have no context—you need to set them up. Also, why are they called "Why I Write" and not "Why I Revise"?"

If writing is a thousand infinitesimal commitments to ideas that a writer may or may not yet believe, then those early rough drafts allow the reckless suspension of choice and commitment. They can be the place where a writer discards responsibility, starts to play, takes risks, vamps, vogues, tries out extreme positions, a place where the writer discovers what he or she does not know or does not understand about a topic and admits it. Drafting also marks that process of learning; it is the tangible manifestation of all the choices a writer makes over time. In the third version of my entry on "Revision," I decided to use the first part of my friend's advice, and include both of the earlier versions in the entry. The question she asked me about the title was bothering me, so I added a paragraph which ended up being nearer to the core of what I had really wanted to say all along:

Why I Revise

I revise because I am a slow learner. I revise because it has sunk in over time that the act of writing will teach me what I need to know, will screech out the limitations of an idea, the need for evidence or a stronger thesis, if only I give myself time to learn and a clear enough head to see and to listen to what is actually on the page. I plan to revise because it helps to delay the pain of judgment until I have something on the page. I plan to revise because the promise of future control allows for the immediate risk, the loss of control. Revision has taught me that neither the glories nor the drudgery of writing are quite what they seem at the time; often, what seemed like the quintessential discovery of a paper requires further development, while the words that seemed so tedious to put down yield something valuable.

At this point, I liked the three pieces that I had accumulated. The two versions of "Why I Write" also showed some of more intricate rethinking I had done by changing words and sentences, and the extra piece, "Why I Revise" seemed to offer a reflection on the other two. I labeled the first two pieces "first draft" and "second draft" and call the three pieces together, "Revision." Then I showed the entry to my collaborator on this book. She said, "I like these, but I'm not sure where they come from or how one builds on the other. Also, what do you want your readers to do with them?" "How annoying," I thought. "Why can't she just like what I've got here?" After a day or two, I realized that not only was she right, but her advice was echoing my first reader's question about context, a question I had ignored because I wasn't sure what to do about it. That was when I created the explanatory context for the three versions that you see here.

RELATED WORDS

Assignment 14	Reading 132
Audience 25	Structure 149
Brainstorming 30	Titles 180
Editing 63	Voice 187
Evaluation 72	Workshop 191
Free-Writing 87	Writer's Block 195

EXERCISES

1. Look back through things you have written in any context—including childhood stories or poems, schoolwork, letters, and so on—and assemble a collage of yourself as a writer. Write a paper using quotes from things you have written and analyzing what they reveal about parts of your identity as a writer.

2. In a small group, examine one of the assigned readings looking for evidence of the revision process that produced it. What might have been the assignment, question, or experience that propelled the writer into beginning this essay? Look at all elements of the essay (including endnotes, footnotes, parentheses, evidence, examples, etc.) to speculate about what choices the writer has made after responding to the initial trigger. Present your findings, including the clues from the essay that support your deductions.

3. Create a version of your draft in which you use footnotes, cross-outs, and remarks in brackets to reveal as fully as possible what choices you have made so far in the writing of your essay, any questions you encountered, any dead-ends, any discoveries. Give this annotated ver-

sion to one reader and ask for feedback that takes into consideration your questions and choices. Give the original version of your draft to a different reader (who will thus be unaware of many of the choices you made and questions you had) and ask for feedback. Use the two kinds of feedback to revise the paper.

4. Prepare a one-page handout for the other members of your group in which you present two alternative drafts of a sentence or paragraph from your paper. Then comment on the two versions by, for example, explaining why one is better than the other or explaining why you are unsure about which one to include in your next draft.

Structure
The Stories Essays Tell

We accept easily that a story has a beginning, middle, and an end, a protagonist and an antagonist, symbols, a climax, a resolution, and so on. Indeed, we are so familiar with the conventions of story telling that we often do not know that we know them at all. For example, we accept willingly that fairy tales aren't realistic but some short stories are; in other words, we know about genres and their conventions often without consciously acknowledging them as such. And we, perhaps unconsciously, attune ourselves to the development of the tale as it unfolds; we deeply (in a buried way) understand its structure, rejoice in it, live vicariously through it. Anyone who has read stories to children will know what we mean.

Essays equally have structures. However, most of us do not grow up reading—let alone listening to—essays; so the structure of essays comes less "naturally" (deeply, unconsciously) to us. Yet, the structure of essays has a lot to do with the structure of stories. Just like stories, essays have a beginning, middle, and an end. Just like stories, they have a pace, a climax, a main plot, even protagonists and antagonists of sorts. They are, like fairy tales and stories, economical in form; that is, each part contributes to the whole. Essays, like stories, have individual steps (paragraphs rather than episodes), and they have transitions and guiding elements. But, one might say, essays are not as suspenseful as stories since they state their theses in advance. Yet, the suspense of the essay may well lie in seeing how the thesis works, what it means in the first place, and what it comes to mean and imply in the end. In some ways, that is true of stories, too. We often do know what kind of story is going to be told (who ever doubted, for example, what *Fatal Attraction* is about, and who doesn't know what happened to Cinderella?), but we don't know how and what exactly the story is going to tell. Or we enjoy the repetition and slight variation that each listening or reading brings. Finally, the endings of essays and stories, one might argue, are also not natural matches; stories resolve themselves apparently more clearly than essays. Essays often end in further questions even as they prove their point. But don't stories do that too? While essays often aren't looking for happy resolutions, the resolutions of fairy tales—to use an extreme example—often contain on second sight some complication, a feeling of discomfort that lies behind the comfort of the happily ever after. And, of course, stories famously can end in troubling images and unresolved tensions. The emphases might be slightly different but the purposes are closely related: to give and give not closure, to resolve without erasing, to make us think and to make us feel that we have reached the end of a piece. On the whole then, essays share tremendous structural similarities with stories.

Grimm's fairy tale "Hansel and Gretel" is about seven printed pages long and thus roughly the length of a research essay habitually assigned in college courses. And in those pages it needs to fulfill some demands that it shares with a research essay: hooking a reader, setting up a feasible premise and task, then developing this task, and finally resolving it. Furthermore, the writer or teller needs to orient the reader, letting her know at all moments where she is and what came before and what might be expected after; the tale needs keys and transitions, sign-posts, that lead the reader along as they follow the fate of the characters and discover its meaning.

"Hansel and Gretel" opens:

> Near a great forest there lived a poor woodcutter and his wife and his two children; the boy's name was Hansel and the girl's Gretel. They had very little to bite or to sup, and once, when there was great dearth in the land, the man could not even gain the daily bread. (101)

The opening sets up a landscape, the people involved, and the central problem: There isn't enough food for the parents and the two children. What to do? From here ensues a debate between the parents in which the mother argues that they should bring the children into the forest and leave them there so that they cannot find their way back. The father cannot at first find it in his heart to do so and resists; but the mother persuades him that if they do not do it all four of them will starve, and so the father agrees. Overhearing the parents, Hansel goes out and collects stones that will help them find their way back. When the parents try to implement their plan, Hansel uses the stones to get back to the house and the parents' plan is aborted.

The tale first sets up a problem, a debate, and a proposed solution. Then it works through related episodes: two attempts to abandon the children—one failed, one successful; two birds that "help the children"—one leading them into and the other out of disaster; two women trying to kill them—one by starving them, the other by fattening and eating them; two plots to undermine these plans—leaving markers and offering a bone instead of a finger; and two reversals resolve the plot—the witch gets baked instead of the kids, and the mother dies instead of the children. Thus the tale proceeds by repetition and variation, allowing us to tune into its patterns and understand the story.

The fairy tale ends with a resolution and a quote:

> Then was all care at an end, and they lived in great joy together.
>
> Sing every one
> My story is done
> And look! round the house
> There runs a little mouse.
> He that can catch her before she scampers in
> May make himself a fur-cap out of her skin. (107)

If we think of the fairy tale as an essay for a moment, we can see in it an exploration of the problem it sets up in the first paragraph: How do we survive when there is not enough to eat? The fairy tale proposes and explores in detail several solutions: the father's is that you share until you die; the mother's is that you put your own needs before that of others, giving two people the chance to survive instead of killing all four; the witch's is that you use the hunger of others to trap them and eat them. The happy ending suggests . . . ? Certainly the tale favors in its outcome the father's solution over the mother's and the witch's (and the gender issues here are food for thought as well), but the outcome remains complex. The children now support their father based on the treasures they took from the witch they murdered. And the final quote, addressed to the reader, suggests that the tale applies in some metaphorical sense to all of our lives and offers a rather surprising message. In each of our lives murders are needed to survive and competition for food is an integral part of life: You kill the mouse who wants your food and get a fur-cap in return. So, the tale indeed poses a problem, discusses and explores solutions, and ends with a sense both of resolution and unease. Each episode of the tale is similar and different from the one before, and this pattern of repetition and variation moves us forward and contains the meaning of the tale—a complex discussion on how to survive in desperate poverty, how to negotiate self-interest and solidarity with others when each of us can only survive at the expense of another.

If we can read stories as essays, we can read essays as stories. For example, literary critic Jane Tompkins's essay " 'Indians': Textualism, Morality, and the Problem of History," begins with a place, characters, and a problem; and it, too, tells a story. Tompkins tells how she was always disappointed as a child when she saw "real American Indians" at an event in Inwood Park in New York since they did not match her imagination of Indians (561). Now as an adult, she turns to research to find out about real Indians. From here, as Tompkins puts it, "this essay records the concrete experience of meeting and solving the difficulty I have just described" (563). She tells the story of encountering various sources in her quest for an answer.

Thus, pursuing the initial problem the beginning sets up, Tompkins' essay works with repetition just as "Hansel and Gretel" does; each source Tompkins encounters in her research does not quite give her the right answers; and so the episodes of her essay pile up. And just as the fairy tale highlights repetition to reveal its structure, Tompkins's essay takes stock and highlights relations between each step of the story. And in the best story-telling tradition, Tompkins keeps track of her story, leading it to its climax. Her search, exhausting and frustrating, leaves her at a seemingly disastrous dead end: None of the sources contain the truth about the genocide of the Indians. The climax of her story compares in complication and intensity to that of "Hansel and Gretel" right before Gretel manages to get the witch to crawl into the oven. Finally, a resolution of sorts follows. In the end—perhaps like Hansel and Gretel who plunder the witch's treasures—Tompkins understands that she can still gain knowledge from limited sources as long as she does not expect them to be entirely truthful. And she also realizes that academic thinking itself allows her to emphasize the importance of those limited perspectives over the importance of responding to the moral issues the conquest and murder of Indians entails. So, in that sense, she, too, turns to the audience and involves us in the tale she told; like the mouse in our cellar, our college and scholarly papers are part of the story. What happens in her essay, happens in our house, our study, our desk. The point is larger than the specifics of the tale: When we get entangled in academic critiques of various sources, we might forget the larger moral issues a topic demands as well.

Certainly, this comparison between "Hansel and Gretel" and Tompkins' essay is a stretch, and we want it to be little more than suggestive. Yet fairy tales and stories, which all of us know, can teach us more about developing the structure of an essay than we might think. There is no one structure to essays, but there are common elements to consider. An essay has a beginning, middle, and an end. The beginning needs to draw in the reader, establish a conflict of sorts so that there is something at stake, some work to perform, some risk to take. The opening then serves, just as in stories, to set the scene, to familiarize the reader with the world of the essay, and to establish a conflict. Just as stories consist of scenes, as do plays, the essay consists of paragraphs that tie together to create the plot of the essay. Each paragraph is indeed quite a bit like a scene, building on a scene before and propelling the plot forward, working with both repetition and variation. Through this repetition and variation, this memory pattern, they build up to a climax, a moment of the highest complication and duress, and then move into a resolution. And that resolution, the conclusion to the essay, involves an odd mixture of comfort and discomfort, solution and continuing problem. Here, too, as the story teller looks at his audience, the essayist turns most carefully to his reader leaving them with a way to take the story/essay with them to their homes and lives.

Thinking about essays as stories then is one way of giving them structure, of making them whole (with a beginning, a middle, and an end), giving them focus and development, and of shaping them so that the reader will be hooked, oriented, pleased and instructed. It is also one way of connecting our deep sense of structure in stories to the academic task of shaping an essay. That's exactly the point: without extraordinary experience and talent, we don't get a story right the first time. Have you ever tried to just start telling a story without knowing the end? The same with essays. Structure, in other words, comes for many writers after drafting, not before it, or before and after and after again. Some writers start with a rough structure of a story and then refine it with each revision. Others do better writing a draft and then thinking about what the real story is they want to tell. So when we finally plot out our essays, we read them from back to front, from middle to end and beginning, from paragraph to paragraph—in all directions until all parts respond to each other and build a whole. In a second, third, and fourth draft, in other words, we can place all the elements, determine where our climax is, plot the best structure. We are after all writers and not oral storytellers; we can do it with paper and without a listener (yet). Then we present the story with a beginning, middle, and an end. And all our knowledge of fairy tales and stories helps us to do so in a way that engages a reader.

RELATED WORDS

Argument 9	Paragraphs 114
Conclusions 42	Parallelism 118
Essay 68	Revision 143
Introductions 99	Thesis 176
Key Terms 106	Transitions 183

EXERCISES

1. Identify the beginning, the middle, and the end of an essay (published and/or student essay) by marking the three parts and writing an outline for the essay. How do you recognize and distinguish one from the other? How could the distinctions be improved?

2. Memory: Make notes in a draft where an essay has lost its memory of previous paragraphs. Make revision suggestions that restore memory to that part by suggesting how one paragraph can be made to repeat and vary the previous paragraphs.

3. Plot: Cut up the paper into paragraphs (do this both with published writing and student writing) and reassemble the paper to (a) determine the best order or plot and (b) insert orientation devices where needed. After reassembling it, write down the plot of the essay.

4. Climax: Determine where the climax of a (published or unpublished) essay (or several essays) resides. What makes you think so?

5. Resolution: Looking at a draft or finished academic essay, identify the resolution. What is resolved by it and what is left unresolved? How does the essay's meaning get expanded or complicated in the end? For the draft, make suggestions on strengthening the resolution and on considering remaining unresolved issues.

Subject-Verb
Sentence Squeeze-Play

Once we can identify the subject and the main verb of a sentence we have the keys to its very core, to the essence of what makes it tick. The subject is the noun—the person, place, or concept—that the whole sentence is organized around. The main verb is the central action of the sentence, most often one performed by that subject. These two work in partnership to make a sentence a sentence. Without both of them, the sentence simply does not exist as a complete and autonomous entity—it becomes a fragment of a sentence or a clause that is dependent on some other sentence to make it work. Guidebooks to good writing uphold a vision of this subject-verb relation as an ideal of purity and simplicity. A well-identified subject linked in perfect agreement to a vigorous verb is in truth the key to clarity and conciseness—and no excess words allowed! The guidebooks are mostly right on this one. Yet, what we find in academic writing is an often quite necessary (sometimes admittedly *un*necessary) intricacy of sentence structure that develops according to the complexity and abstraction of the ideas being expressed.

Sports writing seems like a good place to look for the guidebooks' ideal since it is famed for a punchy simplicity of sentence structure, for its clearly designated subjects, and for its active verbs. Think of the typical sports headline, which often consists entirely of a subject and verb—"Seattle Slew Triumphs!"—or a basic subject-verb combination with an object (whoever got beaten) or some other minor addition:

Yankees pummel Red Sox
Notre Dame slaughters Rutgers, 41–3
Iron Mike turns into putty
Squeeze-play lifts Cubbies over Cardinals

Or consider the famous 1938 newspaper headline about a fight between American boxer Joe Louis and German boxer Max Schmeling (who had received an encouraging cable from Hitler earlier in the day): "Louis Knocks Out Schmeling" (Considine 138). We certainly get the point here: Somebody hits somebody else really hard and that's it. In this case, the simple and repetitive subject-verb structure of each sentence works perfectly to describe the simple and concrete action and reaction that took place.

Fortunately, vigorous prose is not limited to sports-writing. In a scholarly essay intended for an educated general audience, "Television and the Twilight of the Senses," naturalist Bill McKibben chooses powerful, active verbs to propel his argument forward, while relying on repetitive subject and sentence structures to drive that argument home, to beat us over the head with his point. In the following excerpt he is using baseball as one instance of the many ways in which television limits our senses and in the end cheats us of the fuller experiences of life. Unlike the sports examples which rely on description, McKibben moves to the slightly more abstract level of analysis, but he holds himself to simple subject-verb sentences.

> Consider the difference between watching a baseball game on TV and watching one at the park. Technology enriches the TV version with close-up and slo-mo and instant replay, but at a great price. It deprives you of the enormous perspective available to anyone in the stadium, the incredible choice of what to look at. TV looks at pretty women on occasion but never at the fight in the stands or the man selling beer or the outfielder hitching his pants. TV filters out most of the familiar sound of the ballpark, too—the sourceless, undifferentiated babble that comes from forty thousand people talking, laughing, rustling sacks of popcorn—a sound that the crack of the bat breaks so cleanly through, refocusing everyone's attention. TV systems are planning to introduce new interactive technology that will allow you to select between, say, three or four camera angles during the course of a game. But this sort of choice only underlines how much TV amputates your senses. . . . (112)

McKibben's main verb choices here are dynamic and attention-grabbing. They drive this paragraph along. At the same time, a single subject is simply repeated in slightly different forms. Once we select out only the subjects and main verbs of these sentences, the pattern becomes even more apparent:

Subject	*Main Verb*
you (implied)	consider
technology	enriches
it	deprives
TV	looks
TV	filters
TV systems	are planning
choice	underlines

Aside from noticing the implied reader or listener in the first sentence, identifying the main subjects and verbs is not difficult here. McKibben's profound belief in the powerful and all-pervasive evils of TV shows up in this paragraph partly because he makes TV the main actor in every sentence; this helps to demonstrate viscerally the *loss* of action, the lack of initiative, it engenders in human beings. Even potentially upbeat verbs like "enriches" are used to reveal the extent of TV's power to fool us into thinking we're better off with it around. McKibben's fairly straightforward subject-verb patterns clearly get the job done—TV acts on our world, and we had better watch out—but the simplicity of his sentence structures also reflects the limited degree of his analysis. In other words, this is slightly less of a profound consideration of the effects of technology on our culture and slightly more of a rant.

As we progress a little deeper into academic writing, ideas become more intricate and more abstract and sentence structures shift accordingly. Writers in specialized fields also build in more qualifiers, not because they are inherently cautious people but because they need to make finer distinctions and because they are maneuvering in a crowd of many other scholars in order to position what they have to say on a particular subject matter. For example, consider the following passage from an essay by feminist theorist Helena Michie. In this section, Michie discusses how feminists have focused on the idea of the mother when thinking about the family:

> For a variety of historical and political reasons which I will not go into here, feminist literary theorists have followed psychoanalysis in recentering their inquiry around the mother. While very early feminist theorists like Kate Millett struggled with the words of literary and academic fathers, more recent critics and theorists on both sides of the Atlantic have begun to turn their attention to maternal figures, maternal discourse. This discourse has taken many forms and has both figured in and figured almost all major feminist projects. Canonical revision has, for example, frequently been articulated as a search for foremothers; feminist poststructuralists have looked for the place of the mother in producing the *jouissance* that for critics from Roland Barthes to Jacques Derrida in turn produces and disseminates meaning, desire, and language; linguistic theorists have scanned literature and language for marks of *écriture féminine*, the mother tongue, what Cixous so famously refers to as "white ink . . . good mother's milk." Perhaps more fundamentally, motherhood and the maternal body have been seen as the location of language and self, the place where the female subject and the female narrative "I" are produced and reproduced. (59)

Here the task of finding the subject and the main verb becomes more difficult (you might try this on your own before checking the list that follows). However, once detected, the subject-verb pattern offers us a kind of map through the complex structure and vocabulary of the passage, and even some possible tools for analysis. We can learn to tell the difference between the *core* of each sentence and the qualifying and modifying phrases that are built around that core.

Subject	*Main Verb*
theorists	have followed
critics and theorists	have begun
discourse	has taken . . . has figured in . . . {has} figured
revision	has been articulated
{;} poststructuralists	have looked
{;} theorists	have scanned
motherhood . . . body	have been seen

In this case, identifying the subject and main verb primarily involves digging the core elements of the sentence out from a morass of preliminary or intervening clauses. In the first sentence, for example, once we eliminate the long prepositional phrase (from "For" up to the first comma) the bones of the main clause emerge. "Eliminate it then," the guides to good writing cry, "too many words!"—and in some cases they are right. Yet Michie is using that opening clause to distinguish the topic she wants to explore from an entire body of scholarship that exists on a deeply related topic, the question of *why* theorists have taken this particular track. The second and last sentences have plural subjects—two nouns functioning together as the subject of the same sentence—and therefore must be partnered with plural verb forms ("motherhood and the maternal body *have* been seen" whereas motherhood alone *has* been seen, for example). The third sentence throws a curve ball because it has multiple verbs all partnering with the same subject. What has discourse done? What actions has it taken? We must track through the entire sentence to piece together that series of actions. The fourth sentence looks the most ominous and is by far the longest sentence in the passage. Yet once we figure out that it is actually three main clauses joined by semicolons, we can look in each of those main clauses for its own subject-verb partnership; because of the semicolons, each of those clauses must be treated equally. "Then why not separate them?" the guidebooks ask. Michie might answer that these three clauses function meaningfully together to show three ways in which scholars have focused on mothers, and in fact, she might argue, by piling them one upon the other in this fashion she is rhetorically backing up her point that many different theorists over time have zeroed in on this topic and ignored other aspects of family.

As with this example, we often can measure the complexity of a sentence by the difficulty of identifying for sure which is the main noun or noun phrase and which is the main verb. Within specialized disciplines, writing also becomes more technical and uses agreed-upon conventions that may not be familiar to others outside the field. For example, writers in the humanities tend to avoid passive voice constructions because they are considered "wordy," dull, indirect, while in scientific writing passive voice constructions are the norm—possibly because scientists value objectivity and want to emphasize the measurable results of studies over the fallible human agents designing and implementing them. "To assess spontaneous excision of genomic islands, LightCycler PCR was done with the

LightCycler-FastStart DNA Master SUBR Green I kit (Roche Diagnostics, Mannheim, Germany) with specific primers designed in and around the genomic islands" (Baba, et al. 3). Who exactly carried out that LightCycler test and who designed those primers?—we will never know. For these scientists the important information is not "who did it" but what methods and equipment were used.

Within these more specialized regions, tracking down the subject and verb can become a rigorous treasure hunt, an exercise in sniffing out the key players and refusing to be distracted by all the minor actors shrieking and waving to get our attention. However, the rewards of a successful hunt are substantial, both in giving access to the central meaning and function of a sentence, and by reminding us that there are sentence structures flexible enough to communicate the most complex, abstract, or bizarre idea.

RELATED WORDS

Coordination and Subordination 45   Parallelism 118
Discipline 57   Punctuation 126
Editing 63   Voice 187
Grammar 90

EXERCISES

1. In a group, choose paragraphs from three different academic essays and create a separate list identifying the subject and main verb in each sentence. (It may also help to consult a grammar handbook during this exercise.) For each example, discuss what that subject-verb pattern tells us about that writer's intention and meaning in the paragraph, his or her stylistic choices, strengths, limitations, even his or her character and values.

2. Choose a passage from an academic essay that seems highly specialized and uses long, complex sentences. Figure out the main subject-verb pattern and then rewrite the passage by simplifying the sentence structure (breaking long sentences down into several short sentences, deleting elaborate qualifying clauses, etc.). Compare the effect of the two passages by getting a reader's response from someone in your group.

3. Find five examples of slightly or wildly different sentence structures; that is, sentences where the subject and verb are simple and up front, sentences where they are separated by clauses, sentences where they are inverted, sentences that use passive voice, and so on. For each of those sentences write a sentence of your own in which you copy the structure of the sentence and the placement of subject and verb, but in which you write about a completely different subject matter.

4. In a group, choose an essay in which the writer describes an incident in his or her life and an essay in which the writer analyzes an abstract idea. Compare the subject-verb patterns and relative complexity of sentence structure in the two essays. Then write a paragraph describing an incident and using a series of completely simple sentences with a repetitive subject-verb pattern. Then rewrite the paragraph analyzing that incident and using the most complex sentences you can come up with. Write a final, balanced version in which you describe *and* analyze the incident using some varied sentence structures.

5. Identify the subject-verb pattern in your own draft or in another writer's draft. Note instances where the subject and verb function particularly well together to add momentum and meaning to the sentence. Note the places where the subject and verb do not function well together (because one is singular and the other is plural, for example, or because one is missing). Look at the pattern overall and identify places where it seems repetitive for no reason and could effectively be varied. Choose one paragraph and rewrite it by using simple active verb structures. Rewrite the same paragraph entirely in the passive voice. Rewrite it once more using some effective variations on subject-verb structure.

Summary
The Continuum of Power

Imagine the writer seated at a table surrounded by all the sources she has read for a particular project: let us say five articles, highlighted, stapled, stacked in order of importance; three books brandishing their post-it marked readiness to be included; a glowing computer screen nearby with two book-marked Websites she plans to use; and a file bursting with quotes from people she has interviewed. By the time she summarizes those sources, condensing many of them to a pithy sentence or two, using key quotes from some, building in extended analyses of a few, the pile of material on that table will account for perhaps a third of her finished essay. This mind-boggling reduction of bulk while retaining the essential substance of some sources and key points or examples from others is the genius of summary.

In this sense, summary can be seen as a kind of manufacturing plant in which a writer chops up an entire roast chicken dinner of sources, strips off the frills and the excess examples, boils the remainder down to a purified essence and then serves them up as a series of meaty source "McNuggets." Indeed the level of reduction involved in summarizing can be taken to absurdist extremes as it is every day in television guides' one-sentence summaries of movies. Consider the following synopsis of the three-hour epic, *Pearl Harbor,* followed by the reviewer's succinct, one-sentence assessment: "Best friends join war effort after Japanese attack. Never have so many spent so much for so little." Even within the limits of this specialized form, however, reviewers often convey a distinctive tone of voice, gauge their readers' level of shared knowledge, even stretch themselves a little in aiming for pith and for laughs, as in this *New York Times* summary of *Rosemary's Baby*: "Devil Worship on the Upper West Side. Humdinger suspense, fabulous Farrow." Or best yet, this succinct preview of *Die Hard*: "Explosions, shootings, hangings, splatterings. Huge hit." What more does a viewer need to know?

To choose an evening's entertainment, the viewer needs little more, and in that sense these summaries are successful. Similarly, the effectiveness of any summary depends on the writer conveying to readers only what they need to know in a particular rhetorical situation. In creating a summary, then, a writer is actually making a series of decisions not just about how to mulch down the argument of an entire essay or book, about what to include and what to leave out, but also about what purpose that summary is supposed to serve. And in order to make these decisions, the writer must necessarily make a series of assessments about the intended audience, how much context or explanatory detail they will need, and above all what slant to give the description so that it best supports or leads into the point that writer wants to make. Summary appears to be merely a condensed characterization of the original source, but that characterization is in fact completely driven by the new context in which it is to function.

Consider for example the subtle contrasts between various summaries of Mario Puzo's 1969 novel *The Godfather* on which the famous series of movies was based. In a 2002 piece on "Discovering Italian American Writers," Nancy Pearl condenses the plot of the novel into a one-sentence synopsis and focuses on its appeal for contemporary readers:

> *The Godfather . . .* is the novel that most people associate with Italian American fiction. Filled with violence, love, betrayal, and deception, this action-packed epic is the story of Vito Corleone, leader of one of the most successful New York Mafia families, who jostles for power in the crime underworld and tries to control his turbulent family, as well. (Rereading this, it's easy to see the parallels between Puzo's novel and the HBO series *The Sopranos*) (152).

By contrast, a summary included as part of Andrew Rosenheim's 1999 obituary of Puzo assumes that readers already know something about the plot and focuses on the qualities of the novel that originally made it a blockbuster:

Certainly much of the credit must go to Puzo's undeniable skill as a writer of narrative. In *The Godfather* he sets what is essentially a family saga against a backdrop of new wealth and power in the putatively glamorous environs of New York City, Las Vegas, and Palm Springs. It is a world more of money than taste, and in his evocation of the delights of the nouveaux riches Puzo is really only following the example of other 'social' best-selling novelists such as Irving Wallace or Harold Robbins (6).

Where Rosenheim foregrounds the novel's connection to a literary context, another reviewer emphasizes its epic historical significance: "It was Puzo's wily conceit that these Mafiosi weren't just criminal bums but Roman emperors and generals in modern garb, fighting over turf and position not for money but for the greater glory of their family names" (Podhoretz 83). In contrast, Pauline Kael's review of the 1972 film takes a completely different slant on the implications of the story, calling it "a wide, startlingly vivid view of a Mafia dynasty, in which organized crime becomes an obscene nightmare image of American free enterprise" (1). From family, Romans, countrymen to a nightmare projection of American greed, notice how the portrayal of the Mafia in each of these summaries shifts depending on the perspective and rhetorical purposes of each reviewer.

This manipulation of the information being conveyed is the key to effective summary; each writer chops and bends the original material to fit a particular context. At the same time, each writer must maintain a kind of fairness to the original source. Thus, Kael can get away with calling *The Godfather* a "nightmare projection of American free enterprise," stretching the spirit of the original to serve her own interpretive vision, but she could not legitimately describe it as a novel about animal abuse even though a horse is beheaded as part of the plot. Every summary thus involves a balancing act between an accurate representation of the source and a deliberate appropriation of it for the writer's own purposes. In academic writing, this balance between responsibility to the source and interpretive manipulation becomes particularly acute: An inaccurate representation of the source is frowned upon as a misreading, yet an overly dogged or detailed account of the source can bog a paper down and detract from the writer's interpretive momentum and control. At the same time, academic writers have an enormous range of techniques for relating to their sources ranging from direct quotation to careful paraphrase to summary to close analysis and interpretation. Often writers will use some combination of these methods to taper the account of a source to fit the needs of a particular argument without misrepresenting the original.

In *Ethnic Passages*, literary critic Thomas Ferraro studies the way certain kinds of immigrant novels like *The Godfather* have been undervalued or skewed by traditional critical interpretations of them. Ferraro uses a combination of summary and direct quotation to characterize the work of previous critics, sometimes to show how they have misrepresented the novel and sometimes to approve of and build on their work as in the following example:

> In her discussion of *The Godfather*, Rose Basile Green comes the closest of any critic to unpacking what she calls the "socio-economic ethnic image" of the Corleone crime syndicate. Unlike almost everyone else, Green takes seriously Puzo's portrayal of the syndicates—not as historical fact about actual gangsters but as a treatise (however romanticized) "dealing with the contemporary strategy of gaining and securing power." Yet Green's analysis splits into typical parallel paths: crime as a means for social mobility versus the family as a locus of traditional Southern Italian responsibility. (22)

In this passage we can see Ferraro moving between summary and direct quotation in building toward an analysis of Green's work. He characterizes Green's approach in relation to other critics but does not take the time to give us a complete account of her book; instead, he focuses only on the part of her work that is relevant to his own discussion. In the middle of this quick overview, he drops twice into a direct quotation, first to give us one of Green's key terms and in the second case perhaps to reassure us that he is accurately representing her argument. Toward the end of the passage he is already moving the summary toward the point he wants to make—that Green like other previous critics fails to identify the power that comes not from organized crime but from the internal hierarchy of the immigrant family itself.

Since all these decisions about when and how much to summarize depend on a writer's assessment of his or her own purpose and audience, the number and length of the summaries in an essay will change as the drafts of it mutate from one stage to another, as the writer's sense of what he or she needs from those sources develops. Looking at a completed work like Ferraro's, we can only speculate about some of the choices he made along the way, the ruthless discards, the changes he made in how he characterized particular sources as he developed his own argument, the juggling of that delicate balance between the source's original intent and the needs of the moment. In the second sentence of the passage, for example, Ferraro might easily have chosen to paraphrase Green instead of quoting her directly. By restating Green's idea in his own words instead of allowing her to speak for a second time, Ferraro might have retained a greater sense of authority in this passage (as it stands, he seems to interrupt himself to quote her). Thus for instance a paraphrase might read something like: "Unlike almost everyone else, Green takes seriously Puzo's portrayal of the syndicates—not as historical fact about actual gangsters but as a treatise (however romanticized) on larger societal methods for establishing and maintaining power." On the other hand, because he goes on to show the limitations of Green's argument, to demonstrate how his own interpretation rebuts and triumphs over hers, his use of the second direct quote shows a kind of politeness and argumentative finesse. He allows her to speak directly because he is about to take issue with what she says; by using and responding to the direct quote, he implies that this is a fair and balanced representation of her argument while dramatizing his disagreement with it.

As this sample suggests, the differences between direct quotation, paraphrase and summary indicate a continuum of different positions a writer can take in relation to a source ranging from direct conversation to dependence to manipulation to outright appropriation. A paraphrase differs from direct quotation because it recasts ideas from the source into the vocabulary and context of the summarizing writer rather than allowing the original writer to speak directly. Paraphrase differs from summary in its detailed fidelity to the original source, implying a greater dependency on the source by offering a close translation of a particular passage or idea. Summary differs from paraphrase in its ability to step back and give a condensed overview of the original source or of a larger portion of it. Summary builds toward analysis when the writer uses that condensed synopsis to lead into a more detailed dissection of the original writer's argument. Summary verges on interpretation as it characterizes that source in a particular way to serve the writer's own argument; it is a springboard into interpretation and a balance weight against interpretation's overpowering control. In every case, a writer plays with the continuum of power implied by these differences, choosing to place him or herself at a summarizing distance from the source or up close with a magnifying glass, choosing for a moment to be the faithful representative of the source or allowing it to speak directly, then whipping around to tweak it into a fresh light.

RELATED WORDS

Audience 25	Quotation 130
Citation 32	Reading 132
Counterargument 49	Research 137
Footnotes 81	Synthesis 172
Interpretation 94	

EXERCISES

1. In a group, find three different examples of summary in three academic essays. For each one, analyze why you identified that passage as a summary (rather than as quotation, paraphrase, analysis, or interpretation, for example). How effective is the summary in conveying a meaningful and pithy account of the source? Speculate about the choices the writer made in constructing that summary. How much of the original source seems to be included? Does it appear to be a fair account of that source? Is it accompanied by quotation, paraphrase, analysis, or interpretation?

2. Write a parody in which you summarize an entire well-known book, movie, or essay into a *TV Guide*-style synopsis. Then create a more balanced one to two sentence summary of the source that helps to convey its essence to your colleagues in the class.

3. Using a reading quoted in many of your drafts, have each member of your group summarize the same passage from that reading and use it

to make a point. Discuss how you decided what to leave in, what to leave out, how you each chose to characterize the source in order to make your points, and list some of most effective methods you found for condensing the substance of the original.

4.   Choose one key paragraph from an academic essay and paraphrase it; that is, carefully restate it in your own words. Then summarize that same paragraph for a friend who has never read the essay. Then summarize it for a group of class members who have read the essay. Then summarize it for a person who is unfamiliar with American culture. In your group, compare the four versions and discuss the choices you made in each case.

Syllabus
Social Contract, Utopian Vision, or Draft of the Future?

It is, of course, easy to take the syllabus for granted and at face value; but that would not be in the spirit of this book. The syllabus—as one central academic custom—is actually worth looking at a bit more closely. Why does it exist? What does it mean? The *Oxford English Dictionary* defines *syllabus* as "a concise statement or table of the heads of a discourse, the contents of a treatise, the subjects of a series of lectures etc.; a compendium, abstract, summary, epitome"(*OED* online). A syllabus is thus a shorthand version of a larger piece writing, a kind of code. Derived from the Greek—as a "corrupt reading of syllabus or syllable"—its first documented use in English is 1656 where syllabus means "a Table or Index in a Book, to show places or matter by Letters or Figures" (*OED* online). So, the syllabus is writing in code; thus it invites decoding, careful reading, and filling in.

And when leaving common sense behind and pursuing the term further, one is in for a rather astonishing surprise. Consider what the *Encyclopedia Britannica* list as its "10 relevant entries to a query on 'syllabus' " (see Figure 4): How in the world did we get from a college syllabus to the eclectic group of entries with such diverse and seemingly unconnected figures as Pope Pius IX; Gustav Heinrich Adolf Engler, a German botanist; and Zakir Husain, an Indian statesman? When looked at a bit more closely the entries reveal three broad contexts for syllabus, of which each of our figures are representative: one religious, the other scientific, and the third educational. Four densely printed pages into the entry on Pope Pius IX we find out that in 1864, "Pius [decided] to take immediate action against liberalism," the Encyclopedia informs us, by publishing the "famous Syllabus listing 80 of the 'principal errors of our times.' " All of the errors were already known within the church, but the syllabus made them public and explicit, and according to the entry, "undermined the liberal Catholics' position, for it destroyed their following among intellectuals and placed their program out of court." Tapping further into the entry on the German botanist Gustav Heinrich Adolf Engler, we learn that his 1892 "Syllabus of Plant Names" "provided a comprehensive system of classification whose arrangement of plant orders and families became widely accepted" and "is still a standard and indispensable reference book." And what about Zakir Husain, the Indian statesman? He, the encyclopedia informs us, "responded to the nationalist leader Mahatma Ghandi's appeal to Indian youth to shun state-supported institutions; he helped found the Muslim National University in Aligarh (later moved to New Delhi) and served as its vice-chancellor from 1926 to 1948. At Ghandi's invitation, he also became chairman of the National Committee on Basic Education, established in 1937 to design a Ghandian syllabus for schools." Each context reveals something to us about the syllabus. Pope Pius's (anti-intellectual) syllabus looked to define, control, and enforce correct behavior—to list errors so as to eradicate them. Engler's syllabus was used to classify nature and to create a reference that other scholars could use. Zakir Husain's syllabus was created to conceive of a new vision of education, to plan and map out an alternative form of school based in the thought of Mahatma Ghandi. Each syllabus contained a vision: one attempted to regulate social conduct, one classified nature into scholarly concepts, one drafted a vision for education in the future. Each of these functions—the regulatory, the scholarly and taxonomic, and the educational and visionary—can be found in most college syllabi, including Alec Marsh's for his freshman seminar on Love (see Figure 5).

Even the first lines of the syllabus reveal the visionary: "Fall 2001: The Ideology of Love," was written somewhere before Fall 2001 and before Marsh had begun teaching about the ideology of love. Written before its event, a syllabus contains the vision of the instructor of the future course, and that vision is an educational vision (what are the larger educational goals of the class), a thematic vision (what are its key terms and its thematic progression), and a social vision (how will classes be conducted and what is the desired, or even required, relationship between teacher and student). Marsh's syllabus begins, as most syllabi, with the class meeting times and place, the professor's office location and office hours; Marsh also provides his e-mail address and home phone number—something not every professor offers up. The information thus also reveals a vision of the implied relation between professor and student: Is the professor drawing a line between public and private contact (office phone and home phone—Marsh does not),

---

Pius IX
original name GIOVANNI MARIA MASTAI-FERRETTI (b. May 13, 1792, Senigallia, Papal
States—d. Feb. 7, 1878, Rome), Italian head of the Roman Catholic Church whose pontificate
(1846-78) was the longest in history and was marked by a transition from liberalism to conservatism. Notable events of his reign included the declaration of the dogma of . . .

Roman Catholicism: The Age of Reformation and Counter-Reformation:
THE CHURCH IN THE MODERN PERIOD: The reign of Pius IX (1846–78)
Much of the history of Roman Catholicism in the 19th century is identified with the pontificates of
two men: Pius IX, who was pope for a third of a century, and his successor, Leo XIII, who was pope
for a quarter of a century (1878–1903).

Engler, Adolf
in full GUSTAV HEINRICH ADOLF ENGLER (b. March 25, 1844, Sagan, Prussia [now Zagan,
Pol.]—d. Oct. 10, 1930, Berlin, Ger.), German botanist famous for his system of plant classification
and for his expertise as a plant geographer. (see also *Index:* taxonomy)

Angiosperms: The Flowering Plants: ANGIOPERMS: DIVISION MAGNOLIO-
PHYTA: Classification APPRAISAL
Based on both comparative morphology and the fossil record, it appears that the evolutionary di-
versification of the angiosperms began more than 120 million years ago during the Early Creta-
ceous Period (144 to 97.5 million years ago). The ancestors of the angiosperms must by definition
have been gymnosperms, since all the features that . . .

Dupautoup, Felix-Antoine-Philibert
(b. Jan. 3, 1802, Saint-Félix, Fr.—d. Oct. 11, 1878, Lacombe), Roman Catholic bishop of Orléans
who was a clerical spokesman for the liberal wing of French Catholicism during the mid-19th
century.

Figure 4   Syllabus

spoken and written contact (phone numbers vs. e-mail address—Marsh encourages both), formal and more casual contact (appointment vs. office hours—Marsh
offers ample office hours but also suggests a walk-in contact with students)? And
there is not just one teacher, but also a writing assistant, who is available to students as well. This broadens the space for learning. In Marsh's educational vision,
learning seems to be a cooperative process that takes place within and outside of
class, that offers instruction and assistance, and that seems to encourage dialogue.
    From here follows the list of the texts of the course. Listed in chronological
rather than alphabetical order, the texts reveal a narrative through time from Plato
(and, one might assume something like platonic love) to Adrienne Rich and her
critique of heterosexuality. In this list, we can decode a first argument of the
course about the "ideology of love": Love is a historical concept that can be studied by reading texts on "love" from various periods. "The Ideology of Love," as
represented in this list, is also a Western concept, starting with the Greeks and
moving to a current American poet. It is a course on the Western ideology of love
as seen through the eyes of white Western writers and thinkers.

Publishing: Book publishing: MODERN PUBLISHING PRACTICE: Educational Publishing
A particular branch of editorial work that has grown to be of cardinal importance since World War II concerns the conception, planning, and publication of the hundreds of books needed for educational programs at every level. Throughout the world editors specializing in school books visit teachers and lecturers to promote the writing of the . . .

Pacific Islands: MAJOR POLITICAL UNITS OF MELANESIA: New Caledonia: Administration and social conditions
As a French overseas territory, New Caledonia is fully integrated into the French Republic, is subject to its laws, and sends parliamentary representatives to Paris. Special legislation is required, however, to introduce laws for the government of the territory and in areas such as education, health, and labour. Authority over defense, . . .

Husain, Zakir
(b. Feb. 8, 1897, Hyderabad, India—d. May 3, 1969, New Delhi), Indian statesman, the first Muslim to hold the largely ceremonial position of president of India. His fostering of secularism was criticized by some Muslim activists.

Israel: Physical and human geography: ADMINISTRATION AND SOCIAL CONDITIONS: Education
By enactment, education is obligatory and free for children between the ages of 5 and 15 and free but not compulsory for those 16 and 17. Young people between the ages of 14 and 18 who have not completed schooling are obliged to attend special classes. Parents may choose among state lay education, state religious education, and private . . .

Roman Catholicism: History of Roman Catholicism: THE CHURCH OF THE LATE MIDDLE AGES
The 12th century, or, more correctly, the century 1050–1150, has been called the first Renaissance. A more accurate title would be the adolescence of Europe, in which higher education, techniques of thought and speech, and a fresh attack upon the old problems of philosophy and theology appeared for the first time in postclassical Europe. All . . .

Query Report for this Search

Copyright © 1994–1999 Encyclopaedia Britannica, Inc.

The course description then summarizes the goals and nature of the course; but it is also the first piece that lets the voice of the teacher speak to the student. It might imply an overall narrative, it might expand on a methodology, it might situate the course within the larger curriculum, it might pose some of the key questions around which the course will revolve, it might supply the reader with the key terms of a course. It might furthermore reveal the passions of the teacher, even the pedagogy. In some cases the course description functions as a reiteration of an earlier advertisement of the course—as it was posted in the catalogue—a document students browse not unlike other catalogues to explore and gratify their desires for particular

Marsh/Clark

Tues. Thurs. 11:00–12:15 CA 43
Marsh office
Office phone: xxx-xxx-xxxx
Home phone: xxx-xxx-xxxx
e-mail xxxx.edu
Office Hours: Mon., Tues. Wed. 1–3 PM

Writing Asst. Clark:
Home Phone
e-mail: xxxx.com

Texts:

Plato. The Symposium. Penguin. Christopher Gill trans.

Stone, Bruce ed. Sir Gawain and the Green Knight. Penguin.

Shakespeare, Williams. Romeo and Juliet.

(recommended) Shakespeare, William, Romeo & Juliet. Audio tape: BDD Audio version, Kenneth
   Branagh dir.

de Balzac, Honore. Pere Goriot. Norton Critical ed.

Fromm, Erich. The Art of Loving. Harper & Row.

Rich, Adrienne: "Compulsory Heterosexuality and Lesbian Existence." (HANDOUT)

Course Description: We passionately need to believe that love is the most natural thing in the
world. We believe that true love can save us, redeem us, make us happy and solve our problems. In
fact, as we shall see, love is shaped, directed, and largely controlled by social conventions. When we
remark that 'true love conquers all,' we are tacitly acknowledging the pressure that social custom
brings to bear on love and its unruly passions. By social custom, I mean property and financial relations; when Mdm. de Nucingen tells young Rastignac: 'Mixing money and feelings, isn't it aw-
ful. You won't be able to love me' (Balzac 114) in Pere Goriot she puts her finger on a social question that continues to perplex and wound.

Aside from social considerations, the 'normal' forms of love and even the aim of love seems to
change depending on social practices and psychological theories. Hence the importance of the
key term, 'ideology,' for this course. A tough term to define, 'ideology' refers to social practices,
'habits,' and beliefs that one accepts unquestioningly as being 'natural,' or 'just common-sense.' Evidently, even something as 'natural' and special as love, is not independent of unexamined beliefs.

Expectations: You must come to class awake and alert and ready to work, talk, think and write. I
will try to create an atmosphere conducive to open discussion, my expectation is that you will discuss. You cannot roll out of bed at 10:30 and expect to be effective in class. This is a seminar—that
means it depends on discussion. No lectures. Do the reading and be prepared to speak when called
on. Better yet, volunteer to speak—class participation counts. Coffee or tea anyone?

Requirements: Several essays will be assigned. Since this is a course on writing and critical thinking, you will be asked—and often required—to revise these pieces. Significant class time will be
spent on the mechanics of college papers and academic discourse: thesis, topic, argument, quotation, implication, stakes will become familiar terms to you. While formulating effective arguments
will be stressed, you will learn how to quote and cite sources and how to make a bibliography and
footnotes.

Figure 5   Fall 2001: The Ideology of Love

Papers, Revision Policy, Grades Full drafts of all papers will typically be due on the Tuesday before the paper is due. Final drafts will be handed in with the earlier draft on Thursdays in class. Changes from the draft should be highlighted. All papers with grades lower than "C" must be re-written, with revisions highlighted. Since we are teaching you a skill, that is, how to write an academic essay, your grades will not be averaged, rather, the grades will be weighted towards the end of the term. As you improve with practice your grades should get better. Your final grade will reflect your level at the end of the term. Class participation and attendance are significant components of your grade. If you miss more than four classes you risk failing the course.

Syllabus

Part 1 Platonic Love

Week 1 8/28, 8/30 Tues. Intro. For Thurs. read Symposium p. 3–21.

Week 2. 9/4, 9/6 Tues . SHORT PAPER DUE (3 pages) on one of the first three speeches in SYMPOSIUM.. For Thurs. finish SYMPOSIUM.

Week 3 9/11, 913: Discuss SYMPOSIUM: Thinking about thesis, topic, argument.

Week 4 9/18, 9/20: Tues DRAFT OF 5 page SYMPOSIUM paper due. WORKSHOP. Thurs. 5 page SYMPOSIUM PAPER DUE

Part 2 Courtly Love

Week 5: 9/25, 9/27, Tues, SIR GAWAIN 15–63; and Thurs. SIR GAWAIN 64–115.

Week 6 10/2, 10/4 Tues. SIR GAWAIN Thurs. SIR GAWAIN FALL BREAK

Week 7 10/11 Draft Workshop: Courtly Love Paper 5 Pages;

Week 8 10/16 Tues COURTLY LOVE PAPER (5 PAGES) DUE.

Part 3: Love and Marriage Pt. 1

Week 8 Thurs 10/18 ROMEO AND JULIET

Week 9 10/23, 10/25 ROMEO & JULIET Thurs. draft of ROMEO & JULIET paper due

Part 3 Love and Marriage Pt. 2

Week 10/30 ROMEO & JULIET PAPER DUE 11/1 Thurs. PERE GORIOT 5–71 : ;

Week 11 11/6, 11/8 PG 71–217; Tues PG 71–171; Thurs. PG 172–217.

Week 12 11/13, 11/15 Tues Finish PG, THURS. DRAFT WORKSHOP Draft of PG paper (5 pages) due.

Week 13 11/20 PERE GORIOT PAPER DUE

THANKSGIVING BREAK: Read Rich essay (handout)

Part 4 Sex, Psychoanalysis and Ideology

Week 14 11/27: Rich "Compulsory Heterosexuality etc." Thurs. FROMM vii–74;

Week 15 12/4, 12/6 Finish Fromm WORKSHOP SEX, LOVE & IDEOLOGY paper (15 PAGES).

FINAL PAPER DUE FRIDAY 12/7

Figure 5   (*continued*)

forms of knowledge and experience. In that function, tone plays a significant role in such a description. What drew you to the course? What made you choose it? How was the course "advertised"? Consider Marsh's voice: How does he speak? What does he stress? Marsh moves his reader, the student, from a familiar way of thinking about love—one we are all passionately invested in—to a less familiar, more critical view of love not as nature but as historical construction. By including himself and the student in a "we," he indicates that he, too, shares a belief or hope for love that the reading will question and problematize. He promises a journey together. In the second paragraph, he explains the key term "ideology" as it relates to "nature" and "social conventions"; ideology, he explains, makes us see social conventions as nature. The course description thus offers so far an educational vision and the beginning of a scholarly taxonomy or language: a view of a community (a vision of a we), a problem or question that will be explored (love is not what we want it to be), and the key terms (love, ideology, nature, social custom, habits) and method of exploration (questioning of beliefs through reading and key terms, examining the unexamined, moving from common sense to investigation).

The description of the course is, to Marsh, distinct from his expectations, his requirements, and his rules and policies. Here the visionary slowly turns towards the regulatory. Expectations are strongly urged hopes, but they are not requirements. In his expectations, Marsh paints the ideal class—a utopian vision of a community in which everyone is punctual, prepared, ready to contribute; he envisions an open community of intellectual exchange in which all participants work, talk, think, and write together. While the expectations are uttered in a flirtatious enticing tone (Coffee or tea anyone?), even they reflect a certain urgency that shows that Marsh has not encountered many utopian spaces. The regulatory creeps in: "You must come to class awake," "You cannot roll out of bed at 10:30," "volunteer to speak." The demand for voluntary participation perhaps best captures the mixture of visionary and regulatory thinking that goes into Marsh's description of his expectations. The visionary part of the syllabus slowly gives way to the regulatory part as the syllabus moves from description, to expectations, to requirements, to policies.

The requirements describe a social system rather than a social gathering. They define the social contract that everyone enters into: Students are required to revise and they will learn the conventions of writing in an academic community (quotation, citing sources, bibliography, and footnotes). From here, we move to the entirely regulatory part (the policies and grades)—from legislature to judiciary, if you wish. Consider the change in voice again: Now the passive voice dominates the language ("will be handed in," "should be highlighted," "must be re-written"). These laws are impersonal and unnegotiable. Marsh switches his rhetoric, mitigating the depersonalizing effect, by returning to the fact of teaching ("we are teaching you a skill"); but the mitigation only cushions the move towards the climax of the policies—the potential of failing the class. In a way, we see a move here from Zakir Husain (the visionary) to Gustav

Heinrich Adolf Engler (the academic taxonomist) to Pope Pius the IX (the voice of regulation and punishment).

At this point, we enter the segment called "syllabus," by which Marsh, and most professors, mean the actual class by class vision of the course. The syllabus shows that Marsh envisions four thematic parts to the course: platonic love; courtly love, love and marriage (in two parts); and sex, psychoanalysis, and ideology. A la Gustav Heinrich Adolf Engler, love will be studied through a taxonomy of love as well as through historic time.

There are actually two times encoded in the syllabus: Historical moments as well as the actual teaching time, the schedule: the latter is the common time all participants need to adhere to and that defines the course. This time is contractual, and it is extraordinarily important for the student, who needs to match his or her busy life to the dates and deadlines of the class. It is perhaps the hardest part of learning that one cannot learn just on one's own time—but as part of a machinery. So, here it is important to find a way to adjust one's own clock and timing to the timing and clock of the class. Ideally, each student should write a personalized syllabus—a utopian and regulatory vision of his or her own schedule—that is adopted to the class. If all papers are due on Thursday, when should I write them? How many pages can I read in an hour? How can I adhere to the rhythm of the class within the rhythm of my own life?

The syllabus is a significant custom or ritual establishing relations and structures for the conduct of the community formed and implied by them. Like many rituals, it is an expected social custom that is rarely questioned or thought about, yet it is rather complex. Social contract, utopian vision, and draft for the future, it tries to define a common experience not yet lived. It is one of the most important reading materials assigned in the class—assigned reading about assignments, a contract, an outline of a larger endeavor, a first key to its author, a preview of the story to follow, a reflection on the fact that classroom learning is institutional learning and that the classroom itself, the course, is an institution. For better or worse, the syllabus is the key to understanding a course and a form of citizenship in a course. It defines duties and privileges, relations between students and professors, goals and departure points, expectations and fears—it defines the form of the course. But it also often encodes the intellectual, academic foundations of a course, the way in which it wants to pursue a story, the materials it deems necessary for that story, a way of reading and thinking—the content of the course, if you wish. It brings out that all professors, as they design classes within academic institutions, have a bit in common with Pope Pius IX, Gustav Heinrich Adolf Engler, and Zakir Husain. To analyze how they fit into this group is a good academic exercise to figure out the class to follow.

RELATED WORDS

Academic Thinking 1	Research 137
Discipline 57	Structure 149
Key Terms 106	Workshop 191

EXERCISES

1. Read an assigned syllabus and, in a journal entry, assess the regulatory, taxonomic, and visionary elements of the course. What atmosphere and relation to the teacher do you envision from the syllabus? What behavior is required from you? (Which regulations will be easy for you and which might be a challenge?) What are the key terms and concepts of the course?

2. Put next to the syllabus a calendar of your own schedule and life. Translate the syllabus given to you into your own personal syllabus, adjusting your time to the times given in the syllabus.

3. Compare two syllabi you have received in two different classes. Analyze the differences in light of this entry. Where do you see significant differences, where similarities? For example, two syllabi from different disciplines might share a pedagogical vision, or two syllabi from the same discipline might have contrasting visions. Reflect on how you will handle the differences and how you can best respond to each syllabus in each class. For example, you might conclude that one course will be a good opportunity to learn note-taking skills while another may offer opportunities to work on verbal presentations, and so on.

Synthesis
The Alchemy of Interpretation

Some writers view synthesis as the most pedestrian of all the interpretive arts. It is seen as the place where a writer doggedly compiles a group of sources on a particular topic and demonstrates their internal linkages. Others recognize, on the contrary, that in this act of fusing meaningful relationships between often disparate sources, the writer is a magician, an alchemist, who transforms the raw materials of ideas into gold. Synthesis is the melding of disparate parts into a transcendent whole. Where analysis is all about breaking a seemingly harmonious whole down in order to study its principle parts, synthesis is all about drawing all those elements together, composing a meaningful harmony. One could say that analysis undoes the work of synthesis by unmasking the basic ingredients and methods through which the final artwork was com-

The example of hooks' somewhat controversial thesis statement raises another point: A thesis must be debatable. In fact, another way to describe a thesis is that it establishes the terms of a debate and sets that debate in motion. If the thesis is indisputable—such as "the Columbus legacy is an important component of American history"—why would a reader want to continue reading? Further, the thesis will be more effective if the terms of that debate are contextualized, if the thesis statement refers to the specific subject and source materials the writer plans to use. If hooks had set her essay up with an uncontextualized thesis—arguing that we are a nation of white supremacists— she would certainly have a debate on her hands, but one likely to turn away more readers than it attracts. By setting up the specific issue of the Columbus legacy as the subject and the source material within which this issue will be studied, she generates more interest and conveys a more accurate set of expectations about the essay's actual content.

Having said all this, one would think that a writer should sit down, compose a thesis, drape some source materials, some evidence, and some close readings on the structure provided by that thesis and be done with it. Although this can happen, most often the thesis emerges from the writer's close, exploratory work with the source material, from a preliminary idea examined and tested in the context provided by the evidence. The thesis is the design of the essay but it is most often discovered in the process of writing and revising that essay. In fact, many writers work back and forth between reading, summarizing, analyzing, and synthesizing sources before they develop an interpretation, an approach of their own to the material, and a thesis, an argument they want to make about the material, a place to stand in relation to it. Because of these interrelated processes, writers often don't know what the thesis will be until they have written and thought about the topic in some detail, until they have identified the positions others have taken on the debate clearly enough to know where they stand. For example, hooks describes some of the train of thought, some of the reading, the synthesis, the classroom discussions, the analysis, and the previous writing she has done on the subject of Columbus in order to show how she reached her current position.

Yet having a thesis in mind provides an invaluable sense of direction, helps the writer choose potential evidence, and reveals the significance of that evidence in regards to a particular issue or set of questions. Having a thesis often helps a writer discover something new about that evidence. Because of this, many writers set out with a preliminary thesis developed from their initial reading and rough, exploratory writing on a subject. This might be a particular problem or question that cropped up along the way; it might be a hunch, a hypothesis, about where the evidence will lead. Hooks may have begun with the question of why she herself felt so eager to escape the Columbus debates: "Again and again, I would hear myself saying, 'I don't really ever think about Columbus.' Critically interrogating this assertion, I unpacked the levels of untruth it holds" (244). Or she may have worked from the supposition that the Columbus materials would provide a revealing basis for examining American attitudes toward race and toward historical memory.

An example from a college history classroom may help to track this process of constructing a preliminary thesis in clearer terms. One frequently used assignment question asks students to classify Columbus as either "hero, villain, victim, [or] product of his time" and, as a writing exercise designed to help students analyze excerpts from Columbus' diaries, a teacher encouraged her students to choose one of those classifications as their preliminary thesis.* A writer tackling this assignment would begin with a general topic (Columbus), source materials (Columbus' diaries), and a question to answer (was Columbus a hero or a villain, etc.?). Working from readings, discussions, and some initial writing about the diaries, the writer might choose a preliminary thesis statement—Columbus' diaries show that he was a hero—and then look for the particular evidence in the diaries that would help to support that supposition. After citing and working with that evidence in an initial draft, the writer would likely be ready to go back to that preliminary thesis and add some further specifications. Words that help to identify the relationships between ideas, such as "because," "although," "however," and "therefore" can be useful tools in this process. For example, this writer might elaborate the original thesis using "because": "Columbus' diaries show that he was a hero because he took on the risks of leading an expedition into unfamiliar territory and because he was working from a powerful Christian belief system."

Further exploration of the evidence and the counterevidence might lead the writer to an additional development of the thesis: "Although Columbus was clearly motivated in part by profit, and shared the prevailing racist attitudes of his time toward the native inhabitants of the New World, his diaries reveal the powerful ideological role of Christianity in motivating and giving meaning to his actions." At this point, the writer's thesis statement has far outgrown the preliminary, "Columbus was a hero," to embrace the real complexity of the problem: Here is a man who can be vilified by twenty-first century standards but is a fascinating and in many ways admirable representative of his time. This is a genuinely troubling and still heavily debated problem, one well worth writing (or reading) another five pages on. Finally, if the writer has read hooks or other critics who have weighed in on this debate, he or she might characterize that debate and show where his or her essay was positioned in relation to that debate: "bell hooks argues for the necessity of opposing romanticized views of Columbus' mission to the new world because that mission was a

---

*With thanks to Monica Teztlaff who used this exercise from Elliot Gorn, Randy Roberts, and Terry D. Bilhartz's history textbook, *Constructing the American Past*, in her history class.

clear example of genocidal white supremacist attitudes. However, a close analysis of Columbus's own diaries helps to demonstrate the ahistorical one-sidedness of that argument by providing a context of religious fervor and entrepreneurial zest that helps to explain if not justify his actions." In arriving at this thesis, the writer has a place to stand, a way to organize the essay and give it momentum, a set of criteria for choosing evidence, and a reference point for using and shaping that evidence to make the thesis grow.

RELATED WORDS

Argument 9	Introductions 99
Claims 38	Key Terms 106
Counterargument 49	Structure 149
Evidence 77	Synthesis 172

EXERCISES

1. In a group, analyze two academic essays. In each case, what seems to be the writer's thesis statement and where does it appear? What may have been the preliminary issue, problem, question, debate, or hypothesis that helped the writer choose and work with evidence and that led eventually to this thesis?

2. Choose an academic essay with a clear thesis statement that appears somewhere in the first page or two of the essay. Working in a group, track how that thesis statement gets developed by the evidence in at least three places in the essay. Identify what the writer's argument has become by the end of the essay and compare that full argument to the initial thesis statement. What changes, shifts, additions have occurred?

3. Analyze the rough draft of an essay you are writing: What is the general topic? What source materials will you be using? What problem or question are you focusing on? What kinds of evidence have you been looking at and what has it taught you about the topic? From that analysis write a preliminary thesis statement. Then, following the history classroom example in this chapter, try expanding that thesis statement using words like "because," "although," "however," and "therefore." Build in some account of how the source materials you are using relate to the thesis and to each other.

4. Read through another writer's draft noting all the places where a thesis, an argument, or an indication of the writer's central purpose seem to emerge. Then turn the paper over and write out a thesis statement for that draft in your own words. List any questions that come up during this process and bring them to the writer's attention.

Titles
Why They Matter

People take titles to cars and houses very seriously since they are documents that attest to ownership. In many ways, the titles of academic essays are no different; they, too, have to do with ownership. The title of a car or deed is the last thing one receives, the final evidence of the transactions that have transpired. When one has the title, as a piece of writing, one also owns it completely and thoroughly; one becomes the author of "_____." Titles are serious business.

Titles do not only allow authors to own their writing by naming it and by distinguishing it from writing by others, but they also fix the essay into its final shape; they define the essay, its central concern, its key terms, its main goal and attitude. One should never title an essay lightly or in haste because one might deprive it of its nature, its main goal, its best possible incarnation of itself.

In the second capacity, as the final name for the most important aspect of the essay, titles become inspiring writing tools that can be used in all stages of writing. As imagined titles, for a paper proposal or in a first response to an assignment, they can serve to paint a picture of the kind of essay one may want to write—an ideal of kinds. Then later in the writing process they can capture what a draft has actually achieved. One might for example, after a first completed draft, try out three different titles for an essay to figure out how the essay may be crystallized, what versions of itself it already contains. The final choice of a title has to do with the final polish of an essay and its final designation. What is its most important feature, its most enticing aspect, its most immediate context?

This final thought, of course, reveals one of the most important functions of the final title: that imagining, defining, reaching, and hooking of an audience. While often last in the process, that final title is the first way to reach the reader. It strives to establish a first connection: it needs to interest and inform; it needs to promise, but not the wrong thing; it needs to capture both the essay and the reader. Titles then are not only serious things but also useful and complicated things.

As a result there are many different strategies and genres of titles. The following assortment of titles from an interdisciplinary academic essay collection entitled *Exhibiting Cultures* exhibits a large variety of title strategies and forms—even though the titles are all written for the same audience:

- The Museum as a Way of Seeing
- Exhibiting Intention: Some Preconditions of the Visual Display of Culturally Purposeful Objects
- Resonance and Wonder

- The Poetics of Exhibition in Japanese Culture
- Art Museums and the Ritual of Citizenship
- Locating Authenticity: Fragments of a Dialogue
- Noodling Around with Exhibition Opportunities
- Why Museums Make Me Sad
- How Misleading Does an Ethnographic Museum Have to Be?
- Refocusing or Reorientation? The Exhibit or the Populace: Zimbabwe on the Threshold
- Four Northwest Coast Museums: Travel Reflections
- The World as Marketplace: Commodification of the Exotic at the World's Columbian Exposition, 1893

Each of these titles focuses us on some element of the essay and raises our expectations not only about form but also about content. We sense an author's voice, character, and mood here, ranging from someone who is very personal in his approach, "Why Museums Make Me Sad," to someone who may be a bit contentious or is writing out of a sense of frustration, "How Misleading Does an Ethnographic Museum Have to Be?" to someone who is playful with a tinge of mockery, "Noodling Around with Exhibition Opportunities," to someone who is focused, "professional," and rather neutral, "Exhibiting Intentions: Some Preconditions of the Visual Display of Culturally Purposeful Objects." There are titles that work through the relation between key terms: "Resonance and Wonder" and "Art Museums and the Ritual of Citizenship," for example. And there are titles that imply a thesis: "The museum is a way of seeing" or "the exotic was commodified at the World's Columbian Exhibition in Chicago in 1893." Other titles open up a conflict or puzzle such as " Refocusing or Reorientation? The Exhibit or the Populace," attempting to involve the reader in a mystery or question. Finally, titles may relay form and content such as the title promising "travel reflections" on four northwest coast museums.

The titles of this collection are wonderfully versatile and truly seem to reflect the persona of the writer and to reach out to the reader. That is not always so. Sometimes, titles can also be almost ludicrously similar, a form of fashion trend like platform shoes and bellbottom jeans. Consider the fad for the colon titles in this recent table of contents page of *American Literature,* a foremost journal in its field (Figure 6). These fashionably shaped titles do tell the reader about key terms, key concerns, and key texts. They are informative in that way. But they hide the voice or spirit of the writer, like a business suit tends to hide aspects of the personality of its wearer.

At their best, titles reveal an author and his or her attitude towards an essay as well as the essay's most prominent feature, be it its thesis, topic, key terms, the "text." But sometimes titles betray the essay by hiding all those features behind cliches or formulas. Titles should initiate a dialogue with the writer's most important partner: the reader; they should try to draw in such a reader by being informative, interesting, and an accurate promise for the essay to follow. Like titles to houses and cars, they are serious business, but there is plenty of room to play.

Contents

Book Reviews

Figure 6   Table of Contents Page of American Literature (March 2001)

RELATED WORDS

EXERCISES

1. Looking at academic essays (or our works cited in our "Works Cited" entry), identify three different title strategies and then imitate (or parody) those strategies in designing three different titles for your own essay.

2. After reading a draft of a paper invent three different titles for it that capture some central parts of the essay such as key terms, thesis, attitude, form or tone to name just a few. Use these titles to envision various revisions of the essay.

3. After reading and rereading an assignment given to you, invent a few titles for essays that would respond to the assignment. What would the essay need to do to fulfill the promise of each title? How could the writer revise the essay to make it live up to the title? And which of the titles is in the best interest of the essay? Consider the context of the assignment.

4. Looking only at a title of a published or unpublished essay, discuss what expectations the title raises in the reader. Then, after reading the essay, discuss if and how the essay fulfills those expectations.

Transitions
Miracle Workers or Enforcers?

Transitions are the connective words and phrases that establish working relationships between sentences and between paragraphs. They simultaneously create and help readers to follow the progression of a paper from one idea to the next. They provide the essence and the embodiment of an essay's flow. Transitions are the worker ants transmitting a slice of cake ten thousand times their size from its place under the picnic table to safe storage in the anthill. Tiny, driven words and phrases—"thus," "in this sense," "in other words," "similarly," "consequently," "because of this," "in effect," "rather," "by contrast," "on the other hand," and hundreds more like them—scurry back and forth passing the burden of cake crumbs from mouth to mouth, from one sentence to the next, in a massive joint effort to convey meaning. Without transitions, every sentence is forced to reinvent the world. With transitions, each sentence takes responsibility for the burden of the previous sentence, transmitting and transforming some element of the previous sentence while propelling it into the fresh context of the sentence to come.

Without transitions, ideas are laid out in a seemingly random list or heedlessly stacked one upon the other. For example, consider the following description of a Budweiser commercial developed by a student writer who was summarizing an example from Robert Scholes's "On Reading a Video Text"*:

> There is a Budweiser commercial. It shows an umpire who had to make a tough call. He stood by his call even when the manager of the other team disagreed. This was the umpire's achievement. The manager and others toasted the umpire in a bar. They recognized his achievement. They accepted his "membership" in their community. Scholes discusses the term "narrativity." He describes how the "stories" presented in commercials help to reinforce the message the commercial wants to put across. "By 'getting' the story, we prove our competence and demonstrate our membership in a cultural community" (Scholes 551). The Budweiser commercial presents the story of the umpire. Viewers understand the story. They fill in all the implications that the ad suggests. They fill in background that the ad doesn't actually show. They understand that this is a story of initiation. . . .

While this writer is making some accurate observations about the example and has in mind an important connection between that example and Scholes' term, "narrativity," all those connective linkages are missing in this version because the transitions are missing. As readers, we miss out on the progression of ideas and the relationships between ideas that this writer has in mind. In Scholes' terms, we don't follow the "story" of this paragraph because we have been denied the codes of membership that would help us to fill in the gaps. While we can take note of the writer's observations, access to the larger implications seems restricted, cut off.

By contrast, when the writer revised this paragraph a week later, he consciously built in transitions. Notice the difference when those worker ants take up their burden and the sentences begin to move forward and refer backward, functioning together to mobilize an integrated whole. Not only did the writer add in connective phrases, but the act of defining those relationships helped the writer to push isolated observations a little further so that the content of individual sentences also shifted and developed:

> Scholes uses the example of a Budweiser commercial showing an umpire who had to make a tough call. Because the umpire stood by his unpopular call even when the fans and the manager of the other team disagreed, he demonstrated the knowledge and in-

---

*The "student writer" referred to here actually represents a composite of student responses to this exercise used to dramatize the difference transitions can make.

tegrity demanded by the job. In a strange way, this ability to stand tall against the majority opinion, to withstand rejection, led to the umpire's inclusion in the community he was trying to join. Thus, when the manager and others toasted the umpire in a bar after the game, they were demonstrating their acceptance of his "membership" in their community because he had passed an important test. Further, in presenting this example, Scholes is showing an important aspect of his term "narrativity." He defines this term as the "narratives" or "stories" presented by commercials to help reinforce the messages that advertisers want to put across. These stories become a way to involve the television audience in the commercial and to make them feel supportive of the product: "By 'getting' the story, we prove our competence and demonstrate our membership in a cultural community" (Scholes 551). In other words, by presenting the story of the umpire, the Budweiser commercial gets its viewers to participate by filling in all the implications and background that the ad doesn't actually show. For example, viewers understand that this is a story of initiation, a story about gaining membership. That level of understanding makes viewers feel like they too are members in a valuable cultural community, in the Budweiser community. . . .

In this example, each sentence listens to the previous sentence and propels meaning into the next. Each sentence takes a certain responsibility for the ideas being communicated; it accepts the consequences set in motion by the previous sentence and follows through on them. Using subtle pointing words like "this" and "that," or words like "further" and "thus" that define the logical progression of ideas, or phrases such as "in a strange way" that attempt to capture a particular ironic twist, the writer builds the story of this paragraph in a way that we can follow and engage with.

Yet, in the act of defining the relationship between two sentences, a transition also sets the limits on what that relationship will be. Transitions determine whether one idea is the cause or the effect of another, whether one sentence poses a problem to which the next sentence responds, whether one paragraph is offering a comparison or a contrast to the example given in the preceding paragraph. Transitions decide on the kind of progression a reader will make from one sentence to the next and one paragraph to the next; they decide whether it will it be chronological, narrative, definitional. In doing so, they tend to close off a reader's choices, enforcing a preordained set of moves from one sentence to the next, and thereby freeing the reader from all responsibility; we don't have to imagine the consequences or implications of a particular thought because the writer will demonstrate those implications without a doubt. With this in mind, some writers will occasionally strip a sentence or two of transitions in the effort to encourage the reader to jump in and make the connection, or to provoke readers to take some responsibility for a progression of ideas, or to invite readers to imagine the implications of a particular idea for themselves. For instance, John Berger begins his essay, "Ways of Seeing" with these two sentences: "Seeing comes before words. The child looks and recognizes before it can speak" (50). He doesn't say "For example, the child looks and recognizes before it can speak" or "As evidence of this fact, consider how the child looks and . . ." even though these seem to be the implied relationships between the two sentences. By leaving those relationship undetermined, Berger seems to invite readers' intuitive responses—as if he wants us to participate in and become aware of the links between what we already know (that children see before they can talk) and what we are learning from his essay about the act of "seeing," about taking responsibility for how and what we see. However, few writers can (or should) resist handing over this control ever or for long. And in fact, handing over too much control by refusing to supply readers with those connective movements is, in essence, denying them the codes of membership in the community of the essay.

RELATED WORDS

Argument 9   Parallelism 118
Coordination and Subordination 45   Structure 149
Paragraphs 114

EXERCISES

1. Choose a paragraph from one of the assigned readings and underline every transitional word or phrase the writer uses. In a group, analyze the degree of control the writer is exercising over the reader's progression from sentence to sentence. What kinds of relationships are being suggested by each transitional word or phrase?

2. Try the same analysis suggested by exercise 1, but this time underline only the transitional moves from one paragraph to the next. In a group, analyze the degree of control the writer is exercising over the reader's progression from paragraph to paragraph. What kinds of relationships are being suggested by each transitional word or phrase?

3. Try the same analysis suggested by exercises 1 and 2, this time using your own or another writer's draft.

4. Write a short paragraph in which you try to avoid using any transitional words or phrases. Then rewrite the paragraph making heavy use of transitional connections. Does the content of your sentences also develop and change as you build in the transitions? What kind of participation or involvement are you asking from your reader in each of these versions?

5. Cut a paragraph from a student draft into individual sentences. Have someone else re-assemble the paragraph adding his or her own meaningful transitions as needed. Try the same exercise, this time cutting apart and having someone reassemble the paragraphs of an essay.

Voice
The Sight of Sound

Voice is the identity a writer creates on the page, a sound that leaps into language. The voice that speaks in a particular essay can represent a mood or a pose that the writer inhabited for a few hours, or it can represent a new self that a writer discovered in the act of writing. Above all, though, a voice is a constructed thing. The quality of its sound can be deduced with the listening eye, detected with the watching ear. That sound is constructed in the kinds of sentences a writer puts together, long or short, complex or simple, laden with qualifications and possibilities, modifying clauses and parallel structures, or commandingly pithy. It appears in the layering of those sentences one against the other, the variation or lack of variation from one to the next, and can be detected in the rhythm of those sentences read out loud. The writer's choice of punctuation marks, vocabulary, the connections established within and between sentences, the "ands," "buts," "yets," "becauses," "howevers," "therefores" and "similarlys" all work together to create the particular sound of the person who will appear on that page. Voice inheres in the tone of a piece, its attitude; it filters through the writer's approach to the subject, the amount of context a writer provides or fails to provide, the way a writer thinks about and speaks to his or her readers.

Glancing through a collection of essays with newly attentive ears is like stepping into a room full of voices, each holding forth in its own way, each with its own distinctive sound. The following series of examples are taken from the opening paragraphs of a collection of academic essays and excerpts loosely grouped under the topic of "Schooling."

1. Mark, sixteen and a genial eleventh-grader, rides a bus to Franklin High School, arriving at 7:25. It is an Assembly Day, so the schedule is adapted to allow for a meeting of the entire school. He hangs out with his friends, first outside school and then inside, by his locker. He carries a pile of textbooks and notebooks; in all, it weighs eight and a half pounds. (Theodore R. Sizer, "What High School Is," 111)

2. The national outpouring after the Littleton shootings has forced us to confront something we have suspected for a long time: the American high school is obsolete and should be abolished. In the last month, high school students present and past have come forward with stories about cliques and the artificial intensity of a world defined by insiders and outsiders, in which the insiders hold

sway because of superficial definitions of good looks and attractiveness, popularity, and sports prowess. (Leon Botstein, "Let Teenagers Try Adulthood," 119)

3. "Meritocracy" is a curious word. Invented, by Michael Young, to denote a social
   order that he wanted to hold up as an object of horror, in the United States
   today it is received as the name of an inarguably sacred first principle: that our
   society rewards those who deserve and have earned advancement, rather
   than distributing reward by fiat in some way that involves the circumstances of
   birth. Moreover, people tend to assume casually that the system whose history I've given in these pages and in which we live our lives . . . is the embodiment, and the only possible embodiment, of the principle of meritocracy.
   (Nicholas Lemann, "A Real Meritocracy," 130)

4. My mother withdrew into silence two months before she died. A few nights
   before she fell silent, she told me she regretted the way she had raised me
   and my sisters. I knew she was referring to the way we had been brought up
   in the midst of two conflicting worlds—the world of home, dominated by the
   ideology of the Western humanistic tradition, and the world of a society
   dominated by Mao Tse-tung's Marxism. (Min-zhan Lu, "From Silence to Words:
   Writing as Struggle," 141)

5. Black English is not exactly a linguistic buffalo; as children, most of the thirty-five
   million Afro-Americans living here depend on this language for our discovery of
   the world. But then we approach our maturity inside a larger social body that
   will not support our efforts to become anything other than the clones of those
   who are neither our mothers nor our fathers. (June Jordan, "Nobody Mean
   More to Me Than You and the Future Life of Willie Jordan," 151)

By see-hearing or hear-seeing the voices in these samples, it is astounding
how much we can learn or guess about the writer in each case—or at least
about the persona each writer has chosen to adopt. The voice in the first sample
sounds objective, detail-oriented, precise down to the "half pound." Sentence
structures are even, predictable, lacking in variation. In the third sentence, the
writer slips into the informal diction that Mark might use when "hanging out"
with his friends, but most of the word choices like "genial" and "textbook" have
the more formal sound of the reporter. From this first impression one might
guess that this writer is withholding judgment, even emphasizing the factual
nature of his description to reassure us of the unbiased nature of his viewpoint,
perhaps to lead us by some hidden path to his real view of "What High School
Is." What a contrast this presents to the second writer who comes out with his
opinion immediately and with such a tone of authority—who would dare start
an argument with this voice? In fact, his opening statement, "the American high
school is obsolete and should be abolished" sounds so argumentative, so over
the top, that one wonders if he is joking, or infusing with bitter irony a platform
that he knows will never be accepted. Yet his second long sentence begins to
make a case, attempts with its polished diction, its claim of widespread agreement, to persuade readers to share this view. Notice too the transition, "In the

last month," swinging us easily from the time-frame of Littleton to the time-frame in which the piece was written—quite a contrast to the first writer's list-like repetitiveness, "It is . . . He hangs . . . He carries . . . "

How thoughtful the third voice sounds in comparison to the attention-seeking editorialist we have just heard—this seems more like a wondering voice than one demanding our ear. Yet the variation between that first musing sentence and the longer, more complex one that follows is surely meant to grab our attention. Because the writer sounds knowledgeable and intrigued by his own topic he might draw us along, persuade us to join in his curiosity about this strange word, "meritocracy," and thus follow him into the thicket of the succeeding sentences to find out more about its meaning and history. Perhaps the heavy use of comma signposts and the full stop of the colon suggest an overly anxious effort to guide us along the way. The historical approach to the topic, the tone of thoughtful investigation, the complexity of sentence structure, and the transition, "moreover" signaling the reasoned connection between sentences all combine to characterize this as a typically academic voice, the voice of a trained scholar who speaks from a position he has researched and considered in some depth. Whereas the first writer began to gather authority through his accumulation of observed details and the second simply claimed his authority immediately through tone of voice, Lemann depends on this informative quality (and no doubt his professional credentials as a historian) to win our trust in what he has to say.

By contrast, the fourth voice sounds nonacademic, gentle and self-meditative rather than informative. This writer seems to invite our interest and to base her authority on the grounds of personal experience, knowing that we will tend to accept her account because she has lived it. Yet from the way her simple opening sentence builds toward a more complex sentence structure and vocabulary, toward the "ideology of the Western humanistic tradition," it becomes clear that Lu is not just planning to tell a personal story. She sounds more thoughtful than sad, intent perhaps on lulling her reader in with this poignant personal tale in order to make a larger point about these "conflicting worlds" and (given the topic) perhaps to make some claim about the role of "schooling" in exacerbating or mediating these conflicts. This is a writer who is not afraid to fuse the worlds of the personal and the scholarly essay, to allow one to enrich and enhance the other.

Perhaps she shares this quality with the writer in the last example, whose scholarly choices of sentence structure, punctuation, and diction only call attention to a feeling of overriding urgency—a sense that something powerful and personal is at stake. Unlike the exploratory, informative tone used by Lemann, Jordan's voice seems to throw down a gauntlet, challenging her readers to follow what she means by " linguistic buffalo" and "maturity inside a larger social body," assuming that we will know what she means by "living here," offering little explanatory context. The tone suggests the brisk manner of one who believes there is not a moment more to waste and becomes biting in its indictment of the "clones" Afro-Americans have been forced to become. Her use of "we" and "our" in this context implies that she too is part of this group of

Afro-Americans. She draws her authority both from this insider knowledge and experience and from her informative but also insistent tone (no doubt bolstered like Lemann by her academic credentials). Are her implied readers the others in this group or is she speaking to a less enlightened audience of outsiders to whom this discussion of Black English will be a revelation?

As these five examples suggest, voices can be as nakedly revealing and as complexly concealing as facial expressions. By learning to read for voice, learning to connect the visual and tonal clues that give sound to the written word, we gain access to new layers of meaning available on the page—and new power to create meaning. As writers, we gain power by learning to construct voices, by adapting inflections, strategies of diction, and punctuation from the voices we admire. We gain power by adding new flexibility to the sounds we can make on the page, by learning how to build authority and how to claim it in sound, by learning to write as an insider speaking to an audience who will understand rather than as outsiders trying to break down the barriers to speech.

RELATED WORDS

Academic Thinking 1	Parallelism 118
Audience 25	Punctuation 126
Dash 53	Quotation 130
Editing 63	Subject Verb 154
Grammar 90	Title 180

EXERCISES

1. Choose a passage from an academic essay and circle all the aspects of punctuation, vocabulary, length and variation of sentence structure, transitions, word choice, and so on, that seem to contribute to the sound that writer creates on the page. Write a one-page analysis of that writer's voice citing the evidence you have noted and deducing the identity it reveals. Try this same exercise using another student's essay.

2. In a group, collect samples of four different published essays that are as different as possible in voice. Analyze the details of tone, attitude, context, word choice, transitions, sentence structure, and so on, that make them different. Try this same exercise using student drafts.

3. Read passages from one of the essays out loud first trying to sound as the writer intended and then deliberately reading against the writer's voice. (Try making a very formal, scholarly essay sound like casual talk between friends, for example, or try making a casual story-telling essay sound highly pompous and formal.)

4. Read two academic essays, one written by a man and one written by a woman, but with the names removed so that you have to guess the

gender of the author. List all the clues you might use to guess the writer's gender—approach, interests, subject matter, voice—and specify the reason why that clue might reveal gender difference.

5. Choose a paragraph from a draft of your own essay and rewrite it in a different voice, deliberately manipulating vocabulary, sentence structure, and so on, to give that voice a particular character. Give your essay to another writer and have that person write a few sentences describing the change in voice he or she hears in that paragraph. How does the nature of the relationship that you offer your reader vary with the change in voice?

6. Choose a sentence from a writer you admire based on its sound alone. Read the sentence out loud several times, practicing its sound. Then create a sentence of your own that has nearly that same sound but that meaning-wise could be added into your own draft. Alternatively, try this same exercise using a writer you dislike or one who has a very distinct voice, but this time parody the sound of the sentence, exaggerate its effects.

Workshop
Collaboration and Production

What makes a teacher divide a class into groups or conduct a larger workshop? What "work" exactly is accomplished in a workshop? And in what space does it take place? Literally, *shop* refers to the space in which we produce. And figuratively, Webster's informs us, *shop* is "the source or origin, the place where anything is made" (1677). A workshop in an academic classroom is then a way to get us back to that place of origin; it is perhaps the most realistic reenactment of real academic work in the classroom. It makes students into readers and listeners, colleagues, critics, friends; it stresses the "work" of academic production as well as the collaboration amongst academics. It teaches the nuts and bolts of the trade—the work that goes into the production of academic writing. It also assigns each of us a task and sets up rules for collaboration. It is almost as if students are allowed to move behind the scenes, often literally transforming the classroom from a classical theater setup into a workspace we might imagine behind the stage of a theater;

students are asked to take on a different role, not that of spectators in a fairly mundane surrounding but that of laborers and actors behind the scene, making the production possible.

Consider the workshop of an upholsterer as opposed to the show room. In the show room one sees the brand new and neatly upholstered furniture: clean, elegant, unlived-in, perfect, self-contained. But when one steps behind the show room into the actual workshop, the picture could not be more different. There are all the fragmented and ripped odds and ends of fabrics, fillings, old rusty springs and new shiny ones, hammers, nails and other tools, rough worktables, and often a heap of old skeletal furniture ripped open, sagging, stained, broken. Once we look at the workshop, we see the furniture not as neat objects but as culminations of a long, hard process involving labor, training, and raw materials. Without the workshop behind them, the finished furniture would betray none of the astonishing ripping apart and reassembling, cutting and pasting, the hammering and dirt and calluses that went into their making.

A finished published essay or book is a lot like that newly upholstered furniture in the showroom. It, too, betrays little of the messy work, the odds and ends, the skeletons, the hammering, the rough work that went into its making. Occasionally we see a messy office (perhaps our own), an inkstain on a finger, or—now, in the age of computers—a bandaged hand plagued by tendinitis that hints at the very real labor of academic writing. The workshop in a classroom turns academic thinking into work, into production; academic writing is crafty work that can be learned hands-on and that has loose ends, fragments, as well as hammering involved in it. It is a tough process.

Whether that suits the personalities of scholars and students or not, academic work is by its very nature communal work. It is an immense effort conducted in tribal groups called disciplines, and even smaller units called seminars, writing groups, workshops, courses. Almost all academics are part of such groups; indeed, this co-authored book itself is another example of academic collaboration. Its entire production relied on us believing that together we can accomplish more than each of us alone. And, as our acknowledgments show, many other individuals and institutions are integral parts of this project: editors, students, chairs of departments we worked in, colleagues, friends, spouses, and writers, writers, writers.

The workshop makes this aspect of academic work visible; it is significantly about exchange and mutual dependence, about giving and receiving. The common saying "what goes around comes around" sums up the faith and fear with which people approach workshops.* In writing workshops, for example, it is impossible to forget when someone has given us wonderful criti-

---

*The relation between academic work and gift exchange is taken from Lewis Hyde's marvelous book *The Gift*.

cism on our writing; we remember the respect and engagement that went into such criticism, the way in which the reader truly tried to envision a better version of our essays, the simple fact that a reader spent time and imagination on our work. When we encounter their writing in return, we will most likely do our very best to return the favor. Most writers experience respectful, thoughtful, and constructive criticism as a gift; and they gratefully acknowledge these gifts throughout their writing in dedications, acknowledgments, footnotes, quotes, and citations. Equally, it is wonderful to see oneself acknowledged in someone else's writing; one is given a share of the essay. Indeed, while we immediately relish praise of our work, in the long run we often feel most grateful for those suggestions that made us rethink and reconsider—that is, revise—our essays and thus became integral parts of their growth. Conversely, it is hard not to feel bitter when a workshop member is either lazy or unimaginative in their response to our work; either making no useful comments (positive or negative) or imposing particular concerns on it that seem extraneous to the assignment, purpose, or intent of the writer. The anger over such criticism can be so strong that it never subsides just as the gratefulness over good comments often builds lasting relationships and friendship.

When we enter a workshop, we lay ourselves bare and let others in; we become intensely vulnerable because we transfer authority to a reader and show our work when it is still messy and unfinished. Lewis Hyde writes about how gift exchange challenges the boundaries of our egos and makes us "act as parts of things larger"(17). Such a state is scary and exhilarating at the same time.

Knowing all this, the sometimes reluctant shuffling of chairs in a classroom, the often crawlingly slow process of reconfiguring it into workshop groups is quite understandable. An enforced workshop is a little bit like an enforced office Christmas party—everyone has to give a gift to everyone else, whether they want to or not. One student—an eager, engaged, rather brilliant student, I* might add—once told me that he prefers a root canal to a workshop. I have never had a root canal, but I got the gist of his remark. It is so much easier to be a voluntary member of a workshop, to give a gift out of one's own volition. Yet, it gets easier as one goes along—I heard no further root canal remarks after the first workshop; actually, that particular student was phenomenally good in workshops and seemed to enjoy himself. Analogously, experience confirms that there are quite a few people who have enjoyed office Christmas parties, after all, and even made friends there or met the love of their life. You never know.

Most of all in a workshop, we hope for both affirmation and transformation, and a good workshop will provide both while a bad one may crush us. Everyone has to do their share, imagining concerns of other writers,

---

*The "I" here refers to Hildegard Hoeller.

giving their ideas freely and tactfully, engaging in the essay of someone else without taking it over. In workshops that are assigned a common task this sharing is easier and makes each of us less vulnerable; it amounts to teamwork. But in such workshops too we need to share authority and property of ideas as well as contribute equivalent amounts; we share ideas as gifts and later, according to academic conventions, acknowledge those gifts. Workshops, in other words, are without doubt passionate and difficult places, places in which we can be transformed and in which we can make enemies or friends. They are places where we need to use our imagination and our tact in order to help a writer move to a next step; they are places where we learn how academics work: both their process of production and their reliance on a community no matter how individualistic and competitive their characters might be.

RELATED WORDS

Brainstorming 30	Footnotes 81
Citation 32	Free-Writing 87
Discipline 57	Plagiarism 120
Editing 63	Quotation 130
Evaluation 72	Revision 143

EXERCISES

1. Look for traces of work, production, and gift exchange in a piece of published academic writing by looking for dedication, acknowledgments, footnotes, citations, and quotations. How much can you see of the behind-the-scenes work?

2. Through dedication, acknowledgments, footnotes, citation, and quotations stress the work, production, and community aspect of your essay by encoding in your essay all the help you have been given from other students, teachers, writers, friends.

3. When asked to be in a workshop, analyze what "work" is being asked of you and why that "work" is communal work.

4. Isolate, in an assignment given to you, what part of the academic work asked of you is least clear to you. Ask other to help you understand it.

5. Invent a workshop assignment that might help you learn more about a particular aspect of academic work, for example the part isolated and discussed in exercise 4.

Writer's Block
Lame Excuse or Real Condition?

Haven't you sometimes felt a bit skeptical about writer's block? Perhaps wondered whether it might not be a high-falutin', self-pitying way of saying that one just didn't do one's work? Is the person experiencing writer's block like a "shopoholic" or a gambler who considers, perhaps rightly so, his addiction a disease and himself a modern self-defined victim? Or is it just a lazy person finding an excuse for work not done? While considering it a condition relieves the writer of responsibility, it also makes her powerless to change without treatment. Considering it a lame excuse, on the other hand, puts the responsibility squarely on the writer's already sagging shoulders. Every writer knows how hard writing is, and writer's block is perhaps nothing but an overwhelming, paralyzing, exaggerated, and seemingly unprocessable sense of this fact.

Even the most talkative people experience writer's block. Part of the burden on the shoulders of the writer comes from the tremendous weight print cultures put on writing. "Here it is, in black and white," we say when we *really mean* it. Writing binds us to our statements and thoughts in ways speaking doesn't. Thus, despite the fact that both speaking and writing use the same language, writing is commitment, even entrapment. Yet, at the same time, all writing is preliminary when we do it. So thoughts that are fleeting in our minds become heavy and static on the page. And once they have been seen by a reader, we often feel that we can't play with them, take them back, quite in the same way as we can in a conversation. A love declaration on a romantic evening is not quite the same as a love letter that will be kept, reread, perhaps even quoted or shown to others. Writing stabilizes our thoughts even though our thoughts aren't stable. Writer's block may well be connected to the degree to which we see writing this way. Writers who write with ease often see their drafts as drafts only, almost as fleeting as words spoken; but writers with writer's block may well respond to this transformation of fleeting thoughts into heavy print with anxiety and paralysis.

This transformation is also truly a formal transformation. There can be something very orderly about writing (full sentences, linearity, a stronger sense of grammar) that really jars with our minds, which by no means operate in that fashion. In writing we are not as easily allowed the normal meanderings of our minds, the beautiful ways in which humans contradict themselves, the way in which we let irrationalities and emotions cloud (or better color) our vision when we speak, in which we get fired up into believing things purely by the chemistry of a conversation. Academic writing in particular supposedly stabilizes (i.e., orders, clarifies) our deeply irrational mind into reasonable well-structured and circumspect expositions; the academic writer is expected to be well-rounded, fair, accurate, careful, and lucid. But how often are we lucid? And who loves consistently lucid people? Perhaps then, writer's block is a form of self-protection, a resistance to the death of our wildly irrational (and thus often fascinating and lovable) beings. In that sense, we may think of the resistance to write academically as a healthy response. Feeling better? Can we be proud victims of the condition WB? Yet, here, too, we all know the pleasure of actually getting thoughts onto paper, of achieving such lucidity, of learning about one's own thoughts, of understanding and expanding.

The fact remains, writers want to write. Even nonwriters, if such people could be defined as people who have no consistent inclination to write, often want to write when faced with an assignment or with a dilemma or passion they want to explore and express. Yet, particularly people who do not often write may feel discomfort and fear about writing. Educator Barbara Mellix writes about her early anxieties in writing college papers: "My concern was to use 'appropriate' language, to sound as if I belonged in a college classroom. But I felt separate from the language—as if it did not and could not belong to me"(391). Her feelings, even though partially in her case stemming from her switch from Black English to "standard" English, reflect the fear that most of us have when we begin to write academically. We are at the verge of a transformation that may entail loss, failure, disconnection. Writer's block then is also a mechanism to shield us from those seemingly negative consequences. Yet, this fear prevents us from functioning and learning in a context that we have chosen to enter and that fulfills an important need in our lives: be it to simply learn academically, or to prosper, or to obtain a degree that allows us to pursue the career of our choice.

On the whole then, writer's block could be described as a certain psychological conservatism, a way to delay change, loss, growth, commitment, and self-expression and exposure. It is perhaps neither a lame excuse nor an illness but a symptom of and reaction to the tremendous power of writing. Writer's block makes writing appear monumental, monumentally impossible, and yet writing is neither one of those things. And while we cannot quite offer a twelve-step program, there is a way to get around writer's block. It lies, we believe, in the very definition of writing itself. For there to be a writer's block, writing itself needs to appear monolithic, rocklike. And yet nothing could be further from the truth.

Writing is many different things: reading, taking notes, typing an item into one's works cited page, copying down a quote, writing in a journal and to a friend about not being able to write. There are artful moments in writing and pedestrian moments—both count. Even the most brilliant writers' writing contains an astonishing amount of practical, simple, pedestrian steps: "Bigger said nothing" (194); "Then he went out" (195); "He did not like that look"

(195). These simple sentences are all taken from two pages of Richard Wright's astoundingly novel *Native Son*. They function within the narrative simply to move it along, and anybody could write them. All writing is partially pedestrian, often made up of feasible, non-monumental, instrumental steps.

It seem liberating to think about writing as a large group of activities this way because it helps to dismantle the awesomeness of writing that prevents writers from writing. Turning on the computer and simply typing an item into a bibliography—a completely mindless activity—is nonetheless writing. It can be done while watching a ballgame or a soap opera, and it keeps the writer in touch with his keyboard. Typing in a quote, copying down the words of others, is another way of writing, and it may just lead to a response to the quote. Or simply sending an e-mail to a friend about not being able to write on this d★★★ topic—incidentally the origin of this entry—is a way of writing. In all cases, it is important to remind ourselves that writing has taken place. Writing blocks us most likely when we conceive of it as a block—one dauntingly solid activity— rather than a wide realm of small and large, imaginative and mindless, mental and physical, serious and playful activities. Perhaps writer's block is neither a lame excuse nor a real condition but a missed opportunity to redefine writing itself.

RELATED WORDS

Audience 25   Reading 132
Brainstorming 30   Revision 143
Free-Writing 87   Workshop 191
Metaphor 110

EXERCISES

1. Isolate at least five different activities that are part of writing for you and rank them by order of difficulty for you. Which ones do you dread and which can you bear and which do you enjoy? When faced with writer's block the next time, start with the easiest or most pleasurable activity and do that for as long as you can and then move to the next. Put off the most difficult ones as long as you can continue to "write."

2. The next time you respond to a writing assignment, keep a log of your process and jot down time spent on each phase. Keep that log for future reference and comparison so as to develop patience with each phase.

3. In an academic essay, isolate five different forms of writing such as quotation, interpretation, analysis, citation, title, and so on. Imitate only one of those features at a time in relation to an assignment given to you.

4. In a group discuss a writing assignment given to you by talking out various ways to begin to respond to the assignment. Write down the

various ways in which writers start responding and keep for a future crisis, that is, writer's block.

5.   When faced with writer's block, write an e-mail to a friend about it.

Works Cited
Why This Entry Gets
the Last Word

You may notice that, for once in this book, an entry does not appear in its proper alphabetical position. We do this because a list of "Works Cited" always appears at the end of a book. And although such rules exist to be broken, we do not choose to break this one because the Works Cited or Bibliography pages function as a kind of endpaper to any book, providing the full Rolodex of information on every source included in that book. Those pages identify the entire system of citation that holds that particular book together; in doing so, they verify the exact place where the scholarly references and interchanges included in that book seem to stop short, which is exactly the point at which that book takes up twenty, fifty, one hundred or more conversations with other books, articles, and Websites—or can do so the moment a reader begins to track down one of those sources.

As we explained in our entry on "Citation," this system of noting sources is a fundamental custom in all academic thinking, but it differs in *style* in various disciplines. Our own works cited list follows the style prescribed in the fifth edition of the *MLA Handbook for Writers of Research Papers* and tries to obey its rules. As you look through it, you will be able not only to find what kind of sources informed our writing but also to see how different kinds of sources—books by single authors, essay collections, scholarly journals, reference books, Websites, and so on—are being cited. Since we only list those sources that actually were cited in the book, you will not see those many other sources that inspired and influenced us and which, as the MLA style demands, would be listed in a separate "Works Consulted" or "Selected Bibliography" page; such a page would contain those sources that went into the making of a text without being directly referenced.

If, as we maintain in our entry on discipline, disciplines are different subcultures of the larger academic culture, then it makes sense that each subculture expresses its process of citation in different codes. So, as you hand in papers for various courses, you need to translate your works cited accordingly. How to do that? If you are asked to cite your sources in MLA style, you may simply look at our works cited list below and imitate. Of course, styles go in and out of fashion as we know from platform shoes and double-breasted suits; similarly, the MLA brings out a new style book every few years or so, and in order to stay up-to-date one has to track down the latest style guide—which the Websites listed below will help you to do. If you need to use a style other than MLA, you will have to consult a "style guide" that explains the ins and outs of that particular style. Those style guides—just like the MLA style guide—come in paper form and should be available in the library, or they may also be available on the Internet. Below you will find first, a list of style guides and, second, our works cited list in MLA style.

List of Style Guide Manuals and Websites

- MLA (The Modern Language Association of America):
  Website: http://www.mla.org (Look under "MLA Style" and then under "Frequently Asked Questions").
  Manual: Gibaldi, Joseph. *MLA Handbook for Writers of Research Papers.* 5th ed. New York: MLA, 1999.
- Chicago:
  Website: http://www.press.uchicago.edu/Misc/Chicago/cmosfag.html
  Manual: *The Chicago Manual of Style,* 14th ed. Chicago: U of Chicago P, 1993.
- APA (The American Psychological Association):
  Website: http://www.apastyle.org
  Manuals: *Publication Manual of the American Psychological Association.* 5th ed. Washington DC: APA, 2001.
  Gelfand, Harold and Charles J. Walker. *Mastering APA Style: Student's Workbook and Training Guide.* Washington DC: APA, 2001.

WORKS CITED

Aaron, Jane E. *The Little Brown Compact Handbook.* 4th ed. New York: Longman, 2001.

Adams, Rachel. *Sideshow U.S.A.* Chicago: U of Chicago P, 2001.

Alexie, Sherman. "Sherman Alexie Website." 12 Jan. 2003. <http://www.thingsfallapart.com/>.

"Assignment." *Oxford English Dictionary Online.* 2nd ed. 1989. 20 August 2001 <http://dictionary.oed.com/>.

Atwood, Margaret. "Nine Beginnings." *The Writer on Her Work: New Essays in New Territory.* Ed. Janet Sternburg. Vol. 2. New York: Norton, 1991. 150–56.

Baba, Tadashi, et al. "Genome and Virulence Determinants of High Virulence Community-Acquired MRSA." *Lancet* 25 May 2002: 1819–28. Ebscohost. Indiana U South Bend, IN. 20 June 2002 <http://ehostvgw4.epnet.com/deliver.asp>.

Barnlund, Dean. "Communication in a Global Village." *Literacies: Reading, Writing, Interpretation.* Ed. Terence Brunk, et al. 2nd ed. New York: Norton, 2000. 47–61.

Barthes, Roland. *Mythologies.* Trans. Annette Lavers. New York: Noonday, 1973.

Berger, John. "Ways of Seeing." *Ways of Reading.* Eds. David Bartholomae and Anthony Petrosky. 5th ed. New York: Bedford/St. Martin's, 1999. 104–27.

Birkerts, Sven. "The Owl Has Flown." *Literacies: Reading, Writing, Interpretation.* Eds Terence Brunk, et al. 2nd ed. New York: Norton, 2000. 72–77.

Bogdan, Robert. *Freak Show.* Chicago: U of Chicago P, 1988.

Botstein, Leon. "Let Teenagers Try Adulthood." *Reading Culture: Contexts for Critical Reading and Writing.* Eds. Diana George and John Trimbur. 4th ed. New York: Longman, 2001. 119–21.

"Brainstorm." *Webster's New Universal Unabridged Dictionary.* 2nd ed. New York: Simon and Schuster, 1983.

Clifford, James. *The Predicament of Culture.* Cambridge, MA: Harvard UP, 1988.

"Common Sense." *Oxford English Dictionary Online.* 2nd ed. 1989. 20 August 2001 <http://dictionary.oed.com/>.

Connors, Robert. *Composition-Rhetoric: Baackgrounds, Theory, and Pedagogy.* Pittsburgh: U of Pittsburgh P, 1997. 233–35.

Considine, Bob. "Louis Knocks out Schmeling." *The Best American Sports Writing of the Century.* Ed. David Halberstam. Boston: Houghton Mifflin, 1999. 138–39.

Cronon, William. "The Trouble with Wilderness; or Getting Back to the Wrong Native." *Uncommon Ground: Toward Reinventing Nature.* Ed. William Cronon. New York: Norton, 1995. 69–90.

"Dash." *Webster's New Universal Unabridged Dictionary.* 2nd ed. New York: Simon and Schuster, 1983.

Davis, Thadious. *Nella Larsen: Novelist of the Harlem Renaissance.* Baton Rouge: U of Louisiana P, 1994.

Derrida, Jacques. *Spurs: Nietzsche's Styles.* Chicago: U of Chicago P, 1978.

Dickinson, Emily. *The Complete Poems of Emily Dickinson.* Ed. Thomas H. Johnson. Boston: Little Brown, 1890.

Didion, Joan. "Why I Write." *Joan Didion: Essays and Conversations.* Ed. Ellen G. Friedman. Princeton, NJ: Ontario Press, 1984. 5–10.

Douglass, Frederick. "Narrative of the Life of Frederick Douglass, an American Slave." *The Heath Anthology of American Literature.* Ed. Paul Lauter. 4th ed. Vol. 1. Boston: Houghton Mifflin, 2002. 1817–80.

————. "Frederick Douglass to His Former Master, Capt. Thomas Auld." *Letters of a Nation.* Ed. Andrew Carroll. New York: Broadway Books, 1997. 93–101.

Elbow, Peter. *Writing Without Teachers.* London: Oxford UP, 1973.

"Engler, Gustav Adolf Heinrich." *Encyclopedia Britannica.* CD-ROM. 1999 ed. Chicago: Encyclopedia Britannica, 1999.

Felski, Rita. "On Confession." *Women, Autobiography, Theory: A Reader.* Eds. Sidonie Smith and Julia Watson. Madison: U of Wisconsin P, 1998. 83–95.

Ferraro, Thomas J. *Ethnic Passages: Literary Immigrants in Twentieth-Century America.* Chicago: U of Chicago P, 1993.

Fishman, Stephen M. "Student Writing in Philosophy: A Sketch of Five Techniques." *Writing to Learn: Strategies for Assigning and Responding to Writing Across the Curricu-*

lum. Eds. Mary Deane Sorcinelli and Peter Elbow. *New Directions for Teaching and Learning* 69 (Spring 1997). San Francisco: Jossey-Bass, 1997. 53–66.

Freire, Paolo. "The 'Banking' Concept of Education." *Ways of Reading.* Eds. David Bartholomae and Anthony Petrosky. 2nd ed. Boston: Bedford/St. Martin's, 1990. 206–22.

Frost, Robert. *Robert Frost Poetry and Prose.* Eds. Edward Connery Lathem and Lawrance Thompson. New York: Rinehart, 1972.

Gabler, Neil. *Life, the Movie.* New York: Knopf, 1998.

Garber, Marjorie. *Academic Instincts.* Princeton: Princeton UP, 2001.

Geertz, Clifford, "Deep Play: Notes on the Balinese Cockfight." *Ways of Reading.* Eds. David Bartholomae and Anthony Petrosky. 2nd ed. Boston: Bedford/St. Martin's, 1990. 363–98.

———. *The Interpretation of Cultures.* New York: Basic, 1973.

———. *Local Knowledge.* New York: Basic, 1983.

Gorn, Elliot, Randy Roberts, and Terry D. Bilhartz, eds. *Constructing the American Past: A Source Book of a People's History,* 4th ed. Vol. 1. New York: Longman, 2002.

Greenblatt, Stephen. "Resonance and Wonder." *Exhibiting Cultures.* Eds. Steven D. Lavine and Ivan Karp. Washington, DC: Smithsonian, 1991. 42–56.

"Grammar." *Oxford English Dictionary Online.* 2nd ed. 1989. 22 May 2001 <http://dictionary.oed.com/>.

Grimm, Brothers. "Hansel and Gretel." *Grimm's Complete Fairy Tales.* New York: Barnes & Noble, 1993. 101–107.

Goldman, Marion S. *Gold Diggers and Silver Miners: Prostitution and Social Life on the Comstock Lode.* Ann Arbor: U of Michigan P, 1981.

hooks, bell. "Columbus: Gone But Not Forgotten." *Mind Readings: An Anthology for Writers.* Ed. Gary Colombo. Boston: Bedford/St. Martin's, 2002. 237–45.

Hyde, Lewis. *The Gift.* New York: Random House, Vintage Books, 1983.

Jasanoff, Sheila. "The Eye of Everyman: Witnessing DNA in the Simpson Trial." *Social Studies of Science* 28.5 (October–December 1998): 713–40.

Jordan, June. "Nobody Mean More to Me Than You and the Future Life of Willie Jordan." *Reading Culture: Contexts for Critical Reading and Writing.* Eds. Diana George and John Trimbur. 4th ed. New York: Longman, 2001. 151–61.

Kael, Pauline. Review of *The Godfather. Microsoft Cinemania.* CD-ROM. 1997 ed. Microsoft, 1996.

Karp, Ivan and Steven D. Lavine, eds. *Exhibiting Cultures.* Washington D.C.: Smithsonian, 1991.

Kaye-Smith, Sheila. "Mrs. Adis," *Century Magazine* 103. 3 (January 1922): 321–26.

Kuhn, Thomas. "The Historical Structure of Scientific Discovery." *Ways of Reading.* Eds. David Bartholomae and Anthony Petrosky. 2nd ed. Boston: Bedford/St. Martin's, 1990. 384–96.

Larsen, Nella. "Sanctuary," *Forum* 83 (January 1930): 15–18.

———. "Our Rostrum," *Forum* 83 (January 1930): 41.

Latour, Bruno and Steve Woolgar. *Laboratory Life : The Social Construction of Scientific Facts.* Beverly Hills: Sage Publications, 1979.

Lemann, Nicholas. "A Real Meritocracy." *Reading Culture: Contexts for Critical Reading and Writing.* Eds. Diana George and John Trimbur. 4th ed. New York: Longman, 2001. 130–35.

Lu, Min-zhan. "From Silence to Words: Writing as Struggle." *Reading Culture: Contexts for Critical Reading and Writing.* Eds. Diana George and John Trimbur. 4th ed. New York: Longman, 2001. 141–50.

Malinowski, Bronislaw. "Tribal Economics in the Trobriands." *Tribal and Peasant Economies: Readings in Economic Anthropology.* Ed. George Dalton. Austin: U of Texas P, 1967. 185–223.

———. *A Diary in the Strict Sense of the Term.* New York: Harcourt, 1967.

Mallon, Thomas. *Stolen Words: Forays into the Origins and Ravages of Plagiarism.* New York: Penguin Books, 1989.

Manguel, Alberto. *A History of Reading.* New York: Viking, 1996.

McDowell, Deborah E. Introduction. *Quicksand and Passing.* By Nella Larson. New Brunswick, Rutgers UP, 1986: ix–xxxvii.

McKibben, Bill. "Television and the Twilight of the Senses." *Mind Readings: An Anthology for Writers.* Ed. Gary Colombo. Boston: Bedford/St. Martin's, 2002. 109–16.

Mellix, Barbada. "From Outside, In." *Literacies: Reading, Writing, Interpretation.* Eds. Terence Brunk, et al. 2nd ed. New York: Norton, 2000. 385–95.

"Metaphor." *Encyclopedia Britannica.* CD-ROM. 1999 ed. Chicago: Encyclopedia Britannica, 1999.

Michie, Helena. "Not One of the Family: The Repression of the Other Woman in Feminist Theory." *Feminisms.* Eds. Robyn R. Warhol and Diane Price Herndl. New Brunswick, NJ: Rutgers UP, 1991. 58–68.

Miller, Mark Crispin. "Getting Dirty." *Ways of Reading.* Eds. David Bartholomae and Anthony Petrosky. 2nd ed. Boston: Bedford/St. Martin's, 1990. 397–406.

Milner, Clyde A. et al., eds. *The Oxford History of the American West.* New York: Oxford UP, 1994.

Mumford, Laura Stemple. "Plotting Paternity: Looking For Dad on the Daytime Soaps." *Signs of Life in the USA: Readings on Popular Culture for Writers.* Eds. Sonia Maasik and Jack Solomon. 3rd ed. New York: Bedford/St. Martin's, 2000. 249–59.

Norton, Anne. "The Signs of Shopping." *Signs of Life: Readings on Popular Culture for Writers.* Eds. Sonia Maasik and Jack Solomon. Boston: Bedford, 2000. 62–69.

Pearl, Nancy. "Discovering Italian American Writers." *Library Journal* 127. 16 (Oct. 2002): 152. Ebscohost. Indiana U. South Bend, IN. 12 Jan. 2003. <http://ehostvgw4.epnet.com/deliver.asp>.

Podhoretz, John. "Father of The Godfather." Review. *The Heritage Foundation Policy Review,* Feb. 2000/March 2000. Lexis-Nexis. Indiana U. South Bend, IN. 11 Jan. 2003 <plum.iusb.edu:2064/universe/document?>.

"Pope Pius IX." *Encyclopedia Britannica.* CD-ROM. 1999 ed. Chicago: Encyclopedia Britannica, 1999.

Randall, Marilyn. "Appropriate(d) Discourse: Plagiarism and Decolonization," *New Literary History* 22.3 (Summer 1991): 525–41.

Rich, Adrienne. "When We Dead Awaken: Writing as Revision." *Ways of Reading*. Eds. David Bartholomae and Anthony Petrosky. 5th ed. New York: Bedford/St. Martin's, 1999. 603–16.

Rosenheim, Andrew. Obituary of Mario Puzo. *The Independent (London)* 5 July 1999: 6. Lexis-Nexis. Indiana U. South Bend, IN. 11 Jan. 2003 <plum.iusb.edu:2064/universe/document?>.

Rouse, Irving. *The Tainos: Rise and Decline of the People Who Greeted Columbus*. New Haven: Yale UP, 1992.

Sale, Roger. *On Writing*. New York: Random, 1970.

Sarton, May. "From Journal of a Solitude." *The Norton Reader*. Eds. Linda H. Peterson, et al. 10th ed. New York: Norton, 2000. 98–103.

Schacter, Daniel L. "Building Memories: Encoding and Retrieving the Present and the Past." *Mind Readings: An Anthology for Writers*. Ed. Gary Colombo. Boston: Bedford/St. Martins, 2002. 158–175.

Schmidt, Kristi. "The Shared Power of End-Of-Life Decisions." Unpublished essay, 2000.

Scholes, Robert. "On Reading a Video Text." *Literacies: Reading, Writing, Interpretation*. Eds. Terence Brunk, et al. 2nd ed. New York: Norton, 1997. 619–23.

Silverman, Jay, et al. *Rules of Thumb for Research*. Boston: McGraw-Hill, 1999.

Simon, Richard Keller. *Trash Culture*. Berkeley: U of California P, 1999.

Sizer, Theodore. "What High School Is." *Reading Culture: Contexts for Critical Reading and Writing*. Ed. Diana George and John Trimbur. 4th ed. New York: Longman, 2001. 110–18.

Sontag, Susan. "In Plato's Cave." *Making Sense: Constructing Knowledge in the Arts and Sciences*. Eds. Robert Coleman, et al. Boston: Houghton Mifflin, 2001. 474–90.

———. *Illness as Metaphor and Aids as Metaphor*. New York: Anchor Books Doubleday, 1990.

Spain, Daphne. "Spatial Segregation and Gender Stratification in the Workplace." *Signs of Life in the USA: Readings on Popular Culture for Writers*. Eds. Sonia Maasik and Jack Solomon. 3rd ed. New York: Bedford/St. Martin's, 2000. 771–77.

Stephens, Walter. "Mimesis, Mediation, and Counterfeit." *The Literary and Philosophical Debate*. Vol. 1. Ed. Mihai Spariosu. Philadelphia: Benjamin's, 1984. 238–71.

"Syllabus." *Encyclopedia Britannica*. CD-ROM. 1999 ed. Chicago: Encyclopedia Britannica, 1999.

"Syllabus." *Oxford English Dictionary Online*. 2nd ed. 1989. 4 June 2002 <http://dictionary.oed.com/>.

"Synthesis." *Oxford English Dictionary Online*. 2nd ed. 1989. 4 June 2002 <http://dictionary.oed.com/>.

"Television Highlights." *New York Times* 11 January 2003, Late ed.: B22.

Todorov, Tzvetan. *The Conquest of America*. Norman, OK: U of Oklahoma P, 1999.

Tompkins, Jane. "'Indians': Textualism, Morality, and the Problem of History." *Ways of Reading*. Eds. David Bartholomae and Anthony Petrosky. 5th ed. New York: Bedford/St. Martin's, 1999. 672–92.

Turkle, Sherry. "The Triumph of Tinkering." *Making Sense: An Anthology for Writers*. Ed. Gary Colombo. Boston: Bedford/St. Martin's. 553–65.

Turner, Frederick Jackson. "The Significance of the Frontier in American History, 1893." *Modern History Sourcebook*. Website. 9 July 2003. <www.fordham.edu/halsall/mod/1893turner.html>.

Vidal, Gore. Reply to letter of David Nielsen. *New York Review of Books* 17 December 1981: 8 pars. 7 July 2002 <http://www.nybooks.com/articles/6787>.

Washakie. "Washakie, a Shoshone Indian to Governor John W. Hoyt on Being Forced Off Their Land." *Letters of a Nation*. Ed. Andrew Carroll. New York: Broadway Books, 1997. 25–27.

Wharton, Edith, "Life and I." Appendix. *Novellas and Other Writings*. New York: Library of America, 1990. 1071–96.

Williams, Ben Ames, ed. *A Diary From Dixie*. By Mary Chesnut. Cambridge: Harvard UP, 1980.

Williams, Nigel. *My Life Closed Twice*. London: Faber and Faber, 1977.

Williams, Raymond. *Keywords: A Vocabulary of Culture and Society*. New York: Oxford UP, 1976.

Williams, Rosalind. "The Dream World of Mass Consumption." *Rethinking Popular Culture*. Eds. Chandra Mukerji and Michael Schudson. Berkeley: U of California P, 1991. 198–236.

Willis, Susan. "Disney World: Public Use/Private State." *Signs of Life: Readings on Popular Culture for Writers*. Eds. Sonia Maasik and Jack Solomon. Boston: Bedford, 2000. 744–56.

————. "Learning from the Banana." *American Quarterly* 39:4 (Winter 1987) 586–600.

Woodward, C. Vann, ed. *Mary Chesnut's Civil War*. New Haven: Yale UP, 1981.

Woolf, Virginia. "Streethaunting." *Art of the Personal Essay: An Anthology from the Classical Era to the Present*. Ed. Phillip Lopate. New York: Anchor Books, Random, 1995. 256–65.

Workman, Lynda. "The Experience of Policy." *Literacies: Reading, Writing, Interpretation*. Eds. Terence Brunk, et al. 2nd ed. New York: Norton, 2000. 749–59.

Wright, Joanne H. "Going Against the Grain: Hobbes's Case for Original Maternal Dominion." *Journal of Women's History* 14.1 (Spring 2002): 123–48.

Wright, Richard. *Native Son*. New York: Harper Collins, 1993.

"Zakir, Husain." *Encyclopedia Britannica*. CD-ROM. 1999 ed. Chicago: Encyclopedia Britannica, 1999.

RELATED WORDS

EXERCISES

1. Looking through our works cited list, identify as many different kinds of sources as you can (from books, to articles in collections, to Websites, etc.).

2. Looking through our works cited list, determine how many different disciplines are represented, how many sources are academic, and how many are not.

3. From exercise 1, take examples of different kinds of sources and translate those sources into APA style citation and/or Chicago style citation. Use our entry on citation and the reference tools listed previously for help.

4. In a group, select one complicated item from our works cited list and discuss its elements: codes signaling article, book, or Website, for example, abbreviations, names, dates, numbers, and so on. What does each element of the citation signify?

5. In a library session, choose one item from this works cited list and find out whether your library has it or has access to it. Then choose an obscure source from your library's collection, create a works cited entry for that source, and have some one else in your group track down that source.

6. Looking through our works cited, discuss in a group where our main interests lie. Can you guess?

Index